Java Threads

Java Threads

Scott Oaks and Henry Wong

O'REILLY™

Cambridge · Köln · Paris · Sebastopol · Tokyo

Java Threads
by Scott Oaks and Henry Wong

Copyright © 1997 O'Reilly & Associates, Inc. All rights reserved.
Printed in the United States of America.

Published by O'Reilly & Associates, Inc., 101 Morris Street, Sebastopol, CA 95472.

Editor: Mike Loukides

Production Editor: Mary Anne Weeks Mayo

Printing History:

      January 1997:   First Edition.

This book is printed on acid-free paper with 85% recycled content, 15% post-consumer waste. O'Reilly & Associates is committed to using paper with the highest recycled content available consistent with high quality.

ISBN: 1-56592-216-6   [5/97]

Table of Contents

Preface

When Sun Microsystems released the first alpha version of Java in the winter of 1995, developers all over the world took notice. There were many features of Java that attracted these developers, not the least of which were the set of buzzwords Sun used to promote Java: Java was, among other things, robust, safe, architecture-neutral, portable, object-oriented, simple, and multithreaded. For many developers, these last two buzzwords seemed contradictory: how could a language that is multithreaded be simple?

It turns out that Java's threading system is simple, at least relative to other threading systems. This simplicity makes Java's threading system easy to learn, so that even developers who are unfamiliar with threads can pick up the basics of thread programming with relative ease. But this simplicity comes with some trade-offs: some of the advanced features that are found in other threading systems are not present in Java. However, these features can be built by the Java developer from the simpler constructs Java provides. And that's the underlying theme of this book: how to use the threading tools in Java to perform the basic tasks of threaded programming, and how to extend them to perform more advanced tasks for more complex programs.

Who Should Read This Book?

This book is intended for programmers of all levels who need to learn to use threads within Java programs. The first few chapters of the book deal with the basic issues of threaded programming in Java starting at a basic level: no assumption is made that the developer will have had any experience in threaded programming. As the chapters progress, the information becomes more advanced, both in terms of the information presented and the experience of the developer that the material assumes. For developers who are new to threaded programming, this sequence should provide a natural progression of the topic.

This progression mimics the development of Java itself as well as the development of books about Java. Early Java programs tended to be simple, though effective: an animated image of Duke dancing on a Web page was a powerful advertisement of Java's potential, but it barely scratched the surface of that potential. Similarly, early books about Java tended to be complete overviews about Java with only a chapter or two dedicated to Java's threading system.

This book belongs to the second wave of Java books: because it covers only a single topic, it has the luxury of explaining in deeper detail how Java's threads can be used. It's ideally suited to developers who will target the second wave of Java programs: more complex programs that will fully exploit the power of Java's threading system.

Though the material presented in this book does not assume any prior knowledge of threads, it does assume that the reader has a knowledge of other areas of the Java API and can write simple Java programs.

Versions Used in This Book

Writing a book on Java in the age of Internet-time is hard: the sand on which we're standing is constantly shifting. But we've drawn a line in that sand, and the line we've drawn is at the JDK 1.0.2 from Sun Microsystems. In a few cases, we've guessed at features that will be available in later releases of the JDK based on information that Sun has announced, but it's likely that versions of Java that postdate 1.0.2 will contain some changes to the threading system not discussed in this version of the book. The two most likely areas for this are related to the thread security model (we actually discuss the proposed JDK 1.1 model in our discussion of security), and a change in some versions of the virtual machine that allow Java to use more that one CPU simultaneously on platforms that have multiple CPUs.

We don't believe any of these changes will have a drastic effect on writing threaded programs in Java. At worst, there may be extensions of the Java API that provide some additional functionality not covered in this book, but these changes should be complementary to the existing API.

In addition, some vendors that provide Java—either embedded in browsers or as a development system—are contemplating releasing extensions to Java that provide additional functionality to Java's threading system (in much the same way as the examples we provide in Chapters 5 through 7 use the basic techniques of the Java threaded system to provide additional functionality). Those extensions are beyond the scope of this book: we're concerned only with the reference JDK 1.0.2

from Sun Microsystems. The only time that we'll consider platform differences concerns an area of the reference JDK that differs on UNIX platforms and Windows platforms: these platforms contain some differences in the scheduling of Java threads, a topic we'll address in Chapter 6.

Organization of This Book

Here's an outline of the book, showing the progression of the material we present. The material in the appendixes is generally either too immature to present fully, or it is mostly of academic interest, although it may be useful in rare cases.

Chapter 1, *Introduction to Threading*
> This chapter introduces the concept of threads, and the terms we use in the book.

Chapter 2, *The Java Threading API*
> This chapter introduces the Java API that allows the programmer to create threads.

Chapter 3, *Synchronization Techniques*
> This chapter introduces the simple locking mechanism that Java developers can use to synchronize access to data and code.

Chapter 4, *Wait and Notify*
> This chapter introduces Java's other synchronization mechanism that developers use to synchronize access to data and code.

Chapter 5, *Useful Examples of Java Thread Programming*
> This chapter summarizes the techniques presented in the previous chapters. Unlike the earlier chapters, this chapter is solutions-oriented: the examples give you an idea of how to put together the basic threading techniques that have been presented so far as well as provide some insight as to how to design effectively using threads.

Chapter 6, *Java Thread Scheduling*
> This chapter introduces the Java API that controls how threads are scheduled by the virtual machine and provides some classes that extend Java's basic scheduling model.

Chapter 7, *Advanced Synchronization Topics*
> This chapter discusses various advanced topics related to data synchronization, including designing around deadlock and developing some additional synchronization classes.

Chapter 8, *Thread Groups*

The chapter discusses Java's thread group class, which allows a developer to control and manipulate groups of threads. Java's security mechanism for threads is based on this class and is also discussed in this chapter.

Appendix A, *Miscellaneous Topics*

This appendix presents a few methods of the Java API that are of limited interest: details of interrupting a thread (currently too immature to use in a Java program), methods that deal with the thread's stack, and the Thread-Death class.

Appendix B, *Exceptions and Errors*

This appendix presents the details of the exceptions and errors that are used by the threading system.

Appendix C, *Threading Within the Java API*

This appendix presents some information on the Java core classes that use threads internally to perform their tasks.

Appendix D, *Thread Debugging*

This appendix provides some help in understanding the challenges in debugging threaded programs, although the information here is no replacement for powerful debugging tools (none of which exist as of this writing).

Conventions Used in This Book

`Constant width` font is used for:

- Code examples

```
public void main(String args[]) {
    System.out.println("Hello, world");
}
```

- Method and variable names within the text

`Bold constant width` font is used for:

- Presenting revised code examples as we work through a problem

```
public void main(String args[]) {
    System.out.println("Hello, world");
}
```

- Highlighting a section of code for discussion within a longer code example

Examples of the programs in this book may be retrieved online from *http://www.ora.com/*.

Acknowledgments

As readers of prefaces are well aware, writing a book is never an effort undertaken solely by the authors who get all the credit on the cover. We are deeply indebted to the following people for their help and encouragement: Michael Loukides, who believed us when we said that this was an important topic and who shepherded us through the creative process, David Flanagan for valuable feedback on the drafts, and Reynold Jabbour for supporting us in our work.

Many people in O'Reilly's production and design groups contributed to our project. Mary Anne Weeks Mayo was the production project manager and copy editor. Seth Maislin wrote the index. Chris Reilley expertly put pictures to our words. Quality control was assured by Kismet McDonough-Chan, Clairemarie Fisher O'Leary, and Sheryl Avruch. Mike Sierra contributed his FrameMaker tool-tweaking prowess. The book's interior was designed by Nancy Priest. Eden Reiner created the back cover; Edie Freedman designed the front cover.

Mostly, we must thank our respective families. To James, who gave Scott the support and encouragement necessary to see this book through (and to cope with his writing in a small sublet while their lives were in storage for six months), and to Nini, who knew when to leave Henry alone for the 10 percent of the time when he was creative and kick his butt the rest of the time: thank you for everything!

Feedback for Authors

We've attempted to be complete and accurate throughout this book. Changes in releases of the Java specification as well as differing vendor implementations across many platforms and underlying operating systems make it impossible to be completely accurate in all cases (not to mention the possibility of our having made a mistake somewhere along the line). This book is a work in progress, and as Java continues to evolve, so too will this book.

The authors welcome your feedback about this book, especially if you spot errors or omissions that we have made. You can contact us at *scott.oaks@sun.com* and *henry.wong@sun.com.*

1

Introduction to Threading

This is a book about using threads in the Java programming language and the Java virtual machine. The topic of threads is very important in Java, so important that many features of a threaded system are built into the Java language itself, while other features of a threaded system are required by the Java virtual machine. Threading is an integral part of using Java.

The concept of threads is not a new one: for some time, many operating systems have had libraries that provide the C programmer a mechanism to create threads. Other languages—like Ada—have had support for threads embedded into the language much as the support for threads is built into the Java language itself. Nonetheless, the topic of threads is usually considered a peripheral programming topic, one that's only needed in special programming cases.

With Java, things are different: it is impossible to write all but the simplest Java programs without introducing the topic of threads. And the popularity of Java ensures that many developers who might never have considered learning about threading possibilities in a language like C or C++ need to become fluent in threaded programming.

Java Terms

We'll start by defining some terms used throughout this book. Since Java is a new phenomenon, many terms surrounding it are used inconsistently in various sources; we'll endeavor to be consistent in our usage of these terms throughout the book.

Java

First is the term Java itself. As we know, Java started out as a programming language, and many people today think of Java as being simply a program-

1

ming language. But Java is much more than just a programming language: it's also an API specification and a virtual machine specification. So when we say Java, we mean the entire Java specification: a programming language, an API, and a virtual machine specification that, taken together, define an entire programming and run-time environment. Often when we say Java, it's clear from context that we're talking about specifically the programming language, or parts of the Java API, or the virtual machine. The point to remember is that the threading features we discuss in this book derive their properties from all the components of the Java environment taken as a whole. So while it's possible to take the Java programming language, directly compile it into assembly code, and run it outside of the virtual machine, such an executable may not necessarily behave the same as the programs we describe in this book.[*]

Virtual machine, interpreters, and browsers

The Java virtual machine is another term for the Java interpreter, which is the code that ultimately runs Java programs by interpreting the intermediate byte-code format of the Java programming language. The Java interpreter actually comes in two popular forms: the interpreter itself (called *java*) that runs programs via the command line or a file manager, and the interpreter that is built into many popular Web browsers such as Netscape, HotJava, and the appletviewer that comes with the Java Developer's Kit. Both of these forms are simply implementations of the Java virtual machine, and we'll refer to the Java virtual machine when our discussion applies to both. When we use the term *java interpreter*, we're talking specifically about the command line, standalone version of the virtual machine; when we use the term Java-enabled browser (or, more simply, browser), we're talking specifically about the virtual machine built into these Web browsers.

Programs, applications, and applets

This leads us to the terms that we'll use for things written in the Java language. Generically, we'll call such entities *programs*. But there are two types of programs a typical Java programmer might write: programs that can be run directly by the Java interpreter and programs designed to be run by a Java-enabled browser.[†] Much of the time, the distinction between these two types of Java programs is not important, and in those cases, we'll refer to them as programs. But in those cases where the distinction is important, we'll use the

---

[*] This doesn't refer to programs that are compiled by the Java virtual machine itself; these so-called "just-in-time" compilations still run inside the virtual machine. Rather, it refers to programs that are immediately compiled into assembly code and never run in the virtual machine, which for our purposes is somewhat of an academic exercise.

[†] Though it's possible to write a single Java program so that it can be run both by the interpreter and by a browser, the distinction still applies at the time the program is actually run.

term *applets* for programs running in the Java-enabled browser and the term *applications* for standalone Java programs.[*]

Thread Overview

This leaves us only one more term to define: what exactly is a thread? The term *thread* is shorthand for thread of control, and a thread of control is, at its simplest, a section of code executed independently of other threads of control within a single program.

Thread of Control

Thread of control sounds like a complicated technical term, but it's really a simple concept: it is the path taken by a program during execution. This determines what code will be executed: does the code in the `if` block get executed, or does the `else` block? How many times does the `while` loop execute? If we were executing tasks from a "to do" list, much as a computer executes an application, what steps we perform and the order in which we perform them is our path of execution, the result of our thread of control.

Having multiple threads of control is like executing tasks from two lists. We are still doing the tasks on each "to do" list in the correct order, but when we get bored with the tasks on one of the lists, we switch lists with the intention of returning at some future time to the first list at the exact point we left off.

Overview of Multitasking

We're all familiar with the use of multitasking operating systems to run multiple programs at one time. Each of these programs has at least one thread within it, so at some level, we're already comfortable with the notion of a thread in a single process. The single-threaded process has the following properties which, as it turns out, are shared by all threads in a program with multiple threads as well:

- The process begins execution at a well-known point. In programming languages like C and C++ (not to mention Java itself), the thread begins execution at the first statement of the function or method called `main()`.

- Execution of the statements follows in a completely ordered, predefined sequence for a given set of inputs. An individual process is single-minded in this regard: it simply executes the next statement in the program.

---

[*] Most of the distinction between the two involves issues of security; we'll explore those issues in Chapter 8.

- While executing, the process has access to certain data. In Java, there are three types of data a process can access: *local* variables are accessed from the thread's stack, *instance* variables are accessed through object references, and *static* variables are accessed through class or object references.

Now consider what happens when you sit at your computer and start two single-threaded programs: a text editor, say, and a file manager. You now have two processes running on your computer; each process has a single thread with the properties outlined above. Each process does not necessarily know about the other process, although, depending on the operating system running on your computer, there are several ways in which the processes can send each other various messages: a common behavior is that you can drag a file icon from the file manager into the text editor in order to edit the file. So each process runs independently of the other, although they can cooperate if they so choose. The typical multitasking environment is shown in Figure 1-1.

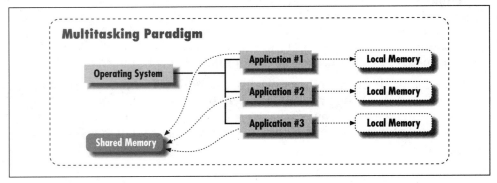

Figure 1-1. Processes in a multitasking environment

From the point of view of the person using the computer, these processes often appear to execute simultaneously, although there are a lot of variables that can affect that appearance. These variables are dependent on the operating system: for example, a given operating system may not support multitasking at all, so that no two programs appear to execute simultaneously. Or the user may have decided that a particular process is more important than other processes and hence should always run, shutting out the other processes from running and again affecting the appearance of simultaneity.

Finally, the data contained within these two processes is, by default, separated: each has its own stack for local variables, and each has its own data area for objects and other data elements. Under many operating systems, the programmer can make arrangements so that the data objects reside in memory that can be shared between the processes, allowing both processes to access them.

Overview of Multithreading

All of this leads us to a common analogy: we can think of a thread just as we think of a process, and we can consider a program with multiple threads running within a single instance of the Java virtual machine just as we consider multiple processes within an operating system, as we show in Figure 1-2.

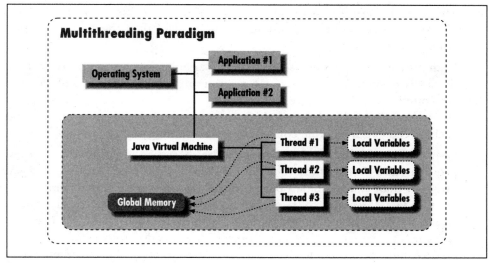

Figure 1-2. Multitasking vs. threading

So it is that within a Java program, multiple threads have these properties:

- Each thread begins execution at a predefined, well-known location. For one of the threads in the program, that location is the main() method;[*] for the rest of the threads, it is a particular location the programmer decides upon when the code is written.

- Each thread executes code from its starting location in an ordered, pre-defined (for a given set of inputs) sequence. Threads are also single-minded in their purpose, always simply executing the next statement in the sequence.

- Each thread executes its code independently of the other threads in the program. If the threads choose to cooperate with each other, there are a variety of mechanisms we will explore that allow that cooperation. Exploiting those methods of co-operation is the reason why programming with threads is such a useful technique, but that cooperation is completely optional, much as the user is never required to drag a file from the file manager into the text editor.

---

[*] This is true even in a Java applet, in which case the main() method was executed by the browser before your applet was created.

- The threads appear to have a certain degree of simultaneous execution. As we'll explore in Chapter 6, the degree of simultaneity is dependent on several factors—programming decisions about the relative importance of various threads as well as operating system support for various features. The potential for simultaneous execution is the key thing you must keep in mind when threading your code.

- The threads have access to various types of data. At this point, the analogy breaks down somewhat depending on the type of data the Java program is attempting to access.

  Each thread is separated, so that local variables in the methods that the thread is executing are separate for different threads. These local variables are completely private; there is no way for one thread to access the local variables of another thread. If two threads happen to execute the same method, each thread gets a separate copy of the local variables of that method.*

  Objects and their instance variables can be shared between threads in a Java program, and sharing these objects is much easier between threads of a Java program than sharing data objects between processes in most operating systems. In fact, the ability to share data objects easily between threads is another reason why programming with threads is so useful. But Java threads cannot arbitrarily access each other's data objects: they need permission to access the objects, and one thread needs to pass the object reference to the other thread.

  Static variables are the big exception to this analogy: they are automatically shared between all threads in a Java program.

Don't panic over this analogy: the fact that you'll be programming with threads in Java doesn't mean you'll necessarily be doing the system-level type of programming you'd need to perform if you were writing the multitasking operating system responsible for running multiple programs. The Java Thread API is designed to be simple and requires little specialized skill for most common tasks.†

Why Threads?

The notion of threading is so ingrained in Java that it's almost impossible to write all but the simplest programs in Java without creating and using threads. And many of the classes with the Java API are already threaded, so that you often are using multiple threads without realizing it.

---

* This is completely analogous to the case where we might run two copies of the text editor: each process would have separate copies of the local variables.

† On the other hand, as you progress to the more advanced uses of Java's thread system, you'll begin to deal with precisely those problems that must be solved by systems programmers.

Historically, threading was first exploited to make certain programs easier to write: if a program can be split into separate tasks, it's often easier to program the algorithm as separate tasks or threads. Programs that fall into this category are typically specialized and deal with multiple, independent tasks. The relative rareness of these types of programs makes threading in this category a specialized skill.[*]

The popularity of threading increased when graphical interfaces became the standard for desktop computers because the threading system allowed the user to perceive better program performance. The introduction of threads into these platforms didn't make the programs any faster, but it did create this illusion of performance to the user, who now had a dedicated thread to service input or display output.

Recently, there's been a flurry of activity regarding a new use of threaded programs: programs that exploit the growing number of computers that have multiple processors.[†] Programs that require a lot of CPU processing are natural candidates for this category, since a calculation that required one hour on a single-processor machine could (at least theoretically) run in half an hour on a two-processor machine, or 15 minutes on a four-processor machine. All that is required is that the program be written to use multiple threads to perform the calculation.

The advent of machines with multiple processors, and operating systems that provide programmers with thread libraries to exploit those processors, has made threading programming a hot topic, as developers move to extract every benefit from these new machines. Until Java, much of the interest in threading centered around using it to take advantage of multiple processors on a single machine.

However, threading in Java has nothing at all to do with multiprocessor machines and their capabilities. At the time of this writing, all implementations of the Java virtual machine are not themselves written as a threaded program, which means that even if you have multiple processors in your computer, the Java virtual machine only uses one processor at a time. So you cannot use Java's threading mechanisms to increase the performance of your program on a machine with multiple processors.[‡]

---

[*] Often, these types of programs were written as separate processes using operating-system dependent communication tools like signals and shared memory spaces to communicate between the processes. This approach increased system complexity.

[†] Very specialized supercomputers have had multiple processors for a while, but only recently have multiprocessor machines been generally available, at least to most corporations.

[‡] This is likely to change at some point in time.

The major reason threading is so important in Java is that Java has no conception of asynchronous behavior. This means that many of the programming techniques you've become accustomed to using in typical programs are not applicable in Java; instead, you must learn a new repertoire of threading techniques to handle these cases of asynchronous behavior.

This is not to say there aren't other times when threads are a handy programming technique in Java; certainly it's easy to use Java for a program that implements an algorithm that naturally lends itself to threading. And many Java programs implement multiple, independent behaviors. So the next few sections cover some of the circumstances in which, due to the need for asynchronous behavior or due to the elegance that threading lends to the problem, Java threads are a required component of the program.

Nonblocking I/O

In Java, as in most programming languages, when you try to get input from the user, you execute a read() method specifying the user's terminal (System.in in Java). When the program executes the read() method, the program will typically wait until the user types at least one character before it continues and executes the next statement. This type of I/O is called blocking I/O: the program blocks until some data is available to satisfy the read() method.

This type of behavior is often undesirable. If you're reading data from a network socket, that data is often not available when you want to read it: the data may have been delayed in transit over the network, or you may be reading from a network server that sends data only periodically. If the program blocks when it tries to read from the socket, then it's unable to do anything else until the data is actually available. If the program has a user interface that contains a button and the user presses the button while the program is executing the read() method, nothing will happen: the program will be unable to process the mouse events and execute the action() method associated with the button. This can be very frustrating for the user, who thinks the program has hung.

Traditionally, there are three techniques to cope with this situation:

I/O multiplexing
> Developers often take all input sources and use a system call like select() to notify them when data is available from a particular source. This allows input to be handled much like an event from the user (in fact, many graphical toolkits use this method transparently to the user, who simply registers a callback function that is called whenever data is available from a particular source).

Polling

Polling allows a developer to test if data is available from a particular source. If data is available, the data can be read and processed; if it is not, the program can perform another task. Polling can be done either explicitly—with a system call like `poll()`—or, in some systems, by making the `read()` function return an indication that no data is immediately available.

Signals

A file descriptor representing an input source can often be set so that an asynchronous signal is delivered to the program when data is available on that input source. This signal interrupts the program, which processes the data and then returns to whatever task it had been doing.

In Java, none of these techniques is available. When you attempt to read data and none is available, your thread will block until data is available. While certain subclasses of the FilterInputStream class provide a method called `available()` that simulates a poll to determine if data is available, this method is limited in its functionality and doesn't actually implement a true poll.[*]

In order to compensate for the lack of these features, a Java developer must set up a separate thread to read the data. This separate thread can block when data isn't available, and the other thread(s) in the Java program can process events from the user or perform other tasks.

While this issue of blocking I/O can conceivably occur with any data source, it occurs most frequently with network sockets. If you're used to programming sockets, you've probably used one of these techniques to read from a socket, but perhaps not to write to one. Many developers, used to programming on a local-area network, are vaguely aware that writing to a socket may block, but it's a possibility that many of them ignore because it can only happen under certain circumstances, such as a backlog in getting data onto the network. This backlog rarely happens on a fast, local-area network, but if you're using Java to program sockets over the Internet, the chances of this backlog happening are greatly increased; hence the chance of blocking while attempting to write data onto the network is also increased. So in Java, you may need two threads to handle the socket: one to read from the socket and one to write to it.

Alarms and Timers

Traditional operating systems typically provide some sort of timer or alarm call: the program sets the timer and continues processing. When the timer expires, the

---

[*] This is a problem we'll solve in Chapter 5.

program receives some sort of asynchronous signal that notifies the program of the timer's expiration.

In Java, the programmer must set up a separate thread to simulate a timer. This thread can sleep for the duration of a specified time interval and then notify other threads that the timer has expired.

Independent Tasks

A Java program is often called upon to perform independent tasks. In the simplest case, a single applet may perform two independent animations for a Web page. A more complex program would be a calculation server that performs calculations on behalf of several clients simultaneously. In either case, while it is possible to write a single-threaded program to perform the multiple tasks, it's easier and more elegant to place each task in its own thread.

The complete answer to the question "why threads" really lies in this last category. As programmers, we're trained to think linearly and often fail to see simultaneous paths that our program might take. But there's no reason why processes that we've conventionally thought of in a single-threaded fashion need necessarily remain so: when the Save button in a word processor is pressed, we typically have to wait a few seconds until we can continue. Worse yet, the word processor may periodically perform an auto-save, which invariably interrupts the flow of typing and disrupts the thought process. In a threaded word processor, the save operation would be in a separate thread so that it didn't interfere with the work flow. As you become accustomed to writing programs with multiple threads, you'll discover many circumstances in which adding a separate thread will make your algorithms more elegant and your programs better to use.

Summary

The idea of multiple threads of control within a single program may seem like a new and difficult concept, but it is not. All programs have at least one thread already, and multiple threads in a single program are not radically different than multiple programs within an operating system.

As we'll examine in Appendix C, a Java program can contain many threads, all of which may be created without the explicit knowledge of the developer. For now, all you need to consider is that when you write a Java application, there is an initial thread that begins its operation by executing the `main()` method of your application. When you write a Java applet, there is a thread that is executing the callback methods (`init()`, `action()`, etc.) of your applet; we speak of this thread as the applet's thread. In either case, your program starts with what you can consider as a single thread. If you want to perform I/O (particularly if the I/O might block), or start a timer, or do any other task in parallel with the initial thread, you must start a new thread to perform that task. In the next chapter, we'll examine how to do just that.

2

The Java Threading API

In this chapter, we will create our own threads. As we shall see, Java threads are easy to use and well integrated with the Java environment.

Threading Using the Thread Class

In the last chapter, we considered threads as separate tasks that execute in parallel. These tasks are simply code executed by the thread, and this code is actually part of our program. The code may download an image from the server or may play an audio file on the speakers, or any other task; because it is code, it can be executed by our original thread. In order to introduce the parallelism we desire, we must create a new thread and arrange for the new thread to execute the appropriate code.

Let's start by looking at the execution of a single thread in the following example:

```
public class OurClass {
    public void run() {
        for (int I = 0; I < 100; I++) {
            System.out.println("Hello");
        }
    }
}
```

In this example, we have a class called OurClass. The OurClass class has a single public method called `run()` that simply writes a string 100 times to standard output.[*] If we execute this code from an applet as shown below, it runs in the applet's thread:

---

[*] Or to the Java output window on most browsers.

13

```
import java.applet.Applet;

public class OurApplet extends Applet {
    public void init() {
        OurClass oc = new OurClass();
        oc.run();
    }
}
```

If we instantiate an OurClass object and call its `run()` method, nothing unusual happens. An object is created, its `run()` method is called, and the "Hello" message prints 100 times. Just as other method calls, the caller of the `run()` method waits until the `run()` method finishes before it continues. If we were to graph an execution of the code, it would look like Figure 2-1.

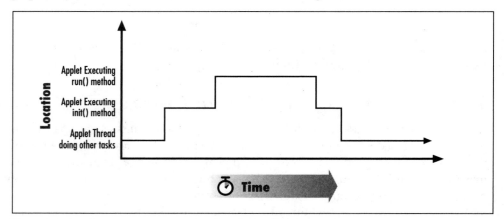

Figure 2-1. Graphical representation of nonthreaded method execution

What if we want the run() method of OurClass to execute in parallel with the init() and other methods of the applet? In order to do that, we must modify the OurClass class so that it can be executed by a new thread. So the first thing we'll do is make OurClass inherit from the Thread class:[*]

```
public class OurClass extends Thread {
    public void run() {
        for (int I = 0; I < 100; I++) {
            System.out.println("Hello");
        }
    }
}
```

---

[*] The Thread class is part of the *java.lang* package and hence is automatically imported into every Java program.

If we can compile this code and run it with our applet, everything works exactly as before: the applet's `init()` method calls the `run()` method of the OurClass object and waits for the `run()` method to return before continuing. The fact that this example compiles and runs proves that the Thread class exists. This class is our first look into the Java threading API and is the programmatic interface for starting and stopping our own threads. But we have not yet created a new thread of control; we have simply created a class that has a `run()` method. To continue, let's modify our applet like this:

```
import java.applet.Applet;

public class OurApplet extends Applet {
    public void init() {
        OurClass oc = new OurClass();
        oc.start();
    }
}
```

In this second version of our applet, we have changed only one line: the call to the `run()` method is now a call to the `start()` method. Compiling and executing this code confirms that it still works and appears to the user to run exactly the same way as the previous example. Since the `start()` method is not part of the OurClass class, we can conclude that the implementation of the `start()` method is part either of the Thread class or of one of its superclasses. Furthermore, since the applet still accomplishes the same task, we can conclude that the `start()` method causes a call, whether directly or indirectly, to the `run()` method.

Upon closer examination, this new applet actually behaves differently than the previous version. While it is true that the `start()` method eventually calls the `run()` method, it does so in another thread. The `start()` method is what actually creates another thread of control; this new thread, after dealing with some initialization details, then calls the `run()` method. After the `run()` method completes, this new thread also deals with the details of terminating the thread. The `start()` method of the original thread returns immediately. Thus, the `run()` method will be executing in the newly formed thread at about the same time the `start()` method returns in the first thread, as shown in Figure 2-2.

Here are the methods of the Thread class we've discussed so far:

Thread()
    Constructs a thread object using default values for all options.

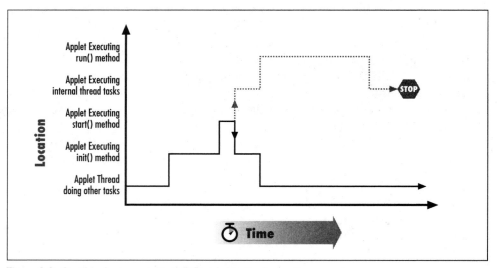

Figure 2-2. Graphical representation of threaded method execution

void run()

> The method that the newly created thread will execute. The developer should override this method with the code they want the new thread to run.[*]

void start()

> Creates a new thread and executes the run() method defined in this thread class.

To review, creating another thread of control is a two-step process. First, we must create the code that executes in the new thread by overriding the run() method in our subclass. Then we create the actual subclassed object using its constructor (which calls the default constructor of the Thread class in this case) and begin execution of its run() method by calling the start() method of the subclass.

Animate Applet

Let's see a more concrete example of this. When you want to show an animation in your Web page, you do so by displaying a series of images (frames) with a time interval between the frames. This use of a timer is one of the most common places in Java where a separate thread is required: because there are no asynchronous signals in Java, you must set up a separate thread, have the thread sleep for a period of time, and then have the thread tell the applet to paint the next frame.

---

[*] If this method is not overridden, the run() method of the Thread class will be executed, which will not do anything useful in this example.

run() vs. main()

In essence, the `run()` method may be thought of as the `main()` method of the newly formed thread: a new thread begins execution with the `run()` method in the same way a program begins execution with the `main()` method.

While the `main()` method receives its arguments from the `argv` parameter (which is typically set from the command line), the newly created thread must receive its arguments programmatically from the originating thread. Hence, parameters can be passed in via the constructor, static instance variables, or any other technique designed by the developer.

An implementation of this timer follows:[*]

```
import java.awt.*;

public class TimerThread extends Thread {
    Component comp;        // Component that need repainting
    int timediff;          // Time between repaints of the component

    public TimerThread(Component comp, int timediff) {
        this.comp = comp;
        this.timediff = timediff;
    }

    public void run() {
        while (true) {
            try {
                comp.repaint();
                sleep(timediff);
            } catch (Exception e) {}
        }
    }
}
```

In this example, the TimerThread class, just like the OurClass class, inherits from the Thread class and overrides the `run()` method. Its constructor stores the component on which to call the `repaint()` method and the requested time interval between the calls to the `repaint()` method.

---

* Appendix C shows another technique to do this where the separate thread is hidden from the programmer.

What we have not seen so far is the call to the `sleep()` method:

static void sleep (long milliseconds)
> Puts the current executing thread to sleep for the specified number of milliseconds. This method is static and may be accessed through the Thread class name.

static void sleep (long milliseconds, int nanoseconds)
> Puts the current executing thread to sleep for the specified number of milliseconds and nanoseconds. This method is static and may be accessed through the Thread class name.

The `sleep()` method is part of the Thread class, and it causes the current thread (the thread that made the call to the `sleep()` method) to pause for the specified amount of time in milliseconds. The try statement in the code example is needed due to some of the exceptions that are thrown from the `sleep()` method.[*] The

---

sleep(long) and sleep(long, int)

The Thread class provides a version of the `sleep()` method that allows the developer to specify the time in terms of nanoseconds. Unfortunately, most operating systems that implement the Java virtual machine do not support a resolution as small as a nanosecond. For those platforms, the method simply rounds the number of nanoseconds to the nearest millisecond, and calls the version of the `sleep()` method which only specifies milliseconds. In fact, most operating systems do not support a resolution of a single millisecond, so that the milliseconds are in turn rounded up to the smallest resolution that the platform supports.

For the developer, we should note that support of nanoseconds may never be available in all versions of the Java virtual machine. As a matter of policy, we should not design applets that require support of nanoseconds (or even exact timing of milliseconds) in order to function correctly.

---

easiest description of the task of the `sleep()` method is that the caller actually sleeps for the specified amount of time. The reason this method is part of the Thread class is because of how the methods accomplish the task: the current (i.e.,

---

[*] Exceptions thrown by the Thread class will be discussed in Appendix A. For now, we'll catch and discard all exceptions.

calling) thread is placed in a "blocked" state for the specified amount of time, much like the state* it would be in if the thread were waiting of I/O to occur.

To return to step 2 of the two-step process: let's take a look at the Animate applet that uses our TimerThread class:

```java
import java.applet.*;
import java.awt.*;

public class Animate extends Applet {
    int count, lastcount;
    Image pictures[];
    TimerThread timer;

    public void init() {
        lastcount = 10; count = 0;
        pictures = new Image[10];
        MediaTracker tracker = new MediaTracker(this);
        for (int a = 0; a < lastcount; a++) {
            pictures[a] = getImage (
                getCodeBase(), new Integer(a).toString()+".jpeg");
            tracker.addImage(pictures[a], 0);
        }
        tracker.checkAll(true);
    }

    public void start() {
        timer = new TimerThread(this, 1000);
        timer.start();
    }

    public void stop() {
        timer.stop();
        timer = null;
    }

    public void paint(Graphics g) {
        g.drawImage(pictures[count++], 0, 0, null);

        if (count == lastcount) count = 0;
    }
}
```

Here we create and start the new thread in the applet's start() method. This new thread is responsible only for informing the applet when to redraw the next

---

* The possible "states" of threads will be discussed in Chapter 6.

frame; it is still the applet's thread that performs the redraw when the applet's `paint()` method is called.[*]

In this example, we've also introduced the Thread class's `stop()` method:

void stop()

    Terminates an already running thread.

As we can guess, the `stop()` method in the Thread class serves to stop and destroy the thread of execution. This is necessary because TimerThread, once started, does not terminate by returning from its `run()` method. Since we do not need `repaint()` requests when the applet is no longer running, there is no need to keep the thread alive. It is not too difficult to set up the program so that the TimerThread can check on whether or not it should call the `repaint()` method; for simplicity, we will just terminate the thread.[†]

The start() and stop() Methods of the Applet Class

It is unfortunate that both the Applet and the Thread classes have a `start()` and a `stop()` method, and that they have the same signature in both classes. This may be a source of confusion when implementing or debugging threaded applets.

These methods serve different purposes and are not directly related to each other.

What does the stop() method accomplish? As we mentioned, when the `run()` method completes, the thread automatically handles the cleanup process and other details of terminating the thread. The `stop()` method simply provides a way of prematurely terminating the `run()` method. The thread will then, as usual, automatically handle the cleanup process and other details of terminating the thread.[‡] Or in other words, the `stop()` method stops the thread.

---

[*] The `init()` method simply loads the image frames from the server; we won't discuss the details of the MediaTracker class here.

[†] Obviously, more complicated programs cannot be controlled by simply starting and stopping the thread on demand.

[‡] Details of the process are given in Appendix B.

Threading Using the Runnable Interface

As simple as it is to create another thread of control, there is one problem with the technique we've outlined so far. It's caused by the fact that Java classes can inherit their behavior only from a single class, which means that inheritance itself is expensive[*] to the developer. In our example, we are threading a simple loop, so this is not much of a concern. However, if we have a complete class structure that already has a detailed inheritance tree and want it run in its own thread, we cannot simply make this class structure inherit from the Thread class as we did before. One solution would be to create a new class that inherits from Thread and contains references to the instances of the classes we need. This level of indirection is an annoyance.

The Java language solves this lack of multiple inheritance with the mechanism known as interfaces.[†] This mechanism is supported by the Thread class and simply means that instead of inheriting from the Thread class, we can simply implement the Runnable interface, which is defined as follows:

```
public interface Runnable {
     public abstract void run();
}
```

The Runnable interface contains only one method: the run() method. The Thread class actually implements the Runnable interface; hence, when you inherit from the Thread class, your subclass also implements the Runnable interface. However, what we want to do in this case is to implement the Runnable interface without actually inheriting from the Thread class. This is achieved by simply substituting the phrase "implements Runnable" for the phrase "extends Thread"; no other changes are necessary in step 1 of our thread creation process.

```
public class OurClass implements Runnable {
    public void run() {
        for (int I = 0; I < 100; I++) {
            System.out.println("Hello, from another thread");
        }
    }
}
```

Step 2 of our thread creation processes has some other changes. Since an instance of the OurClass class is no longer a Thread object, it cannot be treated as one. So in order to create a separate thread of control, an instance of the Thread class is

---

* By "expensive" we mean that inheritance can be considered a scare resource because a class may only inherit from only one other class.

† It can be argued that interfaces cannot accomplish everything that multiple inheritance can, but that is a debate for a different book.

still needed, but it will be instantiated with a reference to our OurClass object. In other words, its usage is slightly more complicated:

```
import java.applet.Applet;

public class OurApplet extends Applet {
    public void init() {
        Runnable ot = new OurClass();
        Thread th = new Thread(ot);
        th.start();
    }
}
```

As before, we have to create an instance of the OurClass class. However, in this new version, we also need to create an actual Thread object. We create this object by passing our Runnable OurClass object reference to the constructor of the Thread using a new constructor of the thread class:

Thread(Runnable target)

Constructs a new thread object associated with the given Runnable object.

The new Thread object's `start()` method is called to begin execution of the new thread of control.

The reason we need to pass the Runnable object to the Thread object's constructor is that the thread must have some way to get to the `run()` method we want the thread to execute. Since we are no longer overriding the `run()` method of the Thread class, the default `run()` method of the Thread class is executed; this default `run()` method looks like this:

```
public void run() {
    if (target != null) {
        target.run();
    }
}
```

Here, `target` is the Runnable object we passed to the Thread's constructor. So the thread begins execution with the `run()` method of the Thread class which immediately calls the `run()` method of our Runnable object.

Interestingly, since we can use the Runnable interface instead of inheriting from the Thread class, we can merge the OurClass class into the applet itself. This is a common technique to spin off a separate thread of control for the applet. Since the applet itself is now Runnable, instance variables of the applet thread and the `run()` method in this newly spun off thread are the same.

```
import java.applet.Applet;

public class OurApplet extends Applet implements Runnable {
```

```
    public void init() {
        Thread th = new Thread(this);
        th.start();
    }

    public void run() {
        for (int I = 0; I < 100; I++) {
            System.out.println("Hello, from another thread");
        }
    }
}
```

This technique can also be used with our Animate class:

```
import java.applet.*;
import java.awt.*;

public class Animate5 extends Applet implements Runnable {
    int count, lastcount;
    Image pictures[];
    Thread timer;

    public void init() {
        lastcount = 10; count = 0;
        pictures = new Image[10];
        MediaTracker tracker = new MediaTracker(this);
        for (int a = 0; a < lastcount; a++) {
            pictures[a] = getImage (
                getCodeBase(), new Integer(a).toString()+".jpeg");
            tracker.addImage(pictures[a], 0);
        }
        tracker.checkAll(true);
    }

    public void start() {
        if (timer == null) {
            timer = new Thread(this);
            timer.start();
        }
    }

    public void paint(Graphics g) {
        g.drawImage(pictures[count++], 0, 0, null);
        if (count == lastcount) count = 0;
    }

    public void run() {
        while (isActive()) {
            try {
                repaint();
```

```
            Thread.sleep(1000);
        } catch (Exception e) {}
    }
    timer = null;
}
}
```

After merging the classes, we now have a direct reference to the applet, so we can call the `repaint()` method directly. Because the Animate class is not of the Thread class, its `run()` method cannot call the `sleep()` method directly. Fortunately, the `sleep()` method is a static method, so we can still access it using the Thread class specifier.

The isActive() Method

We used the `isActive()` method in the last example instead of stopping the thread explicitly. This shows another technique you can use to stop your threads; the benefit of this technique is that it allows the `run()` method to terminate normally rather than the immediate termination caused by the `stop()` method. This allows the `run()` method to clean up after itself before it terminates.

The `isActive()` method is part of the Applet class and determines if an applet is active. By definition, an applet is active between the periods of the applet's `start()` and `stop()` method. Don't confuse this method with the `isAlive()` method of the thread class that we'll discuss later.

As can be seen from this example, the threading interface model allows classes that already have fixed inheritance structures to be threaded without creating a new class. However, there is still one unanswered question: when should you use the Runnable interface and when should you create a new subclass of Thread?

Does threading by the Runnable interface solve a problem that cannot be solved through threading by inheritance or vice versa? At this point, there do not seem to be any significant differences between the two techniques. It is easier to use one technique for certain tasks and the other technique for other tasks. For example, our last Animate class saved us the need to have an extra class definition, via its use of the Runnable interface in the Applet class. In the earlier example, having a separate TimerThread definition may have been both easier to understand and to debug. But these differences are relatively minor, and there do not seem to be any tasks that cannot be solved by either technique.

At this point, we will not worry about the difference between the two techniques. We will use one technique or the other, based on personal preference and the clarity of the solution. Hopefully, as we develop examples throughout this book, you will learn to use either technique on a case-by-case basis.

Inheritance or Interfaces?

As noted, we will choose threading with inheritance or interfaces based on personal preference and the clarity of the solution. However, those of you who are object-oriented purists could argue that unless we are enhancing the Thread class, we should not inherit from the Thread class.

Theorists could insert an entire chapter on this issue. Our concern with this issue is mainly for the clarity of the code, and any other reasons for choosing between threading by inheritance or interfaces is beyond the scope of this book.

This is all there is to writing simple threaded Java programs. We have a class that allows us to define a method that will be executed in a separate thread; this thread can be controlled via its start() and stop() methods. However, as we have seen in the previous chapter, it is not just the ability to have different threads that makes the threaded system a powerful tool; it is that these threads can communicate easily with each other by invoking methods on objects that are shared between the threads. While we've looked at some simple examples of this communication, there are more complicated issues that need to be addressed when programming in a threaded environment. We'll start to look into those issues next, but we won't completely solve them without the tools we introduce in Chapter 3.

Another Example: File IO

The timer thread of the Animate applet is a useful, but simple, example of using threads. Most of the code we eventually create will be more complex than the Animate applet.

One reason the Animate applet is so simple is that the two threads are pretty much independent of each other. The applet thread simply starts the Timer-Thread when it needs the timing to occur and stops the TimerThread when it no longer needs the timer. There is no actual data being passed between the threads even though programs generally need to communicate with other programs, with users, or with the operating system. In other words, input/output is a common requirement of most programs.

Why is threading important for I/O? Whether you are reading from or writing to a file or network socket, a common problem exists. The problem is that the action of reading or writing depends on other resources. These resources may be other programs; they may be hardware, like the disk or the network; they may be the operating system or browser. These resources may become temporarily unavailable for a variety of reasons: reading from a network socket may involve waiting until the data is available, writing large amounts of data to a file may take a long period of time to complete if the disk is busy with other requests, and so on. Unfortunately, the mechanism to check whether these resources are available does not exist in the Java API. This is particularly a problem for network sockets, where data is likely to take a long time to be transmitted over the network; it is possible for a read from a network socket to wait forever.[*]

Why Asynchronous I/O?

The driving force behind asynchronous I/O is to allow the program to continue to do something useful while it is waiting for data to arrive. If I/O is not asynchronous and not running in a thread separate from the applet thread, we run into the problems we discussed in the previous chapter: mouse and keyboard events will be delayed, and the program will appear to be unresponsive to the user while the I/O completes.

The solution to this problem is to use another thread. Since this new thread is independent of the applet thread, it can block without the worry of hanging the applet. Of course, this causes a new problem: unlike the Animate applet example, when this thread finally is able to read the data, this data must be returned to the applet thread. Let's take a look at a possible implementation of a generic socket reader class that will read the socket from another thread.[†]

```java
import java.io.*;
import java.net.*;

public class AsyncReadSocket extends Thread {
    private Socket s;
    private StringBuffer result;
```

---

[*] The InputStream class does contain the `available()` method. However, this is used to check if data is available from the buffers held by the browser. This method does not work well with certain mechanisms, like the network socket.

[†] The AsyncReadSocket class provided here is for pedagogical purposes; it has various flaws. Later, in Chapter 5, we'll develop a robust, usable class called AsyncInputStream that supports the notion of asynchronous I/O.

```
    public AsyncReadSocket(Socket s) {
        this.s = s;
        result = new StringBuffer();
    }

    public void run() {
        DataInputStream is = null;
        try {
            is = new DataInputStream(s.getInputStream());
        } catch (Exception e) {}
        while (true) {
            try {
                char c = is.readChar();
                result.append(c);
            } catch (Exception e) {}
        }
    }

    // Get the string already read from the socket so far.
    // This method is used by the Applet thread to obtain the data
    //  in a synchronous manner.
    public String getResult() {
        String retval = result.toString();
        result = new StringBuffer();
        return retval;
    }
}
```

Here we have a Thread class, AsyncReadSocket, whose run() method reads characters from a socket. Whenever it gets any characters, it adds them to the StringBuffer result. If this thread hangs while reading the socket, it has no effect on the applet thread. The applet can call the getResult() method to get any data that has been received by this new thread; if no data is available, the getResult() method returns an empty string. And if the applet thread is off doing some other tasks, this socket thread simply accumulates the characters for the applet thread. In other words, the socket thread stores the data it receives at any time, while the applet thread can call the getResult() method at any time without the worry of blocking or losing data. An actual run of the two threads may look like the diagram in Figure 2-3.

One of the attractions of threaded programming is that it is simple to write many small independent tasks, and that's just what we've done here. And since these "small tasks" are contained in one program, communication between the tasks (the threads) is as simple as communication between two methods in a single program. We just need a common reference somewhere that both threads can access. That "somewhere" in this case is the result instance variable.

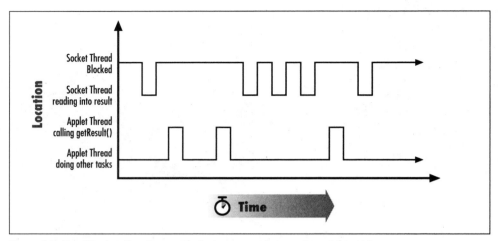

Figure 2-3. Possible time/location graph during a sample execution of the applet

However, there is a problem with this. As you might have already asked, what happens when the applet thread calls the getResult() method at the same time as the readChar() method returns with data? The answer is that we may lose data depending on the exact sequence of events. Specifically:

1. The applet thread enters the getResult() method.

2. The applet thread assigns retval to a new string created from the result StringBuffer.

3. The socket thread returns from the readChar() method.

4. The socket thread appends the character to the result StringBuffer.

5. The applet thread assigns result to a new (empty) StringBuffer.

The data that was appended to the StringBuffer in step 4 is now lost: it wasn't retrieved by the applet thread at step 2, and the applet thread discards the old StringBuffer in step 5. This type of problem is known as a "race condition," and cannot be solved without the tools that we'll learn about in Chapter 3.[*]

As for our AsyncReadSocket class, we created the ability to read a network socket asynchronously with an API that provided no such support to accomplish it. It can be argued that we are still reading the socket synchronously, it is just that we are reading it from another thread that is operating asynchronously. For all intents and purposes, that does not matter; the end result is the same. The data is being delivered to the applet in an asynchronous fashion.

---

[*] There's an additional problem: if two separate threads call the getResult() method at the same time, they could both get copies of the same data from the StringBuffer, and that data would be processed twice.

When Is a Race Condition a Problem?

A *race condition* occurs when the order of execution of two or more threads may affect some variable or outcome in the program. It may turn out that all the different possible thread orderings have the same final effect on the application: the effect caused by the race condition may be insignificant, and may not even be relevant. For example, a character lost in the AsyncReadSocket may not affect the final outcome of the program. Alternately, the timing of the threading system may be such that the race condition never manifests itself, despite the fact that it exists in the code.

A race condition is a problem that is "waiting to happen." Simple changes in the algorithm can cause race conditions to manifest themselves in problematic ways. And, since different virtual machines will have different ordering of thread execution, the developer should never let a race condition exist due to the fact that it is currently not causing a problem on the development system.

Communication operations, whether with a network socket or file, with the browser or the user, are a common reason for starting another thread. Whenever we have to execute some code that may take a long time to accomplish—either because it depends on a resource or is also responsible for doing lengthy parsing of the data—starting another thread makes it possible to accomplish the task without affecting the "reaction time" of the original thread, especially if the original thread handles interaction with the user.

Thread States/Status

While we have been starting and stopping threads in this chapter, we have yet to look at the state of the threads.[*] We simply assumed that when we called the start() method, the thread was running, and that when we called the stop() method, the thread was no longer running. While this assumption is good enough most of the time, certain cases require that we know exactly whether or not a thread is running. It is in these cases that we need to have some kind of indication of the state of the thread.[†] The reason this is necessary is because it may

---

[*] Nor are we really going to examine the states here; we will examine them in detail in Chapter 6. For now, we will take a simple look at that part of the threading API that allows us to control the flow of the threads.

[†] Actually we may need more than just an indication. Just because a thread is in a runnable state doesn't mean that a thread will actually run; we will examine this in detail later when we look at runnable states and scheduling in Chapter 6.

not be possible to be absolutely sure a thread is running. While we know that a thread is not running sometime after the `stop()` method is called, we are not sure of exactly when. And since making the assumption that a thread is not running immediately after its `stop()` method is called is technically a race condition, we should not access any of the methods or instance variables accessed by the stopped thread until we are absolutely sure the thread has stopped.

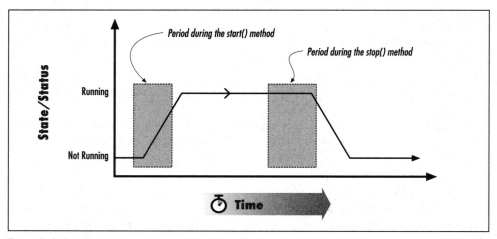

Figure 2-4. Graphical representation of the states of the thread

Why is there a race condition? The reason is because it takes time to actually `start()` and `stop()` a thread; this means that there is a transitional period from when a thread is running to when a thread is not, as shown in Figure 2-4. The `stop()` method actually returns before the thread has stopped; the race condition occurs during this time period. As an application programmer, we technically do not know what is happening during this period, nor should we care. To prevent such a race condition, all we have to do is to wait until the thread is stopped before accessing any of the shared instance variables. Let's modify our MyApplet class to wait until the timer thread stops before finishing:[*]

```
import java.applet.Applet;

public class MyApplet extends Applet {
    Thread t;
    public void start() {
        t = new TimerThread(this, 500);
        t.start();
    }
```

---

[*] This is an academic example; there is no reason to wait for the termination of the timer thread since there's no race condition between the applet thread and the timer thread.

```
public void stop() {
    t.stop();
    while (t.isAlive()) {
        try {
            Thread.sleep(100);
        } catch (InterruptedException e) {}
    }
}
}
```

The Thread class provides the isAlive() method, which is used to find out if a thread can be running:

boolean isAlive()

Determines if a thread is considered alive. By definition, a thread is considered alive sometime before a thread is actually started to sometime after a thread is actually stopped.

Just because a thread has been started does not mean it is actually running, nor that it is able to run; it is this reason that the isAlive() method is more useful in detecting whether a thread has stopped running. For example, let's examine the stop() method of this applet. Just like the earlier versions, we have a Timer-Thread object that is started and stopped when the applet is started and stopped. In this newer version, the applet's stop() method does more than just stop the TimerThread: it also checks to make sure the thread actually has stopped.

In this example, we don't gain anything by making sure the timer thread has actually stopped. But if for some reason we need to deal with common data that is being accessed by both threads, and it is critical to make sure the other thread is stopped, we can simply loop and check to make sure the thread is no longer alive before continuing. For example, in our AsyncReadSocket class, if we do not wait until the thread is stopped and simply access the "final" result being read, we might lose data. More data may actually arrive after the stop() method of the thread is called and before the thread is actually stopped.

There is another circumstance in which a thread can be considered no longer alive. If the run() method completes, the thread will also be considered no longer alive a short time later. Thus, the isAlive() method can be used to determine if the run() method has completed.

This can be thought of as a crude form of communication. We are waiting for information: the indication that the other thread has completed. As another example, if we start a couple of threads to do a long calculation, we are then free to do other tasks. Assume that sometime later we have completed all other secondary tasks and need to deal with the results of the long calculation: we need

to wait until the calculations are finished before continuing on to process the
results.

We could accomplish this task by using the looping `isAlive()` technique we've
just looked at, but there are other techniques in the Java API that are more suited
to this task. This act of waiting is called a *thread join*. We are "joining" with the
thread that was "forked" off from us earlier when we started the thread.* So, modi-
fying our last example, we have:

```
import java.applet.Applet;

public class MyApplet extends Applet {
    Thread t;
    public void start() {
        t = new TimerThread(this, 500);
        t.start();
    }

    public void stop() {
        t.stop();
        try {
            t.join();
        } catch (InterruptedException e) {}
    }
}
```

The Thread class provides the following `join()` methods:

void join()

> Waits for the completion of the specified thread. By definition, `join()`
> returns as soon as the thread is considered "not alive."

void join(long timeout)[†]

> Waits for the completion of the specified thread, but no longer than the
> timeout specified in milliseconds.

void join(long timeout, int nanos)

> Waits for the completion of the specified thread, but no longer than a
> timeout specified in milliseconds and nanoseconds.

When the `join()` method is called, the current thread will simply wait until the
thread it is joining with is no longer alive. This can be caused by the thread being
stopped by yet another thread, or by the completion of the thread itself. The
`join()` method basically accomplishes the same task as the combination of the

---

* Much like a road may fork off to separate paths that may later join back to a single path.

† Note that these timeout values will be subject to the rounding behavior as previously described in
"sleep (long) and sleep (long, int)."

sleep() and isAlive() methods we used in the earlier example. However, by using the join() method, we accomplish the same task with a single method call. We also have better control over the timeout interval, and we don't waste CPU cycles by polling.

Another interesting point about both the isAlive() method and the join() method is that we are actually not affecting the thread on which we called the method. That thread will run no differently whether the join() method is called or not; instead, it is the calling thread that is affected. The isAlive() method simply returns the status of a thread, and the join() method simply waits for a certain status on the thread.

---

this.join() and this.isAlive()

The concept of a thread calling the isAlive() or the join() method on itself does not make sense. There is no reason to check if the current thread is alive since it would not be able to "do anything about it" if it were not alive. As a matter of fact, isAlive() can only return true when it checks the status of the thread calling it. If the thread were stopped during the isAlive() method, the isAlive() method would not be able to return.

The concept of a thread joining itself does not make sense, but let's examine what happens when one tries. It turns out that the join() method uses the isAlive() method to determine when to return from the join() method. In the current implementation, it also does not check to see if the thread is joining itself. In other words, the join() method returns when and only when the thread is no longer alive. This will have the effect of waiting forever.

Thread Naming

The next topic we will examine concerns the thread support classes that are used mainly for thread "bookkeeping." First, it is possible to assign a String name to the Thread object itself:

void setName(String name)
> Assigns a name to the Thread instance.

String getName()
> Gets the name of the Thread instance.

Provided with the Thread class is a method that allows us to attach a name to the thread object and a method that allows us to retrieve the name. The system does not use this string for any specific purpose.* The developer who assigned the name is free to use this string for any purpose desired. For example, let's assign a name to our TimerThread class:

```java
import java.awt.*;

public class TimerThread extends Thread {
    Component comp;           // Component that need repainting
    int timediff;             // Time between repaints of the component

    public TimerThread(Component comp, int timediff) {
        this.comp = comp;
        this.timediff = timediff;
        setName("TimerThread(" + timediff + " milliseconds)");
    }

    public void run() {
        while (true) {
            try {
                comp.repaint();
                sleep(timediff);
            } catch (Exception e) {}
        }
    }
}
```

In this version of the TimerThread class, we assigned a name to the thread. The name that is assigned is simply "TimerThread" followed by the number of milliseconds used in this timer thread. If the getName() method is later called on this instance, this string value will be returned.

Uses for a Thread Name?

Using the thread name to store information is not too beneficial. We could just as easily have added an instance variable to the Thread class (if we're threading by inheritance), or to the Runnable type class (if we're threading by interfaces), and achieved the same results. The best use of this name is probably for debugging. With an assigned name, the debugger displays thread information in terms of a "logical" name instead of a number.

By default, if no name is assigned, the Thread class chooses a unique name. This name is generally "Thread-" followed by a unique number.

---

* At this point, this string may be used by certain debuggers and development systems. Also, if you print a thread object, the name of the thread will be part of the information that is printed.

The naming support is also available as a constructor of the Thread class:

Thread(String name)

Constructs a thread object with a name that is already assigned. This constructor is generally used when threading by inheritance.

Thread(Runnable target, String name)

Constructs a thread object that is associated with the given Runnable object and is created with a name that is already assigned. This constructor is generally used when threading by interfaces.

Just like the setName() method, setting the name via the thread constructor is simple to use. One constructor is provided for threading by inheritance and another for threading by interfaces. In our TimerThread example, since we are setting the name in the constructor, we could just as easily have used the Thread constructor instead of the setName() method:

```
import java.awt.*;

public class TimerThread extends Thread {
    Component comp;          // Component which need repainting
    int timediff;           // Time between repaints of the component

    public TimerThread(Component comp, int timediff) {
        super("TimerThread(" + timediff + " milliseconds)");
        this.comp = comp;
        this.timediff = timediff;
    }

    public void run() {
        while (true) {
            try {
                comp.repaint();
                sleep(timediff);
            } catch (Exception e) {}
        }
    }
}
```

Thread Access

The currentThread() method is the next method of the Thread class that we'll examine:

static Thread currentThread()

Gets the Thread object that represents the current thread of execution. The method is static and may be called through the Thread class name.

This is a static method of the Thread class, and it simply returns a Thread object that represents the current thread.[*] The object returned is the same thread object first created for the current thread.

But why is this method important? The Thread object for the current thread may not be saved anywhere, and even if it is, it may not be accessible to the called method. For example, let's assume that in our AsyncReadSocket class, what is returned in the getResult() method depends on which thread calls the method. If we only wanted to allow certain types of threads, deemed *reader* threads, to get the result we read asynchronously, a possible implementation would be as follows:

```java
import java.io.*;
import java.net.*;

public class AsyncReadSocket extends Thread {
    // Constructor and variables not shown

    public void run() {
        // run() method not shown
    }

    // Get the string already read from the socket so far.
    //   Only allows "Reader" threads to execute this method
    public String getResult() {
        String reader = Thread.currentThread().getName();
        if (reader.startsWith("Reader")) {
            String retval = result.toString();
            result = new StringBuffer();
            return retval;
        } else {
            return "";
        }
    }
}
```

In this version of the AsyncReadSocket class, we are assuming that reader threads are threads whose name starts with "Reader." This name could have been assigned by the setName() method earlier or when the threads are constructed. To obtain a name, we need simply to call the getName() method. However, since we do not have the Thread object reference of the caller, we must call the current-Thread()[†] method to obtain the reference. In this case, we are using the name of the thread, but we could just as easily have used the thread reference for other purposes. Other uses with the thread reference could be priority control or thread groups. These and other services are described in upcoming chapters

---

* The "current thread" is the thread that made the call to the currentThread() method.

† Because the AsyncReadSocket class is a subclass of the thread class, we could have called the current-Thread() method without the Thread qualifier.

Also provided with the Thread class are methods that allow you to obtain a list of all the threads of the program:

static int enumerate(Thread threadArray[])

Gets all the Thread objects of the program and stores the result into the thread array. The value returned is the number of thread objects stored into the array. The method is static and may be called through the Thread class name.

static int activeCount()

Returns the number of threads in the program. The method is static and may be called through the Thread class name.

This list is retrieved with the `enumerate()` method. The developer simply needs to create a Thread array and pass it as a parameter. The `enumerate()` method stores the thread references into the array and returns the number of thread objects stored.[*]

In order to size the array for the `enumerate()` method, it is possible to determine the number of threads in the program. With the `activeCount()` method, we can determine the number of threads in the applet. This value sizes the Thread array to exactly the number of threads in the program. For example, we could add a support method to our Animate applet that prints all the threads[†] in the applet as follows:

```
import java.applet.*;
import java.awt.*;

public class Animate extends Applet {
    // Instance variables and methods not shown

    public void printThreads() {
        Thread ta[] = new Thread[Thread.activeCount()];

        int n = Thread.enumerate(ta);
        for (int i = 0; i < n; i++) {
            System.out.println("Thread " + i + " is " +
                    ta[i].getName());
        }
    }
}
```

---

[*] In general, the `enumerate()` method returns either the number of threads in the program or the size of the array, whichever is smaller.

[†] "All" the threads in the applet is a somewhat misleading term. We'll clear that up in Chapter 8.

In this example, we are instantiating a Thread array; the size of the array is determined by the `activeCount()` method of the Thread class. Once we have an active count, we call the `enumerate()` method to obtain references to all the thread objects in our applet. In the rest of the method, we simply print the name assigned to each thread by calling the `getName()` method on the Thread reference.

Trivia: When Is a Thread Active?

When is a thread active? At first glance, this seems to be a simple question. Using the `isAlive()` method, a thread is considered alive during the period between the call to the `start()` method to a small time period after the `stop()` method is called. We might consider a thread active if it is alive.

However, if the definition of a active thread is a thread whose Thread reference appears in the active count returned by the `activeCount()` method, we would have a different definition of active. A thread reference first appears in the thread array returned by the `enumerate()` method, and is counted by the `activeCount()` method, when the Thread object is first constructed and not when the thread is started.

The thread is removed from the thread array when the thread is either stopped or when the `run()` method has completed. This means that if a Thread object is constructed but is not started, the thread object will not be removed from the enumeration list, even if the original reference to the object is lost.

More on start(), stop(), and join()

Consider this revision to the MyApplet example:

```
import java.applet.Applet;

public class MyApplet extends Applet {
    Thread t;
    public void start() {
        if (t == null)
            t = new TimerThread(this, 500);
        t.start();
    }

    public void stop() {
        t.stop();
        try {
            t.join();
```

```
            } catch (InterruptedException e) {}
        }
    }
```

In our last version of the MyApplet applet (see the section "Thread States/Status"), the start() method of the applet created a new TimerThread object and started it. But what if we had only created the TimerThread once? In the example above, we once again create a new TimerThread in the start() method of the applet; however, since we know the thread will be stopped in the stop() method, we try to restart the stopped thread in the start() method. In other words, we only create the TimerThread once, and use this one thread object to start() and stop(). By starting and stopping a single TimerThread, we do not need to create a new instance of TimerThread every time the applet is started, and the garbage collector will not need to clean up the TimerThread instance that's left when the applet is stopped and the TimerThread de-referenced.

But will this work? Unfortunately, the answer is no. It turns out that when a thread is stopped, the state of the thread object is set so that it is not restartable. In our case, when we try to restart the thread by calling the TimerThread's start() method, nothing happens. The start() method won't return an exception condition, but the run() method also won't be called. The isAlive() method also won't return true. In other words, never restart a thread. An instance of a thread object should be used once and only once.

More Details for Restarting a Thread

What happens when you try to restart a thread? The answer is that it actually depends on when you restart it. When the stop() method is called on a thread, it actually takes time for the thread to stop. Hence, what happens when the start() method is called depends on a race condition.

If the start() method is called before the stopping thread actually stops, an error condition exists, and an exception will be thrown. The same is true if you call start() on a thread object that has not been stopped.

If the start() method is called after the stopping thread has actually stopped, nothing happens: the thread object is in a state where it cannot be restarted.

Can an already stopped thread be stopped? At first glance, this may seem an odd question. But the answer is yes, and the reason is that it avoids a race condition that would occur otherwise. We know there are two ways a thread can be stopped, so you could stop a thread that has already exited because its run() method terminated normally. If the Thread class did not allow the `stop()` method to be called on a stopped thread, this would require us to check if the thread was still running before we stopped it, and we'd have to avoid a race condition where the `run()` method could terminate in between the time when we checked if the thread was alive and called the `stop()` method. This would be a big burden on the Java developer, so, instead, you're allowed to call the `stop()` method on a thread that has already stopped.

The Stopping Thread and the Garbage Collector

The thread object, like any other object, is a candidate for garbage collection when it gets dereferenced. As developers, we should just note that the garbage collector behaves with the threading system correctly and not worry about the exact details. However, for those of us who are detail-oriented, here is how the garbage collector behaves with the threading system.

In all the examples so far, the garbage collector cannot collect the thread object even when the thread has completed or stopped. This is because we still have a reference to the TimerThread object after we called the `stop()` method. To be complete, we should manually dereference the thread object after we call the `stop()` method. However, this is necessary only to free the memory that stores the thread object. The threading system automatically releases any thread-specific resources (including those tied to the operating system) after the thread has completed or stopped whether or not we dereference the object.

Dereferencing a thread object for a running thread is also not a problem. The threading system keeps references to all threads that are running in the system. This is needed in order to support the `currentThread()` and `enumerate()` methods of the Thread class. The garbage collector will not be able to collect the thread object until the threading system also dereferences the object, which won't happen until the thread is no longer alive.

What happens when we call the join() method for a thread that was stopped a long time ago? In the examples so far, we assumed the usage of the `join()` method was to wait for a thread to complete or to stop. But this assumption is not necessary; if the thread is already stopped, it will return immediately. This may seem obvious, but it should be noted that a race condition would have resulted if the `join()` method had required that the thread be alive when the method was first called.

What would be the best way to join() with more than one thread? Let's look at the following code:

```
import java.applet.Applet;

public class MyJoinApplet extends Applet {
    Thread t[] = new Thread[30];
    public void start() {
        for (int i=0; i<30; i++) {
            t[i] = new CalcThread(i);
            t[i].start();
        }
    }

    public void stop() {
        for (int i=0; i<30; i++) {
            try {
                t[i].join();
            } catch (InterruptedException e) {}
        }
    }
}
```

In this example, we start 30 CalcThread objects. We have not actually defined the CalcThread class, but for this example, we assume it is a class that is used to calculate part of a large mathematical algorithm. In the applet's `stop()` method, we execute a loop waiting for all the started threads to be finished. Is this the best way to wait for more than one thread? Since it is possible to `join()` with an already stopped thread, it is perfectly okay to `join()` with a group of threads in a loop, even if the threads finish in a different order than the order in which they were started. No matter how we could have coded the `join()` loop, the time to complete the `join()` will be the time it takes for the last thread to finish.

Of course, there may be cases where a specific joining mechanism is desired, but this depends on details other than the threading system. For all intents and purposes, there should be little performance penalty to pay for joining in an order that is not the order of completion.

Summary

Here's a list of the methods of the Thread class we introduced in this chapter:

Thread()
> Constructs a thread object using default values for all options.

Thread(Runnable target)
> Constructs a new thread object associated with the given Runnable object.

Thread(String name)
> Constructs a thread object with a name that is already assigned. This constructor is generally used when threading by inheritance.

Thread(Runnable target, String name)

Constructs a thread object that is associated with the given Runnable object and is created with a name that is already assigned. This constructor is generally used when threading by interfaces.

void run()

The method that the newly created thread will execute. The developer should override this method with the code they want the new thread to run.

void start()

Creates a new thread and executes the run() method defined in this thread class.

void stop()

Terminates an already running thread.

static void sleep (long milliseconds)

Puts the current executing thread to sleep for the specified number of milliseconds. This method is static and may be accessed through the Thread class name.

static void sleep (long milliseconds, int nanoseconds)

Puts the current executing thread to sleep for the specified number of milliseconds and nanoseconds. This method is static and may be accessed through the Thread class name.

boolean isAlive()

Determines if a thread is considered alive. By definition, a thread is considered alive sometime before a thread is actually started to sometime after a thread is actually stopped.

void join()

Waits for the completion of the specified thread. By definition, join() returns as soon as the thread is considered "not alive."

void join(long timeout)

Waits for the completion of the specified thread, but no longer than the timeout specified in milliseconds.

void join(long timeout, int nanos)

Waits for the completion of the specified thread, but no longer than a timeout specified in milliseconds and nanoseconds.

void setName(String name)

Assigns a name to the Thread instance.

String getName()

Gets the name of the Thread instance.

static Thread currentThread()

> Gets the Thread object that represents the current thread of execution. The method is static and may be called through the Thread class name.

static int enumerate(Thread threadArray[])

> Gets all the Thread objects of the program and stores the result into the thread array. The value returned is the number of thread objects stored into the array. The method is static and may be called through the Thread class name.

static int activeCount()

> Returns the number of threads in the program. The method is static and may be called through the Thread class name.

In this chapter, we have had our first taste of creating, starting, and stopping threads. This is achieved through the methods of the Thread class. However, there are other issues that must be dealt with when it comes to threads: most notably, that communication between the individual threads must avoid the race conditions we outlined. This issue of communication, or synchronization, will be discussed in the next chapter.

We have also examined a simple form of communication that involves waiting for the completion of other threads. Using certain methods of the Thread class API, we can check if another thread is alive or simply wait until another thread has finished its execution before continuing.

3

Synchronization Techniques

The previous chapter covered a lot of ground. We used threads to solve some significant problems, including adding a timer to an animation applet and reading from a network socket asynchronously. The only problem that we left unresolved was a race condition that existed in the AsyncReadSocket class. This condition occurred when two separate threads needed to pass data between each other.

In this chapter, we examine a mechanism that solves this race condition. We will see how this mechanism can be used not only to coordinate access to data, but also for many problems in which *synchronization* is needed between threads. Before we start, let's introduce a few concepts.

A Banking Example

As an application designer for a major bank, we are assigned to the development team for the automated teller machine (ATM). As the first assignment, we are given the task of designing and implementing the routine that allows a user to withdraw cash from the ATM. A first and simple attempt at an algorithm may be as follows:

1. Check to make sure that the user has enough cash in the bank account to allow the withdrawal to occur. If the user does not, then go to step 4.

2. Subtract the amount withdrawn from the user's account.

3. Dispense the cash from the teller machine to the user.

4. Print the result/receipt for the user.

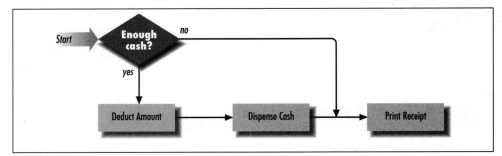

Figure 3-1. Algorithm flowchart for ATM withdrawal

Given this very simple algorithm, an implementation may be as follows:

```
public class AutomatedTellerMachine extends Teller {
    public void withdraw(float amount) {
        Account a = getAccount();
        if (a.deduct(amount))
            dispense(amount);
        printReceipt();
    }
}

public class Account {
    private float total;
    public boolean deduct(float t) {
        if (t <= total) {
            total -= t;
            return true;
        }
        return false;
    }
}
```

Of course, we are assuming that the Teller class along with the `getAccount()`, `dispense()`, and `printReceipt()` methods have already been implemented. For our purposes, we are simply examining this algorithm at a high level, so they will not be implemented here.

During our testing, we run a few simple and short tests of the routine. These tests involve withdrawing some cash. In certain cases, we withdraw a small amount. In other cases, we withdraw a large amount. We withdraw with enough in the account to cover the transaction, and we withdraw without enough cash in the account to cover the transaction. In each case, the code worked as desired. Being proud of our routine, we send it to a local branch for beta testing.

As it turns out, it is possible for two people to have access to the same account (e.g., a joint account). One day, a husband and wife both decided to empty the same account, and purely by chance, they emptied the account at the same time. Just as in the last chapter, we have a race condition: if the two users withdraw from the bank at the exact same time, causing the methods to be called at the exact same time, it is possible for the two ATMs to confirm that the account has enough cash and dispense it to both parties. In the last chapter, we wanted to solve the race condition caused by two threads; it is no different here. The two users are causing two threads to access the account database at the same time.

Definition: Atomic

Related to the atom, once considered the smallest unit of matter possible, unable to be broken into separate parts. When a routine is considered *atomic*, it means that the routine cannot be interrupted during its execution. This can either be accomplished in hardware or simulated in software. In general, atomic instructions are provided in hardware that is used to simulate atomic routines in software.

In our case, we define an atomic routine as one that can't be found in an intermediate state. In our banking example, if the acts of "checking on the account" and "changing the account status" were atomic, it would not be possible for another thread to check on the same account until the first thread had finished changing the account status.

The reason that there is a race condition is because the action of checking the account and changing the account status is not *atomic*. Here we have the husband thread and the wife thread competing for the account:

1. The husband thread begins to execute the `deduct()` method.
2. The husband thread confirms that the total in the account is less than the amount to deduct.
3. The wife thread begins to execute the `deduct()` method.
4. The wife thread confirms that the total in the account is less than the amount to deduct.
5. The wife thread performs the subtraction statement to deduct the amount, returns true, and the ATM dispenses her cash.

6. The husband thread performs the subtraction statement to deduct the amount, returns true, and the ATM dispenses his cash.

As it turns out, the Java specification provides certain mechanisms that deal specifically with this problem. The Java language provides the synchronized keyword; compared to other threading systems, this keyword allows the programmer access to a resource that is very similar to a *mutex lock*. For our purposes, it simply prevents two or more threads calling our deduct() method at the same time.[*]

```java
public class Account {
    private float total;
    public synchronized boolean deduct(float t) {
        if (t <= total) {
            total -= t;
            return true;
        }
        return false;
    }
}
```

By declaring the method as synchronized, if two users decide to withdraw from the ATM at the exact same time, the first user executes the deduct() method while the second user waits until the first user completes the deduct() method. Since only one user may execute the deduct() method at a time, there cannot be a race condition.

Definition: Mutex Lock

Also known as the *mutually exclusive lock*. This type of lock is provided by many threading systems as a means of synchronization. Basically, it is only possible for one thread to grab a mutex at a time: if two threads try to grab a mutex, only one succeeds. The other thread has to wait until the first thread releases the lock; it can then grab the lock and continue operation.

With Java, there is a lock created with every object in the system. When a method is declared synchronized, the executing thread must grab the lock assigned to the object before it can continue. Upon completion of the method, the mechanism automatically releases the lock.

Under the covers, the concept of synchronization is simple: when a method is declared as synchronized, it must have a *token*, which we call a *lock*. Once the

---

[*] We are just introducing the "synchronized" keyword here; by no means is this example an efficient use of this keyword.

method has this token checked out, acquired, or grabbed, it executes the method and returns or releases the token once the method is finished.[*] There is only one lock per object, so if two separate threads try to call synchronized methods of the same object, only one can execute the method immediately; the other thread has to wait until the first thread releases the lock before it can execute the method.

AsyncReadSocket Class Revisited

Let's return to our AsyncReadSocket example. Can we use the Java synchronization primitives we just introduced to solve our race condition problem? Yes, we can. Let's review the problem with our AsyncReadSocket class: as you may recall, the race condition occurred in the access of the `result` variable. Not only was it a problem for two separate threads to get the `result` variable at the same time, but the AsyncReadSocket thread also appended data to the `result` string itself. If the `run()` method is appending data when the `getResult()` method is called, data may also be lost.

If all actions on the `result` variable were atomic, our race condition problem would be solved. In other words, in order to solve our race condition problem, all access to the `result` variable should be placed in separate methods that are declared synchronized. A new implementation of the AsyncReadSocket class follows:

```
import java.net.*;
import java.io.*;

public class AsyncReadSocket extends Thread {
    private Socket s;
    private StringBuffer result;

    public AsyncReadSocket(Socket s) {
        this.s = s;
        result = new StringBuffer();
    }

    public void run() {
        DataInputStream is = null;
        try {
            is = new DataInputStream(s.getInputStream());
        } catch (Exception e) {}
        while (true) {
            try {
                char c = is.readChar();
```

---

[*] There are many ways to return from a method—including by throwing an exception. In every case, the lock is released when the method returns.

```
                    appendResult(c);
            } catch (Exception e) {}
        }
    }

    public synchronized String getResult() {
        String retval = result.toString();
        result = new StringBuffer();
        return retval;
    }

    public synchronized void appendResult(char c) {
        result.append(c)
    }
}
```

Applying the Java synchronization primitive, our new version of the AsyncRead-Socket class no longer has the race conditions we've been talking about. The getResult() method is now synchronized because we need to change the value of the result instance variable. A new method, appendResult(), has also been created. This method is needed is because the run() method needs to append characters to the result instance variable. Since synchronizing the run() method creates a lock scope (see Definition) that prevents the getResult() method from running, a new method is created for the purpose of grabbing the lock only for the scope that we need locked. At this point, we might have introduced more questions than answers. So before we continue, let's try to answer some of these questions.

Definition: Scope of a Lock

The *scope of a lock* is defined as the period of time between when the lock is grabbed and released. In our examples so far, we have used only synchronized methods; this means that the scope of these locks is the period of time it takes to execute these methods. This is referred to as *method scope*.

Later in this chapter, we examine locks that apply to any block of code inside a method or that can be explicitly grabbed and released; these locks have a different scope. We'll examine this concept as locks of various types are introduced.

How does synchronizing two different methods prevent the two threads calling those methods from stepping on each other? As stated earlier, synchronizing a method has the effect of making the method atomic. This means that it is not possible to execute the same method in another thread while the method is already running. However, the implementation of this mechanism is done by a lock that is assigned to the object itself. The reason another thread cannot execute the same method at the same time is because the method requires the lock that is already held by the first thread. If two different synchronized methods of the same object are called, they also behave in the same fashion. The reason is because they both require the lock of the same object, and it is not possible for both methods to grab the lock at the same time. In other words, even if two or more methods are involved, they will never be run in parallel in separate threads. This is illustrated in Figure 3-2: when thread 1 and thread 2 attempt to acquire the same lock (L1), thread 2 must wait until thread 1 releases the lock before it can continue to execute.

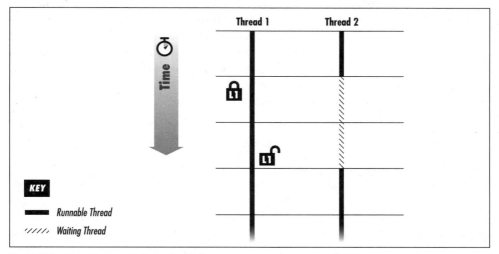

Figure 3-2. Acquiring and releasing a lock

The point to remember here is that the lock is based on a specific object and not on any particular method. Assume that we have two AsyncReadSocket objects called a and b that have been created in separate threads. One thread executes the `a.getResult()` method while the other thread executes the `b.getResult()` method. These two methods can execute in parallel because the call to `a.getResult()` grabs the object lock associated with the instance variable a, and the call to `b.getResult()` grabs the object lock associated with the instance variable b. Since the two objects are different objects, two different locks are grabbed by the two threads: neither thread has to wait for the other.

Why does synchronizing the run() method in the example yield a lock scope that is too large? The scope of the `run()` method is infinite, since the `run()` method executes an infinite loop. If both the `run()` method and `getResult()` method are synchronized, they cannot run in parallel in separate threads. Since the `run()` method has the task of opening the network socket and reading all the data from the socket until the connection is closed, it needs the object lock for the duration of the read. This means that for the duration of the read, it's not possible to execute the getResult() method. This is not a desired effect for a class that is supposed to read the data asynchronously.

How does a synchronized method behave in conjunction with a nonsynchronized method? Simply put, a synchronized method tries to grab the object lock, and a nonsynchronized method doesn't. This means it is possible for many nonsynchronized methods to run in parallel with a synchronized method. Only one synchronized method runs at a time.

Synchronizing a method just means the lock is grabbed when that method executes. It is the developer's responsibility to ensure that the correct methods are synchronized. Forgetting to synchronize a method can cause a race condition: if we had only synchronized the getResult() method of the AsyncReadSocket class and forgot to synchronize the appendResult() method, we would not have solved the race condition, since any thread could call the appendResult() method while the getResult() method was executing.

The Synchronized Class

Why do we need a new keyword to solve a race condition? Could we reengineer the algorithm so that the race condition does not exist? Let's see if we can solve this problem using trial and error.[*] At first glance, the easiest way to make sure that the two threads do not try to change the result variable, or any buffer at the same time, is to use the concept of a busy flag: if a thread needs to access the result variable, it must set the flag to busy. If the flag is already busy, the thread must wait until the flag is free, at which point it must set the flag to busy. The thread is then free to access the buffer without fear of it being accessed by the other thread. Once the task is completed, the thread must set the flag to not busy.

Here's a possible implementation of the busy flag:

```
public class BusyFlag {
    private Thread busyflag = null;

    public void getBusyFlag () {
        while (busyflag != Thread.currentThread()) {
            if (busyflag == null)
                busyflag = Thread.currentThread();
            try {
                Thread.sleep(100);
```

---

[*] Obviously, not a good programming technique; but hopefully, useful for our purposes.

```
                        } catch (Exception e) {}
                }
        }

        public void freeBusyFlag () {
                if (busyflag == Thread.currentThread()) {
                        busyflag = null;
                }
        }
}
```

This BusyFlag class contains two methods. The method getBusyFlag() sits in a loop until it is able to set the busyflag to the current thread. As long as the busyflag is set to another thread, our thread waits for 100 milliseconds. As soon as the flag is set to null, our thread sets it to the current thread. The other method, freeBusyFlag(), frees the flag by setting it back to null. This implementation seems to solve the problem and solve it simply and elegantly. But it does not.

First, why do we need to sleep for 100 milliseconds? Because there seems to be no way to detect changes in the flag without a polling loop. However, a polling loop that does not sleep() simply wastes CPU cycles that can be used by other threads.[*] On the other extreme, it takes a minimum of 100 milliseconds to set the busy flag even if no thread is holding the flag in the first place. A possible enhancement that addresses this problem may be as simple as making the sleep time a variable, but no matter what we configure the time to be, we will be balancing whether we want to be able to set the flag in a decent amount of time versus the CPU cycles wasted in a polling loop.

Second, why do we sleep for 100 milliseconds even if the flag is not set? This is actually intentional. There is a race condition between the check to see if the flag is null and setting the flag. If two threads find the flag is free, they can each set the flag and exit the loop. By calling the sleep() method, we allow the two threads to set busyflag before checking it again in the while loop. This way, only the second thread that sets the flag can exit the loop, and hence exit the getBusyFlag() method.

Of course, this is still a problem. As unlikely as it seems, it is still possible that this order of execution might occur:

1. Thread A detects that the busyflag is free.

2. Thread B detects that the busyflag is free.

3. Thread B sets the busyflag.

---

* It is actually a little more complicated than that due to issues surrounding the scheduling of threads that we'll discuss in Chapter 6.

4. Thread B sleeps for 100 milliseconds.

5. Thread B wakes up, confirms that it has the busyflag, and exits the loop.

6. Thread A sets the busyflag, sleeps, wakes up, confirms it has the busyflag, and exits the loop.

This is an extremely unlikely occurrence, but a possible occurrence nonetheless, and hence this code is not one most programmers are willing to accept.

Finally, what if multiple threads set the busyflag at the exact same moment? Is the act of setting the busyflag variable atomic? In this example, there is an explicit guarantee within the Java specification that states it must be atomic. At the present time, the guarantee does not apply to variables that are doubles or longs, but that may change in the future.

We could use the BusyFlag class to replace the synchronized method in our Account class like this:

```
public class Account {
    private float total;
    private flag = new BusyFlag();

    public boolean deduct(float t) {
        boolean succeed = false;
        flag.getBusyFlag();
        if (t <= total) {
            total -= t;
            succeed = true;
        }
        flag.freeBusyFlag();
        return succeed;
    }
}
```

The vast majority of the time, this BusyFlag class works. However, even if you ran a huge beta test across 100 bank ATMs for a period of one year without a single problem, would you be willing to bet your career on a AutomatedTeller class that uses our BusyFlag class?

Can we fix our BusyFlag class with the synchronization primitives? The problems that we encountered in the BusyFlag class are the same problems the BusyFlag class was meant to solve in the first place. This means that we can fix the problems in the BusyFlag class by using the synchronization primitives; we could use the BusyFlag class to solve other race conditions without worrying that it might break under certain conditions. The implementation (still not optimal) that solves this problem follows:

```
public class BusyFlag {
    private Thread busyflag = null;
    public void getBusyFlag() {
        while (tryGetBusyFlag() == false) {
            try {
                Thread.sleep(100);
            } catch (Exception e) {}
        }
    }

    public synchronized boolean tryGetBusyFlag() {
        if (busyflag == null) {
            busyflag = Thread.currentThread();
            return true;
        }
        return false;
    }

    public synchronized void freeBusyFlag() {
        if (busyflag == Thread.currentThread()) {
            busyflag = null;
        }
    }
}
```

In this implementation of the BusyFlag class, we introduced a new method called tryGetBusyFlag(). It is essentially the same as the getBusyFlag() method except that it does not wait until the flag is free. If the flag is free, it sets the flag and returns true. Otherwise it returns false. You'll notice that this method is declared as synchronized. This means the system makes sure the thread that makes the call to the tryGetBusyFlag() method has grabbed the object lock during the execution of the method.

The freeBusyFlag() method is also declared as synchronized: the thread that made the method call must also grab the object lock before it can continue. Since there is only one object lock for each instance of the class, the lock freeBusy-Flag() will try to grab is the same lock tryGetBusyFlag() will grab. This means that there will be no race condition between threads trying to get the busyflag and the thread that frees the busyflag.

The Synchronized Block

Notice that the original getBusyFlag() method is not declared as synchronized. This is because it's not necessary: it does not try to access the busyflag variable. Instead, it calls the tryGetBusyFlag() method, which accesses the busyflag and is, of course, synchronized. Let's take another look at the getBusyFlag()

method, one that does not call the `tryGetBusyFlag()` method. Instead, this version gets the `busyflag` directly:

```
public synchronized void getBusyFlag() {
    while (true) {
        if (busyflag == null) {
            busyflag = Thread.currentThread();
            break;
        }
        try {
            Thread.sleep(100);
        } catch (Exception e) {}
    }
}
```

Let's assume that we do not want the inefficiency of an extra method call to the `tryGetBusyFlag()` method. In our new version of the `getBusyFlag()` method, we now access the `busyflag` directly. The `getBusyFlag()` method simply loops waiting for the flag to be freed, sets the flag, and returns. Since we are now accessing the `busyflag` directly, we must make the method synchronized, or we will have a race condition.

Why Have the BusyFlag Class at All?

Fixing the race conditions in the BusyFlag class seems more like an academic exercise at this moment. While using the synchronization mechanism is perfectly valid for fixing the problem in the BusyFlag class, why would you then want to use the BusyFlag class in place of the synchronization mechanism?

For all the cases we encountered so far, we wouldn't. One of the answers lies in the scope of the lock: the synchronization mechanism does not allow us to lock code at certain scopes. We will encounter cases where the scope of the lock cannot be solved by the synchronized mechanism. In addition, the concepts of the BusyFlag class will be useful to implement other mechanisms that we'll be exploring throughout the rest of this book. For now, we will have to take it on faith that this exercise is not in vain.

Unfortunately, there is a problem when we declare this method to be synchronized. While declaring the method synchronized prevents other `getBusyFlag()` and `tryGetBusyFlag()` methods from being run at the same time (which prevents a race condition), it also prevents the `freeBusyFlag()` method from running. This means that if the flag is busy when `getBusyFlag()` is called, `getBusyFlag()` waits until the flag is freed. Unfortunately, since the freeBusy-

Flag() method will not run until the getBusyFlag() method frees the object lock, the busyflag will not be freed. This Catch-22 situation is termed *deadlock*.[*]

Example of Deadlock

We examine the concept of the deadlock in detail later in this chapter and again in Chapter 7. But before we continue, let's examine this concept.

Let's assume that we are waiting on line in a bank. I am in front of the line, waiting to withdraw some cash. Let's assume that the bank is out of cash, and I am actually willing to wait for some cash to be deposited. Let's also suppose that the bank only has one teller, and there is a policy of not handling another transaction until the current transaction is finished. Since I am still waiting to receive my money, my transaction is not finished.

Suppose that you are behind me with a million dollars to deposit. Obviously, you cannot deposit the money until I am finished, and I will not be finished until you deposit the money. This is, of course, a very contrived situation, and simple common sense can resolve it. However, this is exactly what is happening in a less contrived way in our BusyFlag class example. Furthermore, because this is a subtle problem, we might not have noticed it during testing, much the same as the bank, with an ample amount of cash, wouldn't have noticed the potential deadlock when it tested its policy.

We have a problem in this implementation of getBusyFlag() because the scope in which we used the object lock was too large. All we need to do is hold the lock for the period during which we need to change the data (i.e., check and get the busyflag); it doesn't need to be held during the entire method. Fortunately, Java also provides us the ability to synchronize a block of code instead of synchronizing the entire method. Using this block synchronization mechanism on our getBusyFlag() method, we now obtain:

```
public void getBusyFlag () {
    while (true) {
        synchronized (this) {
            if (busyflag == null) {
                busyflag = Thread.currentThread();
                break;
            }
        }
        try {
```

---

[*] This deadlock is a problem between a lock and a busyflag. More commonly, deadlock occurs between two or more locks, but the idea is the same.

```
            Thread.sleep(100);
        } catch (Exception e) {}
    }
}
```

In this new implementation of the getBusyFlag() method, we only synchronized the period between checking the flag and setting it if it is not busy. This
usage is very similar to the synchronized method usage, except that the scope
during which the lock is held is much smaller. Interestingly, this usage not only
gives us more precise control over when the object lock is held, but it also allows
us to select which object's lock to grab. In this case, since we want to grab the
same object lock as in the tryGetBusyFlag() and freeBusyFlag() methods,
we chose "this" as the object on which to obtain the lock. For synchronized
methods, the lock that is obtained is the object lock of the class in which the
method exists; in other words, the "this" object.

Object or Reference?

With the introduction of the synchronized block, we can also choose the object
to lock along with synchronizing at a block scope. Care must now be taken to
distinguish between a physical object and an instance variable that refers to an
object.

In our BusyFlag class, we could have used the synchronized block mechanism
in the getBusyFlag(), tryGetBusyFlag(), and freeBusyFlag() methods. This allows us to pick any object as the lock object.

The busyflag variable would not a good choice. This variable may change
values during execution of the three methods, including taking the value of
null. Locking on null is an exception condition, and locking on different objects defeats the purpose of synchronizing in the first place.

This might be obvious, but since picking inappropriate locks is a common mistake, let us reiterate it:

> Synchronization is based on actual objects, not references to objects.
> Multiple variables can refer to the same object, and a variable can change
> its reference to a different object. Hence, when picking an object to use as a
> lock, we must think in terms of physical objects and not references to
> objects.

As a rule of thumb, don't choose to synchronize a block on an instance variable that changes value during the scope of the lock.

Synchronized Method vs. Synchronized Block

It is actually possible to use only the synchronized block mechanism, even when we need to synchronize the whole method. For clarity in this book, we will synchronize the whole method with the *synchronized method* mechanism, and use the *synchronized block* mechanism otherwise. We leave it up to the personal preference of the programmer to decide on when to synchronize on a block of code, and when to synchronize the whole method.

Picking the whole method is the simplest to use, but as we have seen, it is possible to have a deadlock condition due to the scope being too large. It may also be inefficient to hold a lock for the section of code where it is actually not needed.

Using the synchronized block mechanism may also be a problem if too many locks are involved. As we shall see, it is possible to have a deadlock condition if we require too many locks to be grabbed. There is also an overhead in grabbing and releasing the lock, so it may be inefficient to free a lock, just to grab it again a few lines of code later.

Theorists could probably insert a whole chapter on this issue. Our concern is mainly for the clarity of the code, and we decide which to use on a case-by-case basis. Any other reasons for choosing between the two mechanisms is beyond the scope of this book.

Nested Locks

Let's examine our BusyFlag class yet again. Suppose we add another method that finds out which thread owns the lock. This method getBusyFlagOwner() simply returns the busyflag, which just so happens to be the thread object that owns the lock. An implementation is as follows:

```
public synchronized Thread getBusyFlagOwner() {
    return busyflag;
}
```

You could make the argument that this method does not need to be synchronized; after all, it makes no changes to the busyflag. And since the lock is freed when the method returns, there is no guarantee that the result is correct after returning from the method. Of course, since we cannot guarantee that the access to the busyflag is atomic, we should make sure the method is synchronized. So while we don't care if the owner changes right after the method returns, we do want to return a valid Thread object. If the getBusyFlagOwner() method reads the busyflag in the middle of a change, its value may be an invalid intermediate value.

Furthermore, let's make a modification to the freeBusyFlag() method to use this new getBusyFlagOwner() method:[*]

```
public synchronized void freeBusyFlag () {
    if (getBusyFlagOwner() == Thread.currentThread()) {
        busyflag = null;
    }
}
```

In this version of the freeBusyFlag() method, we make a call to the getBusyFlagOwner() method to see if the current thread is the owner before freeing the busyflag. What is interesting here is that both the freeBusyFlag() and the getBusyFlagOwner() methods are synchronized. So what happens? Does the thread hang at the getBusyFlagOwner() method while waiting for the freeBusyFlag() method to free the object lock? If not, and the getBusyFlagOwner() method is allowed to run, what happens when that method completes? Does it free the object lock even though the freeBusyFlag() method still needs it? The answer to all these questions is that it all works the way you want it to.

A synchronized area (by which we mean a synchronized block or method) does not blindly grab the lock when it enters the code section and free the lock when it exits. If the current thread already owns the object lock, there is no reason to wait for the lock to be freed or even to grab the lock. Instead the code in the synchronized area merely executes. Furthermore, the system is smart enough not to free the lock if it did not initially grab it upon entering the synchronized area. This means that the freeBusyFlag() method can call the getBusyFlagOwner() method without any problems.

Unfortunately, our version of the locking mechanism, the BusyFlag class, is not so smart. It hangs waiting for the lock that it is currently holding to be freed. To solve this problem, we must reimplement the BusyFlag class with a counter. The object now checks to see if it already owns the lock and increases the count by one if it does. In the corresponding freeBusyFlag() method, it only frees the busyflag if the count is zero. This way a thread within the scope of a BusyFlag lock directly or indirectly (through method calls) enters other areas that are locked with the same BusyFlag instance:[†]

```
public class BusyFlag {
    private Thread busyflag = null;
    private int busycount = 0;
```

---

[*] There is actually no reason to make this modification since it makes the example more complicated, but bear with us.

[†] This is still not the best implementation of the BusyFlag class.

```
    public void getBusyFlag() {
        while (tryGetBusyFlag() == false) {
            try {
                Thread.sleep(100);
            } catch (Exception e) {}
        }
    }

    public synchronized boolean tryGetBusyFlag() {
        if (busyflag == null) {
            busyflag = Thread.currentThread();
            busycount = 1;
            return true;
        }
        if (busyflag == Thread.currentThread()) {
            busycount++;
            return true;
        }
        return false;
    }

    public synchronized void freeBusyFlag () {
        if (getBusyFlagOwner() == Thread.currentThread()) {
            busycount--;
            if (busycount == 0) busyflag = null;
        }
    }

    public synchronized Thread getBusyFlagOwner() {
        return busyflag;
    }
}
```

With this new implementation of the BusyFlag class, we can now lock any section of code without worrying that we may already own the lock. We can also free the lock without worrying. Both the synchronized mechanism and our BusyFlag class can be used as nested locks. (The BusyFlag class is now beginning to resemble another synchronization primitive known as a *semaphore*.)

Deadlock

While it is not too difficult to check if a thread already owns a lock before grabbing it, is it possible to prevent deadlock of any kind? Before we try to answer this question, let's look further into just what deadlock is. Simplistically, deadlock is when two or more threads are waiting for two or more locks to be freed and the circumstances in the program are such that the locks will never be freed. Ironically, these circumstances are caused when the threads wait for a lock. We saw this occur earlier, when we made the getBusyFlag() method synchronized. The fact that the freeBusy-Flag() method was also synchronized made it impossible for the busyflag to be freed until the getBusyFlag() method returned. Since the getBusyFlag() method is waiting for the busy flag to be freed, it will wait forever.

That deadlock was caused by an object lock grabbed by the Java synchronization primitive and our own implementation of a lock mechanism, the BusyFlag class. Can this deadlock situation also be caused only with Java's synchronization primitives? The answer to this question is yes; furthermore, it may be difficult to predict deadlock or to detect deadlock when it occurs. Code that runs correctly every time during testing may contain potential deadlocks that occur only under certain conditions or on certain implementations of the Java virtual machine. To better illustrate this problem, let's examine some possible methods that may exist in any database system:

```
public void removeUseless(Folder file) {
    synchronized (file) {
        if (file.isUseless()) {
            Cabinet directory = file.getCabinet();
            synchronized (directory) {
                directory.remove(file);
            }
        }
    }
}
```

Suppose, in some database class, we have a method called removeUseless(). This method is called during the period when the program needs to clean up the database system. It is passed a folder object; this object represents some folder we have in our database system. There is some indication of uselessness that is calculated by the isUseless() method of the folder object. In order for us to act on the folder, we must make sure that we have the object lock of the folder. If we find that the folder is useless, we can simply remove the folder from the cabinet. The cabinet can be found by the getCabinet() method, and the folder can be deleted with the remove() method. Just as with the folder object, before we can act on the cabinet object, we must obtain its object lock. Now, let's also suppose that we have another method, called updateFolders():

```
public void updateFolders(Cabinet dir) {
    synchronized (dir) {
        for (Folder f = dir.first(); f != null; f = dir.next(f)) {
            synchronized (f) {
                f.update();
            }
        }
    }
}
```

This method is passed a cabinet object that represents a cabinet in our database system. In order for us to act on this cabinet, we must first obtain its object lock. Let's suppose that the act of updating the cabinet is done by cycling through all the folders in the cabinet and calling the update() method on the folders. Again, in order for us to update the folders, we must also grab the folder lock.

Neither one of these methods is extraordinary; they could exist in one form or another in any database system. However, let's look at a possible run of this implementation as outlined in Figure 3-3. Assume the updateFolders() method is called from thread 1. The method locks the cabinet (L1). Now assume the removeUseless() method is called by thread 2. The removeUseless() method locks the folder (L2), determines that it is indeed useless, and proceeds to lock the cabinet (L1) in order to remove the folder. At this point, thread 2 blocks and waits until the cabinet object lock is freed.

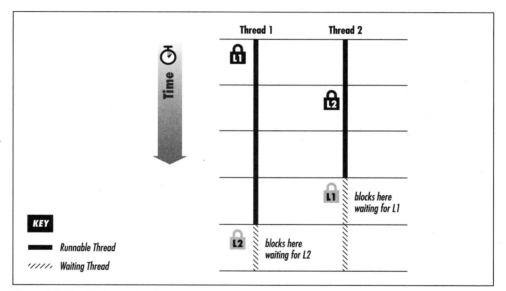

Figure 3-3. Deadlock in a database system

But what happens if the folder on which the removeUseless() method is working is now accessed by the updateFolders() method? When the update-Folders() method reaches this folder, it tries to grab the object lock for the folder (L2). At this point, the removeUseless() method has the folder lock and is waiting for the cabinet lock to be freed; the updateFolders() method holds the cabinet lock and is waiting for the folder lock to be freed. This is the classic deadlock situation, and it illustrates the problem that deadlock can be easy to program and hard to detect: both methods involved use a simple, straightforward algorithm, and there are no obvious signs in the code that deadlock can occur.[*]

Can the system somehow resolve this deadlock, just as it was able to avoid the potential deadlock when a thread tries to grab the same lock again? Unfortunately, this problem is different. Unlike the case of the nested locks, where a single thread is trying to grab a single lock twice, this case involves two separate threads trying to grab two different locks. Since a thread owns one of the locks involved, it may have made changes that make it impossible for it to free the lock. To be able to fix this problem, we can either redesign the program so that it doesn't run into this deadlock condition, or provide a way for this deadlock to be avoided programmatically. In either case, it involves some sort of redesign. Given the complexity of the original design, this may involve a major overhaul of the database system.

How could you expect the Java system to resolve this deadlock automatically when even the developer may not be able to do so without overhauling the design? The answer is that you can't, and it doesn't. We will look at the design issues related to deadlock prevention in Chapter 7.

Return to the Banking Example

So, we just survived the ATM withdrawal problem. It turns out that this problem occurred so infrequently that the total cash involved with the problem transactions was only a few thousand dollars. Luckily, the bank kept records that were good enough to recover the cash. While our manager did not like the fact that we caused a major panic among the upper-level managers, she was somewhat impressed that we were able to track down the problem. While she still does not trust us completely, we still have a job and are able to design and enhance different parts of the ATM system.

The first thing we do is to look at our existing ATM code: we check and double check every piece of code for race conditions, using the synchronized mechanisms that we've learned so far to resolve the problems. Everything seems to be going well until one day, the president of the bank receives a phone call from an irate customer. This customer did a balance inquiry at the ATM that showed a balance of $300. Immediately, he attempted to withdraw $290, but could not.

It turns out that in the very short period of time between when the customer checked his balance and attempted to withdraw the money, his wife withdrew

---

[*] Consider that this code was probably developed by two engineers with no knowledge of each other's work. A decent program design might have prevented the deadlock, but even that would not guarantee deadlock prevention.

$100 from another ATM. Even though the "correct" thing happened, it turned into a big political problem for the bank when the husband threatened to remove his $1 million business account from the bank if the bank "couldn't keep their records straight." So the bank established a new policy that only one ATM could operate on an account at the same time.

This means that we need a new lock scope for the account: the ATM class must be able to lock the account for the duration of a session with a user. This session could comprise transactions that span multiple methods in the ATM class, so the synchronized blocks and synchronized methods that we've learned about so far aren't sufficient to solve this problem: we need a lock that spans multiple methods.

Fortunately, we've already developed the BusyFlag class, so we're in position to solve this problem with little effort:

```
public class AutomatedTellerMachine extends Teller {
    Account a;

    public boolean synchronized login(String name, String password) {
        if (a != null)
            throw new IllegalArgumentException("Already logged in");
        a = verifyAccount(name, password);
        if (a == null)
            return false;
        a.lock();
        return true;
    }

    public void withdraw(float amount) {
        if (a.deduct(amount))
            dispense(amount);
        printReceipt();
    }

    public void balanceInquiry() {
        printBalance(a.balance());
    }

    public void synchronized logoff() {
        a.unlock();
        a = null;
    }
}

class Account {
    private float total;
    private BusyFlag flag = new BusyFlag();
```

```
public synchronized boolean deduct(float t) {
    if (t <= total) {
        total -= t;
        return true;
    }
    else return false;
}

public synchronized float balance() {
    return total;
}

public void lock() {
    flag.getBusyFlag();
}

public void unlock() {
    flag.freeBusyFlag();
}
```

By using a BusyFlag lock, we're now able to lock at a "session" scope by grabbing the `busyflag` when the user logs into the ATM and releasing the `busyflag` when the user logs off the ATM. Locking at this scope cannot be directly achieved with the synchronization primitives within Java.

Being proud of the BusyFlag class, we now place the code into a class library, where it is accepted by the whole development team for the ATM project. Although it is a very simple class, it is also one of the most functional and is used in practically every part of the ATM system.[*]

Static Methods (Synchronization Details)

Throughout this chapter on synchronization, we kept referring to "obtaining the object lock." But what about static methods? When a synchronized static method is called, which object are we referring to? A static method does not have a concept of the "this" reference. It is not possible to obtain the object lock of an object that does not exist. So how does synchronization of static methods work? To answer this question, we will introduce the concept of a class lock. Just as there is an object lock that can be obtained for each instance of a class (object), there is a lock that can be obtained for each class. We will refer to this as the *class lock.*[†]

---

[*] But there are still problems with the BusyFlag class that we'll solve in the next chapter.

[†] In terms of implementation, there is really no such thing as a class lock. The idea of a class lock is used to help us understand locking of static methods.

When a static synchronized method is called, the program obtains the class lock before calling the method. This mechanism is identical to the case in which the method is not static; it is just a different lock. The same rules applies: if a synchronized static method calls another synchronized static method of the same class, the system is smart enough to support the nesting of class locks.

But how is the class lock related to the object locks? Apart from the functional relationship between the two locks, they are not operationally related at all. These are two distinct locks. The class lock can be grabbed and released independently of the object lock. If a nonstatic synchronized method calls a static synchronized method, it acquires both locks. Achieving deadlock between these two locks is a little difficult[*] to accomplish since a static method cannot call a nonstatic method.

If a synchronized static method has access to an object reference, can it call synchronized methods of that object or use the object to lock a synchronized block? Yes: in this case the program first acquires the class lock when it calls the synchronized static method and then the object lock of the particular object:

```
public class MyStatic {
    public synchronized static void staticMethod(MyStatic obj) {
        // Class Lock acquired
        obj.nonStaticMethod();

        synchronized (obj) {
            // Class and Object Locks acquired
        }
    }
    public synchronized void nonStaticMethod() {
        // Object Lock acquired
    }
}
```

Can a nonstatic method grab the static lock without calling a synchronized static method? In other words, can a synchronized block apply to the class lock?

```
public class ClassExample {
    synchronized void process() {
        synchronized (the class lock) {
            // Code to access static variables of the class
        }
    }
}
```

The main reason for a nonstatic method to grab a class lock is to prevent a race condition for variables that apply to the class (i.e., static variables). This can be accomplished by calling a static synchronized method of the class. If for some

---

[*] However, it is not impossible to deadlock any two locks.

The Class Lock and the Class Object

In this last example, we used the object lock of the Class object as a common lock for the class. The reason we are using this object is because there is a one-to-one correspondence of Class objects and classes in the system. We have also mentioned that when a synchronized static method is called, the system will grab the class lock.

It turns out that there is actually no such thing as a class lock. When a synchronized static method is called, the system grabs the object lock of the Class object that represents the class. This means the class lock is the object lock of the corresponding Class object. Using both static synchronized methods and synchronized blocks that use the Class object lock can cause confusion.

---

reason, this is not desired, we can also use the synchronized block mechanism on a common static object.[*] For example, we could use an object stored in a common location that can be accessed by all objects of a particular class type:

```
public class ClassExample {
    private static Object lockObject = new Object();
    synchronized void process() {
        synchronized (lockObject) {
            // Code to access static variables of the class
        }
    }
}
```

Finally, if creating a new object is not desired, you may also obtain the Class object[†] that represents the class itself. The Java system has a class called "Class." Objects of this class are used to represent classes in the system. For our purposes, we are using this class because there is a one-to-one ratio of classes and objects of the Class class that represents the classes. This Class object can be obtained as follows:

```
public class ClassExample {
    synchronized void process() {
        synchronized (Class.forName("ClassExample")) {
            // Code to access static variables of the class
        }
    }
}
```

---

[*] Using a static instance variable would probably be the best technique for storing this common object.

[†] Java has instances of the Class class that are used to represent the different classes in the system. The purpose of this class is for run-time type information and checking. We simply note that there is one Class object for each class type in the system; complete details of the Class class are not in the scope of this book.

A call to the `forName()` method of the Class class returns this object. We can then use this Class object as the locking object via the synchronized block mechanism.

Summary

In this chapter, we introduced the synchronized keyword of the Java language. This keyword allows us to synchronize methods and blocks of code.

We've also developed a synchronization primitive of our own: the BusyFlag, which allows us to lock objects across methods, and to acquire and release the lock at will based on external events. These features are not available with Java's synchronized keyword, but they are useful in many situations.

This concludes our first look at synchronization. As you can tell, it is one of the most important aspects of threaded programming. Without these techniques, we would not be able to share data correctly between the threads that we create. While these techniques are good enough for many of the programs we will be creating, there are other techniques that we introduce in the next chapter.

4

Wait and Notify

In the previous chapter, we took our first look into issues of synchronization. With the synchronization tools introduced, we now are able to have our own threads interoperate with each other. It is possible for threads to share data without any race conditions. However, as we shall see, synchronization is more that avoiding race conditions: it includes a thread-based notification system that we'll examine in this chapter.

Back to Work (at the Bank)

Having just completed a sweep of all the code in the ATM system—synchronizing any potential problems using the techniques of Chapter 3—we have made the system much more robust. Many little hiccups that used to occur no longer show up. But most important, our BusyFlag class allows us to quickly make the modifications required by our president. The use of the BusyFlag class in this situation allows it to be adopted as a corporate standard and used throughout the whole ATM system.

As far as our manager is concerned, we're heroes—until another problem occurs: it turns out that a portion of the ATM system is facing performance problems. This portion of the system was developed by a coworker who made extensive use of the BusyFlag class. Since it is our class, we are given the task of trying to correct the problem. We start by revisiting the entire BusyFlag class:

```
public class BusyFlag {
    private Thread busyflag = null;
```

```
private int busycount = 0;

public void getBusyFlag() {
    while (tryGetBusyFlag() == false) {
        try {
            Thread.sleep(100);
        } catch (Exception e) {}
    }
}

public synchronized boolean tryGetBusyFlag() {
    if (busyflag == null) {
        busyflag = Thread.currentThread();
        busycount = 1;
        return true;
    }
    if (busyflag == Thread.currentThread()) {
        busycount++;
        return true;
    }
    return false;
}

public synchronized void freeBusyFlag () {
    if (getBusyFlagOwner() == Thread.currentThread()) {
        busycount--;
        if (busycount == 0) busyflag = null;
    }
}

public synchronized Thread getBusyFlagOwner() {
    return busyflag;
}
}
```

Upon revisiting the BusyFlag class, we notice the call to the sleep() method. This was originally used by us to avoid eating up too many CPU cycles. At the time, we considered this an open issue. If the getBusyFlag() method slept for a long period of time, this might cause the method to wait too long and hence cause the performance problem. Conversely, if the method does not sleep enough, it might eat up too many CPU cycles and hence cause the performance problem. In either case, this has to be fixed: we have to find a way to wait only until the lock is freed. We need the getBusyFlag() method to grab the busyflag the moment the flag is freed and yet not eat any CPU cycles in a polling loop. We'll solve this problem in the next section.

Wait and Notify

Just as each object has a lock that can be obtained and released, each object also provides a mechanism that allows it to be a waiting area.* And just like the lock mechanism, the main reason for this mechanism is to aid communication between threads. The idea behind the mechanism is actually simple: one thread needs a certain condition to exist and assumes that another thread will create that condition. When this other thread creates the condition, it notifies the first thread that has been waiting for the condition. This is accomplished with the following methods:

void wait()

   Waits for a condition to occur. This is a method of the Object class and must be called from within a synchronized method or block.

void notify()

   Notifies a thread that is waiting for a condition that the condition has occurred. This is a method of the Object class and must be called from within a synchronized method of block.

---

wait(), notify(), and the Object Class

Interestingly enough, just like the synchronized method, the *wait and notify* mechanism is available from every object in the Java system. However, this mechanism is accomplished by method invocations, whereas the synchronized mechanism is done by adding a keyword.

The `wait()`/`notify()` mechanism works because these methods are methods of the Object class. Since every object in the Java system inherits directly or indirectly from the Object class, it is also an Object and, hence, has support for this mechanism.

What is the purpose of the wait and notify mechanism, and how does it work? The wait and notify mechanism is also a synchronization mechanism, however, it is more of a communication mechanism: it allows one thread to communicate to another thread that a particular condition has occurred. The wait and notify mechanism does not specify what the specific condition is.

---

* Under Solaris threads or POSIX threads, these are often referred to as *condition variables*; on Windows 95/NT, these are referred to as *event variables*.

Can wait and notify be used to replace the synchronized method? Actually, the answer is no. Wait and notify does not solve the race condition problem that the synchronized mechanism solves. As a matter of fact, wait and notify must be used in conjunction with the synchronized lock to prevent a race condition in the wait and notify mechanism itself.

Let's use this technique to solve the timing problem in the BusyFlag class. In our earlier version, the `getBusyFlag()` method would call `tryGetBusyFlag()` to obtain the busy flag. If it could not get the flag, it would try again 100 milliseconds later. But what we are really doing is waiting for a condition (a free `busyflag`) to occur. So we can apply this mechanism: if we don't have the condition (a free `busyflag`), we `wait()` for the condition. And when the flag is freed, we `notify()` a waiting thread that the condition now exists.[*]

```
public class BusyFlag {
    private Thread busyflag = null;
    private int busycount = 0;

    public synchronized void getBusyFlag() {
        while (tryGetBusyFlag() == false) {
            try {
                wait();
            } catch (Exception e) {}
        }
    }

    public synchronized boolean tryGetBusyFlag() {
        if (busyflag == null) {
            busyflag = Thread.currentThread();
            busycount = 1;
            return true;
        }
        if (busyflag == Thread.currentThread()) {
            busycount++;
            return true;
        }
        return false;
    }

    public synchronized void freeBusyFlag() {
        if (getBusyFlagOwner() == Thread.currentThread()) {
            busycount--;
            if (busycount == 0) {
                busyflag = null;
                notify();
```

---

[*] This, finally, is the complete, robust implementation of the BusyFlag class.

```
              }
           }
        }

        public synchronized Thread getBusyFlagOwner() {
            return busyflag;
        }
    }
```

In this new version of the `getBusyFlag()` method, the 100-millisecond sleep is removed and replaced with a call to the `wait()` method. This is the `wait()` for the required condition to occur. The `freeBusyFlag()` method now contains a call to the `notify()` method. This is the notification that the required condition has occurred. This new implementation is much better than the old one. We now `wait()` until the `busyflag` is free—no more and no less—and we no longer waste CPU cycles by waking up every 100 milliseconds to test if the `busyflag` is free.

Wait and Notify and Synchronization

As noted, the wait and notify mechanism has a race condition that needs to be solved with the synchronization lock. Unfortunately, it is not possible to solve the race condition without integrating the lock into the wait and notify mechanism. This is why it is mandatory for the `wait()` and `notify()` method to hold the lock for the object for which it is waiting or notifying.

The `wait()` method releases the lock prior to waiting, and reacquires the lock prior to returning from the `wait()` method. This is done correctly so that no race condition exists. If you recall, there is no concept of releasing and reacquiring a lock in the Java API. The `wait()` method is actually tightly integrated with the synchronization lock, using a feature not available directly from the synchronization mechanism. In other words, it is not possible for us to implement the `wait()` method purely in Java. It is a native method, implemented in C.

This integration of the wait and notify and the synchronized method is actually standard. In other systems like Solaris or POSIX threads, condition variables also require that a mutex lock be held for the mechanism to work.

There is another change. The `getBusyFlag()` method is now synchronized. We'll answer this question as we examine a few details about the wait and notify mechanism.

What happens when notify() is called and there is no thread waiting? This is a valid situation. Even with our BusyFlag class, it is perfectly valid to free the `busyflag` when there is no other thread waiting to get the `busyflag`. Since the wait and notify mechanism does not know the condition about which it is sending notification, it assumes that a notification for which there is no thread waiting is simply a notification that goes unheard. In other words, if `notify()` is called without another thread waiting, then `notify()` simply returns.

What are the details of the race condition that exists in wait and notify? In general, a thread that uses the `wait()` method confirms that a condition does not exist (typically by checking a variable) and then calls the `wait()` method. When another thread sets the condition (typically by setting that same variable), it then calls the `notify()` method. A race condition occurs when:

1. The first thread tests the condition and confirms that it must wait.

2. The second thread sets the condition.

3. The second thread calls the `notify()` method; this goes unheard, since the first thread is not yet waiting.

4. The first thread calls the `wait()` method.

How does this potential race condition get resolved? This race condition is resolved by the synchronization lock discussed earlier. In order to call `wait()` or `notify()`, we must have the lock for the object on which we're calling the `wait()` or `notify()` method. This is mandatory: the methods will not work properly and will generate an exception condition if the lock is not held. Furthermore, the `wait()` method also releases the lock prior to waiting and reacquires the lock prior to returning from the `wait()` method. The developer must use this lock to ensure that checking the condition and setting the condition is atomic, which typically means that the condition is held in an instance variable within the object.

So, the getBusyFlag() method is synchronized because it is mandatory for it to be synchronized. But wasn't there a reason why it could not be synchronized in the first place? Why does it work now? The `getBusyFlag()` method was not synchronized in our earlier examples because the lock scope would have been too large. It would not have been possible for the `freeBusyFlag()` method to be called while the `getBusyFlag()` method held the lock. Now, with the wait and notify mechanism, it is not a problem because the `wait()` method releases and reacquires the lock during the period it is waiting. This means it's possible for the `freeBusyFlag()` method to be called.

Is there a race condition during the period that the wait() method releases and reacquires the lock? The `wait()` method is tightly integrated with the lock mechanism. The object lock is not actually freed until the waiting thread is already in a state where it can receive notifications. This would have been difficult, if not impossible to accomplish, if we had needed to implement the `wait()` and `notify()` methods ourselves. For our purposes, this is an implementation detail. It works, and works correctly. The system takes care of the race condition problems that may occur.

Wait and Notify and the Synchronized Block

In all the wait and notify examples so far, we have used synchronized methods. However, there is no reason we can't use the synchronized block syntax instead. The only requirement is that the object we are synchronizing on is the same object on which we call the `wait()` and `notify()` methods. An example could be as follows.

```
public class ExampleBlockLock {
    private StringBuffer sb = new StringBuffer();
    public void getLock() {
        doSomething(sb);
        synchronized (sb) {
            try {
                sb.wait();
            } catch (Exception e) {}
        }
    }
    public void freeLock() {
        doSomethingElse(sb);
        synchronized (sb) {
            sb.notify();
        }
    }
}
```

Why does the getBusyFlag() method loop to test if the tryGetBusyFlag() method returns false? Isn't the flag going to be free when the wait() method returns? No, the flag won't necessarily be free when the `wait()` method returns. The race condition that is solved internally to the wait and notify mechanism only prevents the loss of notifications. It does not solve the following case:

1. The first thread acquires the `busyflag`.

2. The second thread calls `tryGetBusyFlag()`, which returns false.

3. The second thread executes the `wait()` method, which frees the synchronization lock.

4. The first thread enters the `freeBusyFlag()` method, obtaining the synchronization lock.

5. The first thread calls the `notify()` method.

6. The third thread attempts to call getBusyFlag() and blocks waiting for the synchronization lock.

7. The first thread exits the freeBusyFlag() method, releasing the synchronization lock.

8. The third thread acquires the synchronization lock and enters the getBusy-Flag() method. Because the busyflag is free, it obtains the busyflag, and exits the getBusyFlag() method, releasing the synchronization lock.

9. The second thread, having received notification, returns from the wait() method, reacquiring the synchronization lock along the way.

10. The second thread calls the tryGetBusyFlag() method again, confirms that the flag is busy, and calls the wait() method.

If we had implemented the getBusyFlag() method without the loop:

```
public synchronized void getBusyFlag() {
    if (tryGetBusyFlag() == false) {
        try {
            wait();
            tryGetBusyFlag();
        } catch (Exception e) {}
    }
}
```

then in step 10 the first thread would have returned from the getBusyFlag() method even though the tryGetBusyFlag() method had not acquired the busyflag. All we know when the wait() method returns is that at some point, the condition was satisfied and another thread called the notify() method; we cannot assume that the condition is still satisfied without testing the condition again. Hence, we always need to put the call to the wait() method in a loop.

Wait, Notify, and NotifyAll

What happens when there is more than one thread waiting for the notification? Which thread actually gets the notification when notify() is called? The answer is that it depends: the Java specification doesn't define which thread gets notified. Which thread actually receives the notification varies based on several factors, including the implementation of the Java virtual machine, and scheduling and timing issues during the execution of the program. There is no way to determine, even on a single platform, which of multiple threads receives the notification.

There is another method of the Object class that assists us when multiple threads are waiting for a condition:

void notifyAll()

> Notifies all the threads waiting on the object that the condition has occurred. This is a method of the Object class and must be called from within a synchronized method or block.

The Object class also provides the `notifyAll()` method, which helps us in those cases where the program cannot be designed to allow any arbitrary thread to receive the notification. This method is similar to the `notify()` method, except that all of the threads that are waiting on the object will be notified instead of a single arbitrary thread. Just like the `notify()` method, the `notifyAll()` method does not let us decide which threads get notification: they all get notified. By having all the threads receive notification, it is now possible for us to work out a mechanism for the threads to choose among themselves which thread should continue and which thread(s) call the `wait()` method again.

Does notifyAll() Really Wake Up All the Threads?

Yes and no. All the waiting threads will wake up, but they still have to reacquire the object lock. So the threads will not run in parallel: they must each wait for the object lock to be freed. Thus only one thread can run at a time, and only after the thread that called the `notifyAll()` method releases its lock.

Why would you want to wake up all of the threads? There are a few possible reasons, one of which is if there is more than one condition to wait for. Since we cannot control which thread gets the notification, it is entirely possible that a notification wakes up a thread that is waiting for an entirely different condition. By waking up all the waiting threads, we can design the program so that the threads decide among themselves who should execute next.

Another reason is the case where the notification can satisfy multiple waiting threads. Let's examine a case where we need such control:

```
public class ResourceThrottle {
    private int resourcecount = 0;
    private int resourcemax = 1;

    public ResourceThrottle (int max) {
        resourcecount = 0;
        resourcemax = max;
    }

    public synchronized void getResource (int numberof) {
        while (true) {
```

```
            if ((resourcecount + numberof) <= resourcemax) {
                resourcecount += numberof;
                break;
            }
            try {
                wait();
            } catch (Exception e) {}
        }
    }

    public synchronized void freeResource (int numberof) {
            resourcecount -= numberof;
            notifyAll();
    }
}
```

We are defining a new class called the ResourceThrottle class. This class provides two methods, getResource() and freeResource(). Both of these methods take a single parameter that specifies how many resources to grab or release. The maximum number of resources available is defined by the constructor of the ResourceThrottle class. This class is similar to our BusyFlag class, in that our getResource() method would have to wait() if the number of requested resources is not available. The freeResource() method also has to call the notify() method so that the waiting threads can get notification when more resources are available.

The difference in this case is that we are calling the notifyAll() method instead of the notify() method. There are two reasons for this.

*   It is entirely possible for the system to wake up a thread that needs more resources than are available, even with the resources that have just been freed. If we had used the notify() method, another thread that could be satisfied with the current amount of resources would not get the chance to grab those resources because the system picked the wrong thread to wake up.

*   It is possible to satisfy more than one thread with the number of resources we have just freed. As an example, if we free 10 resources, we can then let four other threads grab three, four, one, and two resources respectively. There is not a one-to-one ratio between the number of threads freeing resources and the number of threads grabbing resources.

By notifying all the threads, we solve these two problems with little work. However, all we have accomplished is to simulate a targeted notification scheme. We are not really controlling which threads wake up; instead we are controlling which thread takes control after they all get notification. This can be very inefficient if there are many threads waiting to get notification, because many wake up only to see that the condition is still unsatisfied, and they must wait() again.

If we really need to control which thread gets the notification, we could also implement an array of objects whose sole purpose is to act as a waiting point for threads and who are targets of notification of conditions. This means that each thread waits on a different object in the array. By having the thread that calls the notify() method decide which thread should receive notification, we remove the overhead of many threads waking up only to go back to a wait state moments later. The disadvantage of using an array of objects is, of course, that we will lock on different objects. This acquisition of many locks could lead to confusion or, even worse, deadlock. It is also more complicated to accomplish; we may even have to write a new class just to help with notification targeting:

```java
public class TargetNotify {
    private Object Targets[] = null;

    public TargetNotify (int numberOfTargets) {
        Targets = new Object[numberOfTargets];

        for (int i = 0; i < numberOfTargets; i++) {
            Targets[i] = new Object();
        }
    }

    public void wait (int targetNumber) {
        synchronized (Targets[targetNumber]) {
            try {
                Targets[targetNumber].wait();
            } catch (Exception e) {}
        }
    }

    public void notify (int targetNumber) {
        synchronized (Targets[targetNumber]) {
            Targets[targetNumber].notify();
        }
    }
}
```

The concept is simple: in our TargetNotify class, we are using an array of objects for the sole purpose of the wait and notify mechanism. Instead of having all the threads wait() on the "this" object, we choose an object to wait() on. (This is potentially confusing: we are not overriding the wait() method of the object class here since we've provided a unique signature.) Later, when we decide which threads should wake up, we can target the notification since the threads are waiting on different objects.

Whether the efficiency of a targeted notification scheme outweighs the extra complexity is the decision of the program designer. In other words, both techniques have their drawbacks, and we leave it up to the implementors to decide which mechanism is best.

wait() and sleep()

The Object class also overloads the `wait()` method to allow it to take a timeout specified in milliseconds:[*]

void wait(long timeout)
>   Waits for a condition to occur. However, if the notification has not occurred in timeout milliseconds, then return anyway. This is a method of the Object class and must be called from a synchronized block or method.

void wait(long timeout, int nanos)
>   Waits for a condition to occur. However, if the notification has not occurred in timeout milliseconds and nanos nanoseconds, then return anyway. This is a method of the Object class and must be called from a synchronized block or method.

These methods are provided in order to support external events.[†] In cases where we are only concerned with when a notification arrives, we normally do not use these methods. However, notifications can be dependent on external conditions, in which case we are also concerned with if, along with when, a notification arrives. A timeout may be needed in case those conditions do not occur. As an example, we might write a program that connects to a stock feed server. The program may be willing to wait 30 seconds to connect to the server (that is, to satisfy the condition of being connected); if the connection does not occur within 30 seconds, the program may try to contact a backup server. We'd accomplish this by calling the `wait(30000)` method in our program.

We may still add a timeout in those cases when we know that a condition will eventually be satisfied so that we can accomplish other tasks. For example, let's assume that we needed to do other tasks in our `getBusyFlag()` method:

```
public synchronized void getBusyFlag() {
    while (tryGetBusyFlag() == false) {
        wait(100);
        doSomethingElse();
    }
}
```

---

[*] See the sidebar "sleep(long) and sleep(long, int)" in Chapter 2 for a note about the timing resolution of these methods.

[†] We define external events as events we cannot control. Such events may be conditions caused by another application via a networked socket or a user event.

In this version of getBusyFlag(), we wait() for the notification for up to 100 milliseconds. If this notification does not arrive within the requested time, we are awoken anyway. In a way, this is actually a very contrived example: we could have easily created another thread that does something else.

If we know that the notification will never arrive, what is the difference between wait(long) and sleep(long)? Let's say, for example, we do not use the notify() method on an object. Then, in theory, there is no reason to wait() on the object. However, the wait(long) method does have an extra benefit: it behaves exactly like the sleep(long) method of the Thread class, except that it also releases and reacquires a lock. This means that if we are not using the wait and notify mechanism, we can still use the wait(long) method as a way of sleeping without holding the lock. For example, if we have the following class:

```java
public class WaitExample {
    public synchronized void ProcessLoop() {
        processOne();
        try {
            wait(1000);
        } catch (Exception e) {}
        processTwo();
    }
}
```

The WaitExample class is a simple example of a method that needs to sleep for one second between two distinct operations, during which time it must give up the lock. If we had to code the exact same class without using the wait(long) method, it would add extra complexity:

```java
public class WaitExample {
    public void ProcessLoop() {
        synchronized (this) {
            processOne();
        }
        try {
            Thread.sleep(1000);
        } catch (Exception e) {}
        synchronized (this) {
            processTwo();
        }
    }
}
```

As we said, this is a simple example: imagine if we had to code the following class without the use of the wait(long) method:

```java
public class WaitExample {
    public synchronized void ProcessLoop() {
```

```
        processOne();
        for (int i=0; i<50; i++) {
            processTwo();
            try {
                wait(1000);
            } catch (Exception e) {}
        }
    }
}
```

In Chapter 6, we'll see a better example of using the wait(long) method to replace the sleep() method.

Static Methods (Synchronization Details)

What about using wait() and notify() in a static method? The wait() and notify() methods are nonstatic methods of the Object class. Since static methods cannot call nonstatic methods without an object reference, static methods cannot call the wait() and notify() methods directly. But there is nothing preventing us from instantiating an object for the sole purpose of using it as a waiting point. This is just like the technique we used earlier when trying to grab an object lock from a static method.

Using an actual object also makes the wait() and notify() methods from static and nonstatic methods interoperate, much like using the synchronized block mechanism on a common object can allow static and nonstatic methods to interoperate. The following versions of staticWait() and staticNotify() could be called from both static and nonstatic methods:

```
public class MyStaticClass {
    static private Object obj = new Object();

    public static void staticWait() {
        synchronized (obj) {
            try {
                obj.wait();
            } catch (Exception e) {}
        }
    }

    public static void staticNotify() {
        synchronized (obj) {
            obj.notify();
        }
    }
}
```

It's rare for threads that are executing static methods to interoperate with threads that are executing nonstatic methods in this manner. Nevertheless, by having a static version of the `wait()` and `notify()` methods, we allow this interoperability to occur. The reason that these methods have different names is because the signature is the same as the `wait()` and `notify()` method.

Summary

Here are the methods we introduced in this chapter:

void wait()

Waits for a condition to occur. This is a method of the Object class and must be called from within a synchronized method or block.

void wait(long timeout)

Waits for a condition to occur. However, if the notification has not occurred in timeout milliseconds, then return anyway. This is a method of the Object class and must be called from a synchronized block or method.

void wait(long timeout, int nanos)

Waits for a condition to occur. However, if the notification has not occurred in timeout milliseconds and nanos nanoseconds, then return anyway. This is a method of the Object class and must be called from a synchronized block or method.

void notify()

Notifies a thread that is waiting for a condition that the condition has occurred. This is a method of the Object class and must be called from within a synchronized method of block.

void notifyAll()

Notifies all the threads waiting on the object that the condition has occurred. This is a method of the Object class and must be called from within a synchronized method or block.

With these methods, we are now able to interoperate between threads in an efficient manner. Instead of just providing protection against race conditions, we now have a mechanism that allows threads to inform each other about situations without resorting to polling and timeouts.

The two default techniques of synchronizing data and threads within Java—the synchronized keyword and the wait and notify methods—provide simple, robust ways for threads to communicate and cooperate. Although we examine some advanced techniques for data synchronization in Chapter 7, these default techniques are good enough for most Java programs.

5

Useful Examples of Java Thread Programming

In the previous chapters, we examined some of the tools necessary to support the synchronization of data between threads. With these tools, we now are able to have our own threads interoperate with each other, with the system threads, or with the threads started by the standard Java libraries.[*] This is possible because the tools allow for a thread to examine and modify shared data in a safe manner without race conditions. The ability to handle data safely provides us with the ability to exchange data, which, in turn, allows us to accomplish tasks in separate threads safely, which ultimately allows us to accomplish our goal.

In other words, we can now say that threading itself is just an implementation detail of our program. Ideally, true threading should just feel like another object that does something. And while threading itself is a powerful tool, in the end all you want to accomplish is to "play the audio clip" or "read the data socket."

In this chapter, we examine some of the uses of threads. We will show how threads solve certain problems, the implementation details of these solutions, the threads themselves, and the mechanisms that are used to control and synchronize the threads. We will examine threads more from the perspective of solving problems instead of examining a feature of the threading system.

Data Structures and Containers

Interestingly, our first set of examples does not require any threads to be created at all. Our first topic is the data types that can be used or passed between threads. When you create a data object, you do not always know how many threads will access that object: while these data objects may be accessed by many threads, they

---

[*] These are listed in Appendix C.

may also only be accessed by a single thread (in which case, synchronization of the object is not necessary). To begin, let's examine some operating-system mechanisms used to pass data between processes.

In the UNIX operating system, the first of the interprocess communications (IPC) techniques provided were message queues, semaphores, and shared memory. While UNIX has added many additional mechanisms, these three are still popular and heavily used in many applications. The IPC mechanisms of Java—the synchronization lock and the wait and notify mechanism—are specifically for synchronization. Unlike the message queue and shared memory, no real data is actually passed between threads: the concern is synchronization, not communication.[*] The theory is that communication is easy if synchronization tools are available. For now, let's take a look at the message queue and shared memory and see if these communication mechanisms are useful for communicating between threads.

The Message Queue

We'll start with message queues:

```
import java.util.*;

public class MsgQueue {
    Vector queue = new Vector();
    public synchronized void send(Object obj) {
        queue.addElement(obj);
    }

    public synchronized Object recv() {
        if (queue.size() == 0) return null;

        Object obj = queue.firstElement();
        queue.removeElementAt(0);
        return obj;
    }
}
```

The implementation of the message queue is incredibly simple once we have the proper synchronization tools. In the multitasking paradigm,[†] the operating system has to deliver the data that is sent into the queue from one application to another, as well as synchronize the communication itself. Since threads share the same address space, data passing is accomplished by using a reference to a

---

[*] This applies to most threading systems. In Solaris or POSIX threads, the main tools are the mutex lock, reader writer locks, semaphores, and conditional variables, none of which actually pass any real data.

[†] Comparison between multitasking and threading is discussed in Chapter 1.

common data object. Once we are able to synchronize access to this data object, sending and receiving data using this message queue is simple. In our version of the message queue, the queue is implemented using the Vector class that is implemented in the Java system. We simply need to make sure that we can safely add and remove from this queue; this is accomplished by making sure that all accesses to this queue are synchronized. This implementation is so easy that we do not even need a MsgQueue class. Instead, we could have used the synchronized block mechanism on the Vector object directly, adding and removing the messages directly to and from the Vector. In other words, the message queue IPC is as simple to implement as any container class.[*]

The Shared Memory

A shared memory implementation may be as follows:

```
public class ShareMemory extends BusyFlag {
    byte memory[];
    public ShareMemory (int size) {
        memory = new byte[size];
    }

    public synchronized byte[] attach() {
        getBusyFlag();
        return memory;
    }

    public synchronized void detach() {
        freeBusyFlag();
    }
}
```

Just like the MsgQueue class, the ShareMemory class is also not difficult and may be unnecessary: we could just as easily have synchronized on the byte array object directly and not needed to implement this class. The only advantage is that since we implemented the ShareMemory class as a subclass of the BusyFlag class, we can attach() and detach() from this shared memory at any scope, including a scope that is bigger than a single method.

The real point behind all this is that, even though threads are somewhat analogous to processes, we have to learn to think about data differently than we would between two processes. To share data between processes requires specialized functions that are implemented in the operating system. But data in a Java program is always shared between threads. The fact that we don't have to do anything special to share this data means that while we don't really need IPCs as we know it, we

---

[*] A container class is a data structure that can contain arbitrary data.

have to constantly think threaded. Every time we develop a class, we should be concerned that it may be used by many threads simultaneously, whether our program actually contains many threads or not.

The Circular Linked List

So what about all the container classes we will develop? The linked list? The B-tree? The graph? Any other data structure we care to invent? When we implement one of these classes, should we implement it such that it can be accessed by multiple threads in parallel? The answer could be personal preference or corporate policy. It is, however, not difficult to make any container class safe for multiple threads. And it is arguably better to make it safe and not worry whether sometime in the future this container might be used across multiple threads. Let's take a look at a container class most of us have implemented at one time or another, the circularly linked list:

```java
public class CircularListNode {
    Object o;
    CircularListNode next;
    CircularListNode prev;
};
```

Just like any other linked list most of us have written, we will use a simple data structure node to store the object. We actually don't care what type of object we have in our list, so all we need is a reference to the Object class. This allows us to hold any type of object in our container.[*] We will also keep a reference to the previous node and to the next node in the circularly linked list. This is, of course, an implementation detail; we merely keep two references for efficiency in our search.

```java
public class CircularList {
    private CircularListNode current;

    public synchronized void insert(Object o) {
        CircularListNode tn = new CircularListNode();
        tn.o = o;
        if (current == null) {
            tn.next = tn.prev = tn;
            current = tn;
        } else {                            // Add Before Current Node
            tn.next = current;
            tn.prev = current.prev;
            current.prev.next = tn;
            current.prev = tn;
```

---

[*] To hold a primitive type, you need to use one of the type wrapper classes: Character, Integer, Float, etc.

```
        }
    }

    public synchronized void delete(Object o) {
        CircularListNode p = find(o);
        CircularListNode next = p.next;
        CircularListNode prev = p.prev;
        if (p == p.next) {          // Last Object on the list
            current = null;
            return;
        }
        prev.next = next;
        next.prev = prev;
        if (current == p) current = next;
    }

    private CircularListNode find(Object o) {
        CircularListNode p = current;
        if (p == null)
            throw new IllegalArgumentException();
        do {
            if (p.o == o) return p;
            p = p.next;
        } while (p != current);
        throw new IllegalArgumentException();
    }

    public synchronized Object locate(Object o) {
        CircularListNode p = current;
        do {
            if (p.o.equals(o)) return p.o;
            p = p.next;
        } while (p != current);
        throw new IllegalArgumentException();
    }

    public synchronized Object getNext() {
        if (current == null)
            return null;
        current = current.next;
        return current.o;
    }
}
```

The implementation of our CircularList class is probably no different from any circularly linked list implementation we may have done before. We simply provide methods to insert() and delete() from the circularly linked list; once that list has the objects, we can pass this list to other methods that may process the list.

This processing is done by simply cycling through the list with the `getNext()` method or by searching for a particular object using the `locate()` method.

How do we make this CircularList class safe for use by multiple threads? It's as simple as declaring all the methods as synchronized. By adding the synchronized keyword, we can now use this CircularList class safely across different threads simultaneously. In other words, by taking a few minutes to make the class safe, we can use this class as a form of inter-thread communication. With enough practice, we should use the synchronization tools without much effort.

Note that the `find()` method is not synchronized: as a private method that is called only by synchronized methods, there is no reason for it to be synchronized, though it wouldn't have hurt had we done so.[*]

Synchronization and Efficiency

It can be argued that synchronizing a class just because it might be used by multiple threads is inefficient: it takes a certain amount of time to acquire the synchronization lock. This is a trade-off a developer must be aware of when designing a large program.

In this book, we've taken the view that it is easier to solve performance problems when they occur rather than finding bugs caused by lack of data synchronization.

A Network Server Class

In the socket networking model, the server side has to read from or write to many sockets that are connected to many clients. We already know that by reading data from a socket in a separate thread, we solve the problem of hanging while we're waiting for data. Threading on the server side has an additional benefit: by having a thread associated with each client, we no longer need to worry about other clients within any single thread. This simplifies our server-side programming: we can code our classes as if we were handling a single client at a time.

In this section, we'll develop such a server. But before we dive right in, let us review some networking basics.

---

[*] Note the subtle difference between the `find()` and `locate()` methods: as in internal method, the `find()` method returns objects of CircularListNode; the `locate()` method returns the actual object that was inserted into the list.

Figure 5-1 shows the data connections between several clients and a server. The server side socket setup is implemented in two steps. First, a socket is used for the purpose of listening on a port known to the client. The client connects to this port as a means to negotiate a private connection to the server.

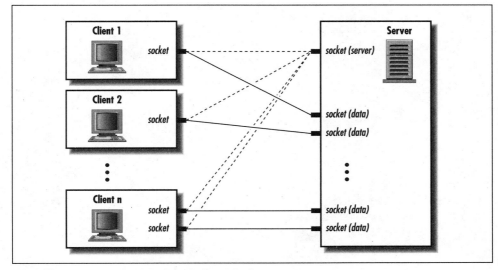

Figure 5-1. Network connections between clients and server

Once a data connection has been negotiated, the server and client then communicate through this private connection. In general, this process is generic: what most programmers are concerned with is the data sockets (the private connection). Furthermore, the data sockets on the server side are usually self-contained to a particular client. While it is possible to have different mechanisms that deal with many data sockets at the same time, generally the same code is used to deal with each of the data sockets independently of the other data sockets.

Since the setup is generic, we can place it into a generic TCPServer class and not have to implement the generic code again. Basically, this TCPServer class creates a ServerSocket and accepts connection requests from clients. This is done in a separate thread. Once a connection is made, the server clone()s (makes a copy of) itself so that it may handle the new client connection in a new thread.[*]

```
import java.net.*;
import java.io.*;

public class TCPServer implements Cloneable, Runnable {
    Thread runner = null;
```

---

[*] In the alpha release of Java, there was a NetworkServer class that accomplished the same thing. This class was later moved to the Sun package and, hence, is not available on all platforms.

```java
        ServerSocket server = null;
        Socket data = null;

        public synchronized void startServer(int port) throws IOException {
            if (runner == null) {
                server = new ServerSocket(port);
                runner = new Thread(this);
                runner.start();
            }
        }

        public synchronized void stopServer() {
            if (server != null) {
                runner.stop();
                runner == null;
                server.close();
            }
        }

        public void run() {
            if (server != null) {
                while (true) {
                    try {
                        Socket datasocket = server.accept();
                        TCPServer newSocket = (TCPServer) clone();

                        newSocket.server = null;
                        newSocket.data = datasocket;
                        newSocket.runner = new Thread(newSocket);
                        newSocket.runner.start();
                    } catch (Exception e) {}
                }
            } else {
                run(data);
            }
        }

        public void run(Socket data) {

        }
    }
```

Considering the number of threads started by the TCPServer class, the implementation of the class is simple. First, the TCPServer class implements the Runnable interface; we will be creating threads this class will execute. Second, the class is Cloneable, so that a copy of this class can be created for each connection. And since the copy of the class is also Runnable, we can create another thread for each client connection. Since the original TCPServer object must operate on the server socket, and the clones must operate on the data sockets, the TCPServer class must be written to service both the server and data sockets.

To begin, once a TCPServer object has been instantiated, the startServer() method is called:

```
public synchronized void startServer(int port) throws IOException {
    if (runner == null) {
        server = new ServerSocket(port);     // Establish socket
        runner = new Thread(this);           // Establish thread
        runner.start();
    }
}
```

This method creates a ServerSocket object and a separate thread to handle the ServerSocket object. By handling the ServerSocket in another thread, the start-Server() method can return immediately, and the same program can act as multiple servers. We could have performed this initialization in the constructor of the TCPServer class; there's no particular reason why we chose to do this in a separate method.

The stopServer() method is the "clean up" method for the TCPServer class:

```
public synchronized void stopServer() {
    if (server != null) {
        runner.stop();      // Stop the thread
        runner == null;
        server.close();     // Terminate socket
    }
}
```

This method cleans up what was done in the startServer() method. In this case, we need to stop() the thread we started and close() the socket the thread was working on. We need to set the runner variable to null to allow the object to be reused: if the runner variable is null, the startServer() method can be called later to start another ServerSocket on the same or different port.

Notice that the stopServer() method also checks to see if the server variable is null before trying to stop the server. The reason for this is because the TCPS-erver object will be cloned to handle the data sockets. Since this clone handles a data socket, we set the server variable to null in the clone. This extra check is done just in case the programmer decides to execute the stopServer() method from the clone instance that is handling a data socket.[*]

The bulk of the logic comes in the run() method:

---

[*] This will be clearer when we finish examining this TCPServer class. The server instance variable determines if we are a thread handling the server socket or one of the data sockets.

```
public void run() {
    if (server != null) {
        while (true) {
            try {
                Socket datasocket = server.accept();
                TCPServer newSocket = (TCPServer) clone();

                newSocket.server = null;
                newSocket.data = datasocket;
                newSocket.runner = new Thread(newSocket);
                newSocket.runner.start();
            } catch (Exception e) {}
        }
    } else {
        run(data);
    }
}
```

What is interesting about this class is that the run() method contains some conditional code. Since the server instance variable is set in the startServer() method, the if statement in the run() method always succeeds. Later we will be cloning this TCPServer object and starting more threads using the clone. The conditional code differentiates the clone from the original.

The handling of the ServerSocket is straightforward. We just need to accept() connections from the clients. All the details of binding to the socket and setting up the number of listeners are handled by the ServerSocket class itself. Once we have accepted a network connection from a client, we once again have a situation that benefits from threading.

However, in this case, instead of using a different Runnable class, we use the TCPServer class: more precisely, we clone() our TCPServer object and configure it to run as a Runnable object in a newly created thread. This is why the TCPServer's run() method checks to see if a ServerSocket object is available or not. The reason we cloned our TCPServer object was so we can have private data for each thread. By making a copy of the object, we make a copy of the instance variables that can then be set to the values needed by the newly created thread.

All this code that handles the ServerSocket is in the while loop of the run() method. The rest of the run() method handles the client data socket:

```
public void run() {
    if (server != null) {
        // code to handle the server socket
    } else {
```

```
            run(data);
        }
    }

    public void run(Socket data) {

    }
```

The newly created thread running with the newly cloned Runnable object first calls the `run()` method; for a data socket, the `run()` method just calls the overloaded `run(Socket)` method. As can be seen from the code, this `run(Socket)` method does absolutely nothing; using the TCPServer class by itself does nothing with the data sockets. To have a useful TCPServer, then, you must extend it:

```
import java.net.*;
import java.io.*;

public class ServerHandler extends TCPServer {
    public void run(Socket data) {
        try {
            InputStream is = data.getInputStream();
            OutputStream os = data.getOutputStream();

            // Process the data socket here !!
        } catch (Exception e) {}
    }
}
```

All we need to do in our subclass is override the `run(Socket)` method; we only need to handle one data socket in the `run(Socket)` method. We do not have to worry about the ServerSocket or any of the other data Sockets. When the `run(Socket)` method is called, it is running in its own thread with its own copy of the TCPServer object. All the details of the ServerSocket and the other data Sockets are hidden from this instance of the TCPServer class.

Once we have developed a specific version of the TCPServer class (in this case, the ServerHandler class), we create an instance of the class and start the server. An example usage of the ServerHandler class is:

```
import java.net.*;
import java.io.*;

public class MyServer {
    public static void main(String args[]) throws Exception {
        TCPServer serv = new ServerHandler();

        serv.startServer(300);
    }
}
```

Using this ServerHandler class is simple. We just need to instantiate a TCPServer object and call its startServer() method. Since the ServerHandler object is also a TCPServer object, it behaves just like a TCPServer object; the only difference is that each data socket will have code that is specific to the ServerHandler class executed on its behalf.

The TCPServer Class and Applets

In our usage of the TCPServer class, we have implemented a standalone "application" whose purpose is to provide a service. This service is available to clients who are either applications or applets (or programs written in any language). The TCPServer example is a standalone application for two reasons.

First, there are few cases imaginable where an applet should provide a network service. The purpose of an applet is to be downloaded to a browser and provide a service to the user. This service is on-demand and may be stopped at any time. There is no service that can be provided in this temporary environment that is useful to other clients on the network.

Second, it is a security violation for applets to instantiate a ServerSocket object. While this may not be true in certain browsers, particularly those which are configurable for the Intranet, this is true for most available Internet browsers.

What other threading issues, most notably synchronization issues, are we concerned with in our TCPServer class? Basically, there are really no issues we have not already seen. The startServer() and stopServer() methods are synchronized because they examine common instance variables that may change. The run() method does not have to be synchronized because the startServer() method is written to guarantee the run() method is called only once. The stopServer() method also stops the thread before closing the server socket, hence preventing a race condition.*

Since all the calls to the run() method in each connection are done in a clone() of the TCPServer object, there is no reason to synchronize the data socket threads because they will be changing and examining different instances of the TCPServer class. The separate threads that handle the data sockets are not sharing data and hence do not need to be synchronized. And if the ServerHan-

---

* To be correct, we probably should have also waited until the thread has completely stopped before closing the ServerSocket. This is left as an exercise for the reader.

dler class needed to share data, then the synchronization that would be done would be the ServerHandler or one of its supporting classes.

In this example, we used the Runnable interface technique. Could we have derived from the Thread class directly instead of using the Runnable interface? Yes, we could have. However, using the Runnable interface makes it possible for the TCPServer class to start another thread with a `clone()` of itself. Deriving from the Thread class requires a different implementation. This implementation probably requires that a new TCPServer class be instantiated, instead of simply cloned.

We are not keeping a reference of the "data socket" threads objects anywhere; is this a problem? It is not a problem. As noted earlier, the threading system keeps an internal reference to every active thread in the system. As long as the `stop()` method has not been called on the thread or the `run()` method has not completed, the thread is considered active, and a reference is kept somewhere in the threading system. While removing all references to a Thread object prevents the TCPServer from calling the `stop()` method for the thread, the garbage collector cannot act on the thread object because the thread system still has a reference to it.

Have you noticed that it is difficult to tell that the ServerHandler class and the MyServer class are threaded? This the goal that we have been trying to achieve. Threads are a tool, and the threading system is a service. In the end, the classes we create are designed to accomplish a task. This class, if designed correctly, does not need to show what tools it is using. Our ServerHandler class just needs to specify code that will handle one data socket, and the MyServer class just needs to start the Server-Handler service. All the threading stuff is just implementation detail.[*]

The AsyncInputStream Class

The AsyncReadSocket class we previously developed had a few problems:

- This class is specific to the network socket. We could also use an Asynchronous I/O class for files, pipes, or any data stream. Ideally, we should have the ability to allow any data source to be asynchronous, not just network sockets.

- There is already a class structure for input from a stream. The top of this hierarchy is the InputStream class. Ideally, we should we should be subclassed from the InputStream class. We can also benefit from the nested support of the FilterInputStream class and its subclasses.

- Unlike the TCPServer class, the AsyncReadSocket class does not do a good job at hiding the threading details.

---

[*] This concept isn't new to those of us who have already accepted the object-oriented paradigm.

Do we need to develop a new class for this? Doesn't the InputStream class have a method that supports asynchronous I/O? Although barely mentioned during the development of the AsyncReadSocket class, the InputStream class has the `available()` method that returns the number of bytes that can be read from the stream without blocking. Although this method sounds useful, it does not suit our purposes because this method returns the number of bytes which have already been read and are available for processing. This data may be available because a previous read received more bytes than it actually wanted. The `available()` method simply returns the number of bytes that have been physically read but not yet returned to the user. There might be bytes available on the network (for a socket) or in the operating system that is running the Java virtual machine (for a file).

Just because the `available()` method returns 0 does not indicate that a call to the `read()` method will block. Since avoiding calls that block is our primary purpose in developing this class, the `available()` method is not suited to our purpose.

What we need is an InputStream class whose `available()` method reports the correct number of bytes that can be actually `read()` without blocking. This new class, the AsyncInputStream class, will be implemented just like our AsyncReadSocket class. It creates another thread that `read()`s from the InputStream. Since reading is done in another thread, the `read()` method is free to block if data is not available. Users of our AsyncInputStream class simply believe that we are an InputStream object. As shown in Figure 5-2, we are actually deriving from the FilterInputStream class, which is the base class for InputStream classes that contains InputStream instances.[*]

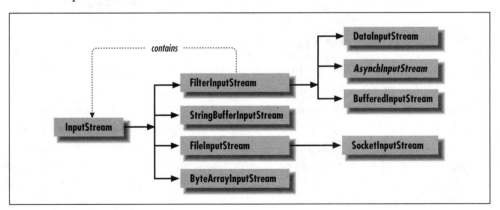

Figure 5-2. The Java InputStream class hierarchy

---

[*] The exact details of this input data model are not within the scope of this book.

The fact that we start another thread to read the data is an implementation detail. Before we examine the policies and other details of our AsyncInputStream class, let's examine the AsyncInputStream class itself:

```java
import java.net.*;
import java.io.*;

public class AsyncInputStream extends FilterInputStream
                                    implements Runnable {
    private Thread runner;              // Async Reader Thread
    private byte result[];              // Buffer
    private int reslen;                 // Buffer Length
    private boolean EOF;                // End-of-File Indicator
    private IOException IOError;        // IOExceptions

    protected AsyncInputStream(InputStream in, int bufsize) {
        super(in);
        result = new byte[bufsize];     // Allocate Storage Area
        reslen = 0;                     // and initialize variables
        EOF = false;
        IOError = null;
        runner = new Thread(this);      // Start Reader Thread
        runner.start();
    }

    protected AsyncInputStream(InputStream in) {
        this(in, 1024);
    }

    public synchronized int read() throws IOException {
        while (reslen == 0) {
            try {
                if (EOF) return(-1);
                if (IOError != null) throw IOError;
                wait();
            } catch (InterruptedException e) {}
        }
        return (int) getChar();
    }

    public synchronized int read(byte b[]) throws IOException {
        return read(b, 0, b.length);
    }

    public synchronized int read(byte b[], int off, int len)
                        throws IOException {
        while (reslen == 0) {
            try {
                if (EOF) return(-1);
```

```java
                if (IOError != null) throw IOError;
                wait();
            } catch (InterruptedException e) {}
        }

        int sizeread = Math.min(reslen, len);
        byte c[] = getChars(sizeread);
        System.arraycopy(b, off, c, 0, sizeread);
        return(sizeread);
    }

    public synchronized long skip(long n) throws IOException {
        int sizeskip = Math.min(reslen, (int) n);
        if (sizeskip > 0) {
            byte c[] = getChars(sizeskip);
        }
        return((long)sizeskip);
    }

    public synchronized int available() throws IOException {
        return reslen;
    }

    public synchronized void close() throws IOException {
        reslen = 0;         // Clear Buffer
        EOF = true;         // Mark End Of File
        notifyAll();        // Alert all Threads
    }

    public synchronized void mark(int readlimit) {
    }

    public synchronized void reset() throws IOException {
    }

    public boolean markSupported() {
        return false;
    }

    public void run() {
        try {
            while (true) {
                int c = in.read();
                synchronized (this) {
                    if ((c == -1) || (EOF)) {
                        EOF = true;         // Mark End Of File
                        in.close();         // Close Input Source
                        return;             // End IO Thread
                    } else {
```

```
                        putChar((byte)c);   // Store the byte read
                }
            }
        }

    } catch (IOException e) {
        synchronized (this) {
            IOError = e;                // Store Exception
        }
        return;
    } finally {
        synchronized (this) {
            notifyAll();                // Alert all Threads
        }
    }
}

private synchronized void putChar(byte c) {
    if (reslen < result.length) {
        result[reslen++] = c;
        notify();
    }
}

private synchronized byte getChar() {
    byte c = result[0];
    System.arraycopy(result, 1, result, 0, --reslen);
    return c;
}

private synchronized byte[] getChars(int chars) {
    byte c[] = new byte[chars];
    System.arraycopy(c, 0, result, 0, chars);
    reslen -= chars;
    System.arraycopy(result, chars, result, 0, reslen);
    return c;
}
}
```

For our purposes, we aren't interested in the details of threading the I/O itself; there is no threading code in this class that we have not already seen in the AsyncReadSocket class. The new thread simply does a blocking read() on the InputStream, and methods are provided so that the original thread can get the data in a nonblocking manner. The InputStream aspect of this class is interesting, but, obviously, learning the Java data input system is not within the scope of this book.

Why is the discussion of this class important? And how is this class different from the Async-ReadSocket class? While this class accomplishes the asynchronous read() in the same fashion as the AsyncReadSocket class, it is also a FilterInputStream, and it is the relationship between the threaded I/O and the InputStream that we are concerned with here. Since this class must behave as an InputStream, we cannot design the behavior of the class as optimally as we would have if all we had been concerned with was communicating with the I/O thread. This is the sort of real-world trade-off that must be made when implementing threaded classes.

In order for the class to function correctly, we need to use practically every synchronization technique that was introduced in the last chapter. Let's start with a look at the instance variables and constructors of the AsyncInputStream class:

```
import java.net.*;
import java.io.*;

public class AsyncInputStream extends FilterInputStream
                             implements Runnable {
    private Thread runner;        // Async Reader Thread
    private byte result[];        // Buffer
    private int reslen;           // Buffer Length
    private boolean EOF;          // End-of-File Indicator
    private IOException IOError;   // IOExceptions

    protected AsyncInputStream(InputStream in, int bufsize) {
        super(in);
        result = new byte[bufsize];  // Allocate Storage Area
        reslen = 0;                  // and initialize variables
        EOF = false;
        IOError = null;
        runner = new Thread(this);   // Start Reader Thread
        runner.start();
    }

    protected AsyncInputStream(InputStream in) {
        this(in, 1024);
    }
}
```

The first three instance variables, runner, result, and reslen, are the important data of the class. runner is the reference to the I/O thread that is started by this class, and result and reslen are the data storage and the length that is being passed back from the I/O thread.[*] The EOF and IOError instance vari-

---

[*] Our AsyncReadSocket class did not support the concept of data size: the getResult() method of the AsyncReadSocket class did not allow the caller to specify the amount to read. Since the InputStream class can read any amount of data, we must keep track of available data in the buffers.

ables are also used for communication. In order to behave as an InputStream class, we must report end-of-file (EOF) conditions and throw exceptions on I/O errors. These EOF conditions and I/O exceptions are generated from the Input-Stream object contained in the AsyncInputStream class. We must save the EOF condition and catch the I/O exception in the I/O thread, and later indicate the EOF condition or throw the exception in the calling thread. If the AsyncInput-Stream class did not have to behave like an InputStream class, we could have designed a simpler error reporting system.

The first constructor of the AsyncInputStream class is straightforward. First, we just allocate[*] and initialize the buffer and variables we will use to communicate with the I/O thread. Second, we instantiate and start() the I/O thread. The other constructor has the same signature of the FilterInputStream class, from which we inherit, and uses a default buffer size. By providing this constructor, we are behaving as all FilterInputStreams.

The InputStream and the End of File

Obviously, in the case of the FileInputStream, the end-of-file indicator is reported when a read() past the EOF is detected. But what does this indicator mean for other data sources?

The EOF can be caused by a number of reasons. The StringBufferInputStream is reporting the end of the string, the ByteArrayInputStream is reporting the end of the array, and the SocketInputStream may be reporting the closure of the network connection.

In any case, we should just use the indicator as the termination of any more data from the source and act appropriately. We should not be concerned with what the actual data source is.

Let's start to look into the details of how data is passed back to the user:

```
public synchronized int read() throws IOException {
    while (reslen == 0) {
        try {
            if (EOF) return(-1);
            if (IOError != null) throw IOError;
            wait();
```

---

[*] The AsyncInputStream class has a fixed buffer size and hence, if the I/O thread reads too far ahead, data might be lost. This is purely a design decision: this class was meant to prevent blocking, not to act as a large I/O buffer. We leave the modification of this class to support an unlimited buffer size as an exercise for the reader.

```
            } catch (InterruptedException e) {}
        }
        return (int) getChar();
    }

    private synchronized byte getChar() {
        byte c = result[0];
        System.arraycopy(result, 1, result, 0, --reslen);
        return c;
    }
```

In the InputStream class, the read() method reads a single byte from the input data stream. If an EOF is detected or an IOException had been caught by the I/O thread, it would have been placed in the EOF and IOError instance variables respectively. The read() method returns a -1 to report an EOF or throws the IOException on behalf of the I/O thread. The lock of the AsyncInputStream object protects these two variables along with the data buffer. The read() method is synchronized to make sure that the I/O thread is not accessing these two instance variables at the same time.

Also, we check for the EOF and the I/O exception only when there is no more data in the buffer. Since the I/O thread is reading ahead, we must delay the EOF indicator or throw the exception in the read() method until the user has drained the input from the buffer: the user should see the EOF or exception at the same point in the data it actually occurred. The I/O thread stops reading when it receives either an EOF or an IOException, so we can safely assume all data in the buffer occurred before either condition happened.

Finally, in order to protect the result data buffer and the reslen length indicator, we use the AsyncInputStream object's synchronization lock. The getChar() method, which returns the next character, is also synchronized.[*] You might ask why we are only using a single lock to protect four different instance variables. This is a design issue; the result and reslen variables are related, and it is unlikely that we would be examining or changing one without the other. The EOF and IOError variables are accessed only once during the lifetime of the I/O thread. It is wasteful to create a new lock for this purpose when a suitable lock is already available.

The AsyncInputStream class allows the reading of an InputStream without blocking. However, what happens when we actually do not have data available when a read is requested? The AsyncInputStream class provides asynchronous support by providing a version of the available() method that works as desired. This

---

[*] The synchronization of the getChar() method is actually not necessary. It is a private method, which means it is not accessible from another class. Since it is only called from the read() method that is already synchronized, synchronization of the getChar() method is not necessary.

allows the user of the AsyncInputStream class to call the read() method only when data is available(). The read() method must still behave correctly if the application still calls the method when data is not available. This means that the read() method must block under such conditions. In other words, the read() method must do what it was designed to avoid in the first place:

```
public synchronized int read() throws IOException {
    while (reslen == 0) {
        try {
            if (EOF) return(-1);
            if (IOError != null) throw IOError;
            wait();
        } catch (InterruptedException e) {}
    }
    return (int) getChar();
}

private synchronized void putChar(byte c) {
    result[reslen++] = c;
    notify();
}
```

Obviously, the read() method cannot block by reading from the InputStream; the InputStream is under the control of the I/O thread and should not be accessed directly by the read() method. In order to simulate this blocking, we use the wait and notify mechanism. The read() method simply wait()s for more data to arrive. When data arrives in the I/O thread, a notification is generated when the data is placed in the buffer. This is done by calling the notify() method in the putChar() method. As can be seen by examining the run() method, the putChar() method is called by the I/O thread to place the data it receives in the data buffer:

```
public void run() {
    try {
        while (true) {
            int c = in.read();
            synchronized (this) {
                if ((c == -1) || (EOF)) {
                    EOF = true;            // Mark End Of File
                    in.close();            // Close Input Source
                    return;                // End IO Thread
                } else {
                    putChar((byte)c);      // Store the byte read
                }
            }
        }
    } catch (IOException e) {
```

```
        synchronized (this) {
            IOError = e;                  // Store Exception
        }
        return;
    } finally {
        synchronized (this) {
            notifyAll();                  // Alert all Threads
        }
    }
}
```

The code for the I/O thread is similar to the code in our AsyncReadSocket class. We simply `read()` from the InputStream, blocking if necessary. When we receive data, we place it in the buffer using the `putChar()` method. Additionally, if we receive an `EOF` indicator or catch an `IOException`, we place that information into the appropriate instance variables. To allow all of these actions to take place safely with the other threads, we grab the same lock that is used by the read thread: the synchronization lock of the AsyncInputStream object.

The only difference in the synchronization locks is that we are now using the synchronization block mechanism. This is because synchronization of the `run()` method would yield too large a lock scope. Synchronizing the `run()` method prevents other threads from calling the synchronized `read()` methods of the AsyncInputStream class since the `run()` method is an infinite loop.

What will happen to all the blocking read threads when an EOF or IOException condition occurs? As we mentioned, we are using the wait and notify mechanism to cause the `read()` method to behave in a blocking manner. However, when an `EOF` or `IOException` condition occurs, there can be no more future notifications, since no more data will be arriving. To solve this, we must use the `notifyAll()` method when these conditions occur. The threads can just wake up in turn, taking the available data from the buffer:

```
public void run() {
    try {
        while (true) {
            // read the data
        }
    } catch (IOException e) {
        synchronized (this) {
            IOError = e;                  // Store Exception
        }
        return;
    } finally {
        synchronized (this) {
            notifyAll();                  // Alert all Threads
        }
    }
}
```

```
    }

    public synchronized void close() throws IOException {
        reslen = 0;
        EOF = true;
        notifyAll();                        // Alert all Threads
    }
```

When no more data is `available()` from the buffer, the remaining threads reading the InputStream return from their `read()` methods the condition that occurred. We also do not have to worry about future `read()` method calls; they simply return the condition that occurred.

The implementation of the `available()` method that works as desired—the method which was the reason for our AsyncInputStream class—is actually anticlimactic:

```
    public synchronized int available() throws IOException {
        return reslen;
    }
```

We simply return the number of bytes we have available in the buffer. Since the I/O thread is actually reading the InputStream, blocking if necessary, we know that there are no more bytes sitting on the network that are unaccounted for. Of course, we have to be synchronized due to the fact that we are accessing the `reslen` variable.

Finally, we made three additional design decisions that we made during the development of the AsyncInputStream class. While these decisions are important to the AsyncInputStream class, they will not be examined here, because they don't pertain to our discussion of threading issues. But to be complete, here is a brief overview:

- The `read(byte[])` method, just like the `read()` method, blocks if data is not available. However, if data is available, but not enough to fill the byte array, the `read(byte[])` method simply reads less than requested, returning the number of bytes actually read. We have chosen this implementation due to the design of the AsyncInputStream class. It works asynchronously, and this implementation best fulfills that design spirit.

- The `skip()` method skips only the number of bytes possible without blocking. This means that if the `skip()` method is called to `skip()` more bytes than are `available()`, it simply skips what is available and returns the number of bytes actually skipped. Again, this implementation best fulfills the design spirit of the AsyncInputStream class.

- The mark and reset feature of the AsyncInputStream class is not supported, even if this feature is supported in the InputStream class that we contain.

There's no real reason why an asynchronous stream would support this, and if users really require this feature, they can always instantiate a BufferedInput-Stream object containing our AsyncInputStream object.

The AsyncOutputStream Class?

One of the main reasons we never implemented an AsyncWriteSocket class is because of usability. With data being buffered at so many places between the two ends of a network connection, there is less reason to worry about blocking for a long time during a `write()` call. However, although it's a rare case, it is possible for a `write()` method to block.

In the case of an AsyncOutputStream class, there is another complication: IOExceptions that are thrown by the `write()` method of the contained Out-putStream cannot be delivered correctly. The call to the AsyncOutputStream's `write()` method would have long since returned. This could be handled by throwing the exception on a later call to the `write()` method or on a call to the `close()` method. That's not a perfect solution, but it's common in cases where data that is written is buffered.

Those developers who want truly robust programs that write data asynchro-nously may consider implementing their own AsyncOutputStream based on the AsyncInputStream we've shown here.

Instances of the AsyncInputStream class behave like any InputStream object. They can be used in cases where an InputStream object is normally used with no changes. While the AsyncInputStream class is also a Runnable type, that is just an implementation detail. Users of the AsyncInputStream class should not even know that a new thread has been started on their behalf when an AsyncInput-Stream object is instantiated.

Using TCPServer with AsyncInputStreams

Let's modify our ServerHandler class to read requests from clients in an asynchro-nous manner:

```
import java.net.*;
import java.io.*;

public class ServerHandler extends TCPServer {
    public void run(Socket data) {
        try {
```

```
            InputStream is =
                new AsyncInputStream(data.getInputStream());
            OutputStream os = data.getOutputStream();

            // Process the data socket here !!
        } catch (Exception e) {}
    }
}
```

With a single line change to our ServerHandler class, we are now reading from the client in an asynchronous manner. We also practically doubled the number of threads started to provide this service. But from examining the source code, there is no indication that even one thread is started, much less two threads per client connected.[*]

Summary

In this chapter, we have taken a look at some real examples of threads in action along with the issues of their synchronization. Unlike the previous chapters, we have now used threads as simply an implementation tool. We have started new threads and communicated between these threads, but users of our classes are not concerned with and may not even know that these threads exist.

We have also examined synchronization issues in cases where we have not started any threads at all. A simple item like a container class must be designed with threading in mind. This is because, while we may not start any threads, we are already threaded in our program. We must think of threading as not only an implementation detail in our classes, but in all other classes in the system. Threading issues like deadlock and race conditions should always be involved in our class designs, whether we actually used threads in our classes at all.

---

* There is also another thread that is started to accept connections.

6

Java Thread Scheduling

At this point, we've covered the fundamental aspects of Java's threading system and are able to write quite complex programs that exploit Java's threads to complete their tasks. We're now going to move into some of the specialized areas of threaded systems. The programming issues and techniques that we'll explore in the next few chapters of this book are not issues that you'll grapple with every day, but when the need arises to have some explicit control over the behavior of your threads, these issues become very important.

To begin, in this chapter we'll look into the topic of how the Java virtual machine decides which thread should be running at any point in time. We predicate this discussion with the assumption that the Java virtual machine is able to run only a single thread at a time. In release 1.0.2 of the Java Developer's Kit and the release of browsers based on that kit (including the 3.0 release of Netscape), this is always the case: even if a Java application or Java-enabled browser is running on a machine that has multiple processors and an operating system that allows programs to use two or more CPUs simultaneously, the Java virtual machine will not take advantage of more than one processor. Hence, only one thread in your program will be running at any instant in time. Determining which of the many threads in your program is running at any one time is the topic of Java thread scheduling.

The key to understanding Java thread scheduling is to realize that the CPU is a scarce resource. When there are two or more threads that want to run, they end up competing for the CPU and it's up to someone—either the programmer or the

Java virtual machine—to make sure that the CPU is shared between these threads. So the essence of this chapter is how to share the CPU between threads that want to access it.

In the earlier examples, we didn't concern ourselves with this topic because, in those cases, the details of thread scheduling weren't important to us. This was because the threads we were concerned with didn't normally compete for the CPU: they had specific tasks to do, but the threads themselves were usually short-lived or only periodically needed the CPU in order to accomplish their task. Consider the thread that is created automatically for you when you call the getImage() method to load an image. Most of the time, this thread isn't using the CPU because it's waiting for data to arrive over the network. When a burst of data does arrive, this thread quickly processes the data and then goes back and waits for more data; since the thread doesn't need the CPU often, there was never a need to concern ourselves with the Java virtual machine's scheduling mechanism.

We need to worry only about how Java threads are scheduled when one or more of the threads is CPU-intensive over a relatively long period of time (the image loading thread is CPU-intensive, but only for short periods of time). We'll look at how the Java virtual machine handles scheduling by default, and then we'll look at various methods to influence the way in which Java virtual machine schedules threads.

Scheduling in the Java Interpreter

Let's start by looking at an example with some CPU-intensive threads. What is the output of the following program?

```
class TestThread extends Thread {
    String id;
    public TestThread(String s) {
        id = s;
    }
    public void run() {
        int i;
        for (i = 0; i < 10; i++) {
            doCalc(i);
            System.out.println(id);
        }
    }
}

public class Test {
    public static void main(String args[]) {
        TestThread t1, t2, t3;
        t1 = new TestThread("Thread 1");
```

Characterizing Programs

Computer programs—written in Java or otherwise—are typically categorized in one of three ways:

CPU intensive

Programs that require many CPU cycles to complete their task. They use the CPU to perform mathematical or symbolic calculations (e.g., manipulation of strings or images) that require a significant amount of time to perform, but need little or no input from the user or from an external data source.

I/O intensive

Programs that spend the vast majority of their time waiting for I/O operations to complete: reading or writing files to disk, reading or writing data on a network socket, or communicating with another program.

Interactive

Programs that perform operations in response to user input. When the user executes a particular action, the program enters a CPU-intensive or an I/O-intensive phase before returning to wait for the next command. The TCPServer we examined in Chapter 5 belongs to this category, though the interaction comes from other (client) programs rather than from user input.

A single program may go through phases that belong to all these categories.

```
            t1.start();
            t2 = new TestThread("Thread 2");
            t2.start();
            t3 = new TestThread("Thread 3");
            t3.start();
        }
    }
```

Assume that the doCalc() method is computationally expensive, requiring three to five seconds per call, and that it makes no calls to any other methods. Clearly, after the program has completed, we'll have 10 lines of output that say "Thread 1," 10 lines that say "Thread 2," and 10 lines that say "Thread 3," but what will be the order of those output lines?

It's common to assume that these output lines will be in some random order, perhaps something like

```
Thread 1
Thread 2
```

```
Thread 2
Thread 3
Thread 1
Thread 2
Thread 3
Thread 3
```

and so on. But it turns out that the order of the output lines is unspecified by Java, and it's just as likely that we'll see 10 lines that say Thread 1 followed by 10 lines that say Thread 2 followed by 10 lines that say Thread 3. The implication is that our first thread (Thread 1) runs to completion before our second thread (Thread 2) ever starts, and that our second thread runs to completion before our third thread ever starts as well.

To understand what's going on here, we need to explore some of the internal aspects of the Java threading mechanism. First, at a conceptual level, every thread in the Java virtual machine can be in one of four states:

Initial

A thread object is in the initial state from the period when it is created (that is, its constructor is called) until the start() method of the thread object is called.

Runnable

A thread is in the runnable state once its start() method has been called. There are various ways in which a thread leaves the runnable state, but the runnable state can be thought of as a default state: if a thread isn't in any other state, it's in the runnable state.

Blocked

A thread that is blocked is one that cannot be run because it is waiting for some specific event to occur. A simple example is the case of a thread that has opened a socket to some remote data server and attempts to read data from that server when data is not available.

Exiting

A thread is in the exiting state once its run() method returns or its stop() method has been called.

Even though the Java virtual machine can only run a single thread at a time, it's frequently the case that more than one thread in a Java program is in the runnable state. When that happens, the Java virtual machine selects one thread from the pool of runnable threads to become the currently running thread. All the other threads in the pool of runnable threads remain in the runnable state, even though they are actually waiting for a chance to run (that is, to become the currently running thread). So the key question is which of the threads from the pool of runnable threads the Java virtual machine will select to become the currently running thread.

Java implements what's known as a pre-emptive, priority-based scheduler among its various threads. This means that each thread in a Java program is assigned a certain priority, a positive integer that falls within a well-defined range. This priority can be changed only by the programmer. The Java virtual machine never changes the priority of a thread, even when a thread changes between any of the various states outlined above, or even after a thread has been running for a certain period of time. So a thread with a priority of 5 will maintain that priority from the time it is created through its various changes between the runnable and blocked states until the thread terminates and enters the exit state.

This priority value is important, because the guarantee made by the Java virtual machine is that the currently running thread will be the thread that has the highest priority among all the threads that are in the runnable state. That's what we mean when we say that Java implements a priority-based scheduler. And the Java virtual machine implements this scheduling in a pre-emptive fashion, meaning that when a high priority thread enters the runnable state, the Java virtual machine interrupts (pre-empts) whatever lower priority thread is running at the time so that the higher priority thread can become the currently running thread.

Scheduling Example: Threads of Different Priorities

An example should make this clearer. Let's look at the following (incomplete) code example:

```java
public class SchedulingExample implements Runnable {
    public static void main(String args[]) {
        Thread calcThread = new Thread(this);
        calcThread.setPriority(4);
        calcThread.start();

        AsyncReadSocket reader;
        reader = new AsyncReadSocket(new Socket(host, port));
        reader.setPriority(6);
        reader.start();

        doDefault();
    }

    public void run() {
        doCalc();
    }
}
```

This Java program has three threads: first, there's the default thread executing the `main()` method which, after creating the other threads, is going to execute the `doDefault()` method. Second, there's the calculation thread (`calcThread`) that is going to execute the `doCalc()` method. And third, there's the reader AsyncReadSocket thread (from Chapter 5) that's reading a socket.

In the following discussion, we assume the threads we created are the only threads in the Java virtual machine, but as we already know, there are many other threads that have been created on our behalf. For simplicity, we'll ignore those threads, since, for the most part, they'll remain in the blocked state and won't affect this discussion. Figure 6-1 shows the transition of the threads in our example between their various states.

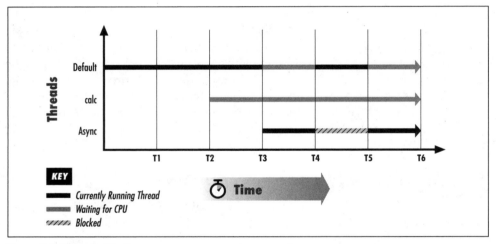

Figure 6-1. Thread state diagram

We start at time T1 with our single default thread executing the `main()` method. The initial thread has a priority of 5 and is the only active thread in the Java virtual machine. So the default thread is in the runnable state and is also the currently running thread. At time T2, the default thread creates the `calcThread`, gives it a priority of 4, and calls its `start()` method. Now there are two threads in the runnable state, but the default thread is still the currently running thread because it has a higher priority than `calcThread`. `calcThread` is in the runnable state, but it is waiting for the CPU.

The default thread continues execution: it creates the `reader` thread, gives it a priority of 6, and then calls the `reader` thread's `start()` method. Immediately after the default thread calls the `reader` thread's `start()` method, the `reader` thread enters the runnable state. Because the `reader` thread has a higher priority than the default thread, the `reader` thread becomes the currently running thread (at the expense of the default thread, which will no longer be running even though it's in the runnable state). These changes in the state of the threads are shown at time T3 in the diagram.

Now the reader thread executes the readChar() method on its socket. If no data is available, the reader thread enters the blocked state (shown at time T4). When this happens, the default thread begins execution from the point at which it was previously interrupted (in fact, the default thread will be completely unaware that it had been interrupted). The default thread continues to be the currently running thread until data becomes available to satisfy the readChar() method. Immediately when this data becomes available (at time T5), the Java virtual machine changes the state of the reader thread to the runnable state. When the Java virtual machine changes the state of the reader thread, it notices that the reader thread now has the highest priority of all the runnable threads, so it interrupts the default thread and makes the reader thread the currently running thread.

Meanwhile, calcThread has been patiently waiting for its chance to run, and it must continue to wait until both the default thread and the reader thread are blocked or have exited (or until some thread raises the priority of calcThread). calcThread is in danger of never becoming the currently running thread at all, a concept known as *CPU starvation*. It is the responsibility of the Java developer to ensure that none of the threads in their Java program starve; the Java virtual machine never adjusts any thread's priority to compensate for that thread's lack of availability to the CPU.

So far this discussion has been very deterministic. At any time, if we know the state and priority of all the threads, we know which thread is the currently running thread. But what would have happened if all the thread had the same priority? This is essentially the question posed by the code example that began this chapter: in that example, all the threads had the same priority. At this point, the behavior of the threaded code becomes nondeterministic.

Scheduling Equal-Priority Threads

In most Java programs, we'll have multiple threads of the same priority; we need to expand our discussion to take this into account. What follows is a description of what happens at a conceptual level within the Java virtual machine. Our intent here is to provide an illustration of how the thread scheduling within the Java virtual machine works, not to provide a blueprint of how the Java virtual machine is actually implemented.

We can conceive that the Java virtual machine keeps track of all the threads in a Java program by means of linked lists; every thread in the Java virtual machine is on a list that represents the state of that thread. There are in the Java virtual machine 10 priority levels a thread can have and we conceive, therefore, of 13 linked lists: one for all threads in the initial state, one for all threads in the blocked state, one for all threads in the exiting state, and one for each priority level. The list of threads at a given priority level represents only those threads that are currently in the runnable state: a thread in the runnable state at priority 7 will be on the priority 7 list, but when the thread blocks, it moves to the blocked linked list.

For simplicity, we conceive of all the blocked threads as being represented on a single list, but there is really no advantage to that: there's really just a pool of threads that are in the blocked state, and there is no ordering between the blocked threads. On the other hand, there definitely is an implied ordering in the runnable threads at a particular level. When it comes time for the Java virtual machine to select a thread to become the currently running thread, it checks the list representing the threads at priority 10. If that list is empty, it then checks the list representing threads at priority 9, and so on until it encounters a nonempty list. It then makes the first thread on that list the currently running thread and also moves that thread to the end of the list.

Let's revisit our last example and this time change the priority of `calcThread` so that it is now the same as the default thread. If these two threads have the same priority, then our state diagram might look like Figure 6-2:[*]

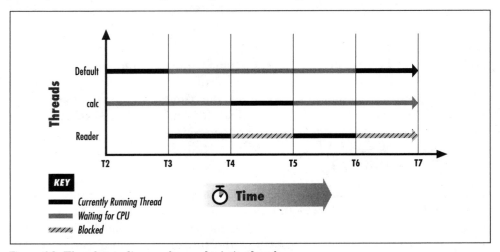

Figure 6-2. Thread state diagram for equal-priority threads

---

* Then again, it might not; see the following discussion of scheduling events when there are equal-priority threads. Also, note that we start here at time T2; things aren't interesting until there are two threads available.

The difference now is that the default thread and `calcThread` have the same priority, so that when the `reader` thread blocks, the Java virtual machine does something different to select the currently running thread. In this example, we're concerned with only three of Java's internal lists: the list of priority 5 threads (the default thread and `calcThread`), the list of priority 6 threads (the `reader` thread), and the list of blocked threads. As the Java virtual machine enters time T2, when `calcThread` is started, those lists look like this:[*]

```
PRIORITY 5:  Default -> Calc -> NULL
PRIORITY 6:  NULL
  BLOCKED:   NULL
```

So the Java virtual machine selects the default thread to be the currently running thread since it is at the head of the nonempty list that has the highest priority. The Java virtual machine also alters the priority 5 list so that as it exits time T2; that list appears as:

```
PRIORITY 5:  Calc -> Default -> NULL
```

At time T3, the default thread starts the `reader` thread, pre-empting the default thread. The Java virtual machine's internal lists now look like this:

```
PRIORITY 5:  Calc -> Default -> NULL
PRIORITY 6:  Reader -> NULL
  BLOCKED:   NULL
```

At T4 when the `reader` thread enters the blocked state, the Java virtual machine searches for a nonempty priority list and finds one at priority 5; the first thread in that list (`calcThread`) becomes the currently running thread and gets moved to the end of the list. So exiting time T4, the internal lists now look like this:

```
PRIORITY 5:  Default -> Calc -> NULL
PRIORITY 6:  NULL
  BLOCKED:   Reader -> NULL
```

And so we continue: every time the reader thread enters the blocked state, the default thread and `calcThread` change positions on the priority 5 list, and they alternate becoming the currently running thread.

So far, we've still had a very deterministic discussion, and the behavior of our threads has still been correspondingly deterministic. But it turns out that there is one complication that introduces a nondeterministic behavior into this scheduling mechanism. We'll discuss this complication by introducing the notion of a

---

* In these diagrams, the currently running thread is always the *last* thread on the highest-priority, nonempty list: that thread was at the head of its list when it was selected to be the currently running thread, at which time it was also moved to the end of the list.

Java scheduling event, which is something that occurs inside the Java virtual machine that causes it to choose the currently running thread.[*]

The complication arises because there are operating-system-specific scheduling events that affect the scheduling of threads of equal priority. We'll postulate the existence of three types of Java scheduling events:

1. *When the currently running thread leaves the runnable state*

   If the currently running thread blocks or exits, the Java virtual machine must select another thread to become the currently running thread. In Figure 6-2, this is the type of scheduling event that occurred at time T4 and at time T6 when the `reader` thread went from the runnable state to the blocked state.

2. *When a thread that has a higher priority than the currently running thread enters the runnable state*

   These events are at the heart of the pre-emption model of the Java scheduler. In Figure 6-2, one of these events occurred at time T3 when the `reader` thread went from the initial state to the runnable state; another occurred at time T5 when the `reader` thread went from the blocked state to the runnable state. In both cases, because the `reader` thread was a higher-priority thread than the currently running thread, a Java scheduling event occurred so that the reader thread became the currently running thread.

3. *Expiration of an arbitrary timer*

   The Java virtual machine arbitrarily creates a scheduling event at some point in time; usually this is at a fixed interval, like 10 times a second.[†] In our example where there are only two threads both at priority 5:

```
PRIORITY 5:  Default -> Calc -> NULL
PRIORITY 6:  NULL
   BLOCKED:  Reader -> NULL
```

   and `calcThread` is the currently running thread, then when one of these timer-based events occurs, the default thread becomes the currently running thread, and they change places in the list:

```
PRIORITY 5:  Calc -> Default -> NULL
PRIORITY 6:  NULL
   BLOCKED:  Reader -> NULL
```

---

[*] Once again, the idea of a Java scheduling event is an abstraction not necessarily corresponding directly to any specific aspect of the Java virtual machine implementation—or even the Java virtual machine specification.

[†] Whether or not this time interval exists, or its size when it does exist, is a platform-specific implementation detail, as we discuss in the next section.

One hundred milliseconds later, another of these timing events may occur, switching the default and calculation threads in their list again and causing `calcThread` to become the currently running thread.

It's important to realize that in all other cases, the change of the state of a thread does not cause a scheduling event; when a thread that has an equal or lower priority than the currently running thread changes state, no scheduling event occurs. In this case, it is not a requirement that a scheduling event occur, since the currently running thread still has the highest priority of all runnable threads in the Java virtual machine. In terms of our concept of the linked lists in the Java virtual machine, consider what happens when there are only two threads in the program, both of which are runnable at a priority level of 5:

```
PRIORITY 5:   Calc -> Default -> NULL
```

So the default thread is the currently running thread. When the default thread creates a new thread (the `reader` thread), the list of threads looks like this:

```
PRIORITY 5:   Calc -> Default -> NULL
  INITIAL:    Reader -> NULL
```

No scheduling event has occurred in this case, so the default thread remains the currently running thread. If the `reader` thread is now put at priority 5 rather than 6, when it moves to the runnable state, it will be added to the beginning of the priority 5 list

```
PRIORITY 5:   Reader -> Calc -> Default -> NULL
```

so that it is the next thread that is run at priority level 5.[*] This still does not cause a scheduling event; the default thread continues to run until the next scheduling event.

Timer-Based Scheduling

There is a lack of consensus regarding scheduling events of type 3, which causes some programs to behave differently in one implementation of the Java virtual machine than in another. On most UNIX implementations of Java, there are no scheduling events of type 3; everything is very deterministic, based on the scheduling events of types 1 and 2. In the example with which we began this section, that would lead to the output where there were 10 lines that said Thread 1 followed by 10 lines that said Thread 2, and so on. On these implementations, once a Java thread becomes the currently running thread, it remains the currently running thread until it exits the runnable state or until a higher priority thread

---

[*] Alternately, it's possible that the new thread is placed at the end of the list so that all other threads have an opportunity to run before it. In practical terms, this distinction is not important.

enters the runnable state. Since in our initial example all threads had the same priority, scheduling events of type 2 never comes into play; since the threads never enter the blocked state, the only time scheduling events of type 1 occur is when the currently running thread enters the exiting state—that is, after it has printed out all 10 lines of its output.

On Windows NT and Windows 95 implementations, scheduling events of type 3 do occur: both these platforms periodically have a Java scheduling event. In the initial example of this chapter, that would mean that the output is mixed: the lines saying Thread 1 will be arbitrarily interspersed with the lines saying Thread 2 and those saying Thread 3. On these platforms, you'll observe a round-robin scheduling effect between threads that have the same priority.

Why Are There Different Java Scheduling Mechanisms?

The difference in Java scheduling mechanisms on different operating systems is somewhat surprising, given Java's strive toward platform independence. In practice, this difference rarely matters, both because in most programs the scheduling mechanism itself rarely matters, and because the time-slicing behavior of Windows 95 and NT platforms is processor specific anyway. Still, in those cases where the behavior does matter, it's inconvenient to have to take this operating-system-specific difference into account.

This difference comes about because the thread mechanism Java uses on some platforms ultimately depends on the thread mechanism of the underlying operating system. Of course, this is not an absolute requirement, since nothing in the Java threads API requires any operating-system involvement. In fact, the implementation of Java 1.0 on Solaris platforms does not use the Solaris operating system's thread library at all; it uses a simpler thread library that is not integrated into the operating system. But there is a trend towards using the native thread libraries on all systems that implement Java.

The move to implement Java threads using the operating system's native thread calls created this difference in scheduling mechanisms, which reflects an ongoing difference in the basic philosophies of the vendors involved. UNIX vendors tend to favor the POSIX threads specification, while Microsoft's implementation favors what their engineers feel is the better model.

Both models have benefits and drawbacks. But for our purposes, the debate over which model is better is academic, since the Java developer wants to avoid any operating-system-specific behavior.

And so the availability (or not) of the scheduling events of type 3 causes the arbitrary output from our initial example: on UNIX platforms there will be no randomness to the output lines, whereas on Windows platforms, the output lines will be somewhat random. This lack of determinism is even greater when platform differences are taken into account. Since the Windows scheduling effect is based on a fixed period of time, the speed of the underlying processor becomes important: a Pentium processor is going to execute each iteration of the doCalc() method much faster than a 386 processor. As a result, the output on a Pentium-based machine is likely to have more clusters of the same line of output (i.e., three lines that say Thread 1 followed by three that say Thread 2 followed by three that say Thread 3 and so on) than will the 386-based machine (where output will more likely be one line of Thread 1 and then one of Thread 2, and so on).

The upshot of this is that if you require the threads in your Java program to execute in a certain order, it is up to you to program the threads to achieve that order. If all your threads have the same priority, then you must make sure that none of your threads starve; you can't count on the time-slicing behavior of the Java implementation on a particular platform to make sure that your threads do not starve. Similarly, if you have threads you would prefer to execute sequentially, you cannot count on the behavior of the UNIX implementations to ensure that equal-priority threads will not interrupt each other. Either way, you must program your threads to have the scheduling behavior you need.

In the remainder of this chapter, we'll look at various ways to do just that, including simple methods to prevent thread starvation and a complete, time-sliced round-robin thread scheduler.

When Scheduling Is Important

If the preceding discussion seems somewhat complicated and esoteric, here's the good news: most of the time, all these scheduling details have no practical impact on your Java program. This is true, in general, of threaded programs under any operating system and with any threading library, but it's particularly true in the case of Java programs.

In a Java program, a thread is most often created because the programmer wants to call a method that may block—usually a read() method on a slow Input-Stream (such as a SocketInputStream) or the Thread.sleep() method to emulate a periodic timer. As a result, threads in the Java virtual machine tend to oscillate between the blocked and runnable states quite often. And as long as every thread in the Java virtual machine is going to block periodically, then they'll all get an opportunity to run: each thread becomes the currently running thread, blocks, exits the blocked state, is placed on the end of the list for its priority, and moves up through the list as other threads go through the same cycle.

Even in those cases where all the threads in the virtual machine do not periodically block, it's usually possible to ignore the issue of scheduling altogether. A Java program usually performs a specific task, and often the completion of that task is all that matters. A Java program that is charged with calculating and displaying four convolutions of a GIF image has to wait for all four convoluted images to be complete before it displays the final image. It's more convenient to program this so that each convolution is performed in a separate thread, but it's going to take the same amount of time to calculate all four convolutions whether each thread calculates its image sequentially or whether there's some sort of round-robin scheduling between the four threads. When the task of our Java program is divided into separate sub-tasks and each sub-task is written as a separate thread, we can ignore the scheduling of those separate threads because, in the end, all we care about is the completed task.

So when do we care about the scheduling mechanism of these threads? When all of these normal cases do not apply; in specific when:

- There are one or more CPU-intensive threads in the program

and either

- Intermediate results of the calculations are interesting (e.g., if we wanted to see one of the four convolved GIF images as soon as possible)

or

- The threads are not performing a joint task; they're providing separate tasks that should, in fairness, employ a round-robin scheduling paradigm (e.g., a server program that is acting on requests on behalf of several different users).

We'll look at these cases in more depth as we discuss the various mechanisms to achieve them.

Scheduling with Thread Priorities

We'll now examine how to manipulate the priority level of Java threads. This is the most useful mechanism available to a Java programmer that affects scheduling behavior of threads; often, a few simple adjustments of thread priorities is all that's required to make a program behave as desired.

Priority-Related Calls in the Java API

In the Java Thread class, there are three static final variables that define the allowable range of thread priorities:

Thread.MIN_PRIORITY
> The minimum priority a thread can have

Thread.MAX_PRIORITY
> The maximum priority a thread can have

Thread.NORM_PRIORITY
> The default priority for threads in the Java interpreter

Every thread has a priority value that lies somewhere in the range between MIN_PRIORITY and MAX_PRIORITY. However, not all threads can have a value anywhere within this range. We'll discuss this further in Chapter 8, but for now you should be aware that the maximum thread priority for a thread within an applet is NORM_PRIORITY + 1.

Symbolic Thread Priority Values

The symbolic definition of priority constants are not necessarily useful. Typically, we like to think of constant values like these in terms of symbolic names, which allows us to believe that their actual value is irrelevant. Using symbolic names also allows us to change the variables and have that change reflected throughout our code.

Unfortunately, that logic doesn't always apply in the case of thread priorities: if we have to manipulate the individual priorities of the threads, we sometimes have to know what the range of those values actually is. If the range between the minimum and maximum priorities were 20, then we could have 20 different threads all at a different priority and, thus, have deterministic behavior among these threads. But if the range were only five, our 20 threads would have to share priorities (on average, four threads at each priority level), and we'd have nondeterministic behavior among the threads. So it's not enough to know that these constants exist; we often have to know that, in fact, the minimum Java thread priority is one, the maximum is 10 (six for applets), and the default is five.

The default priority of a thread is the priority of the thread that created it. This is usually, but not always, NORM_PRIORITY.

There are two methods in the Java thread class that relate to the priority of a thread:

void setPriority(int priority)
>   Sets the priority of the given thread. If `priority` is outside the allowed range of thread priorities, an exception is thrown.

int getPriority()
>   Retrieves the priority of the given thread.

Using the Priority Calls

Let's look at an example of using these calls. Often, simply setting the priority of each of your threads is sufficient to achieve the required scheduling. If you have two threads in your program and one is usually blocked, all you need to do is set the priority of the thread that blocks above the priority of the other thread, and you'll prevent CPU starvation. We'll illustrate this example with a code fragment that is designed to calculate and display fractal images. The calculation of the fractal is very CPU-intensive but has the advantage that it can be done in sections that can be displayed as each is computed. So we'll put the actual calculations into a separate, low-priority thread that calls the `repaint()` method after each section has been calculated. Meanwhile, our applet's initial thread spends most of its time blocked, waiting for an event from the user or for a repaint event.

Here's the skeleton code for our fractal applet:

```
public class Fractal extends Applet implements Runnable {
    Thread calcThread;

    public void init() {
        Thread current = Thread.currentThread();
        calcThread = new Thread(this);
        calcThread.setPriority(current.getPriority() - 1);
    }

    public void start() {
        calcThread.start();
    }

    public void stop() {
        calcThread.stop();
    }

    public void run() {
        while (sectionsToCalculate) {
            doCalc();
            repaint();
        }
    }
```

```
        public void paint(Graphics g) {
            // paint something based on the last fractal section calculated
        }
    }
```

Consider what would happen in this example if we didn't lower the priority of the calculation thread. In that case, the applet would run through its init() and start() methods, and we'd be left with two threads at NORM_PRIORITY: the applet thread and the calculation thread. The applet thread blocks waiting for an event from the windowing system, so the calculation thread is the only runnable thread and hence becomes the currently running thread. The calculation thread calculates a section of the fractal and calls the repaint() method. This creates the necessary event to unblock the applet thread, which moves the applet thread into the runnable state.

However, the calculation thread is still in the runnable state, which means that the calculation thread remains the currently running thread. The applet thread is added to the end of the NORM_PRIORITY list, and as long as nothing creates a scheduling event—which will be the case if we run this program on many UNIX platforms—the calculation thread always remains the currently running thread. Thus, as long as there are sections of the fractal to calculate, the many calls to the repaint() method have no effect: the applet thread never gets the opportunity to become the currently running thread and repaint the screen.

If, however, we set the priority of the calculation thread lower than the priority of the applet thread, then when the calculation thread calls the repaint() method, the applet thread becomes the currently running thread since it is now the runnable thread with the highest priority. The applet thread executes the paint() method and moves again to the blocked state, allowing the calculation thread to become the currently running thread.

When to Use Simple Priority-Based Calls

What are the circumstances in which this technique of setting the priority of certain threads is appropriate? You'll use this technique when

- There is only one CPU-intensive thread

and

- Intermediate results are interesting to the user

That's clearly the case of the fractal calculation: there's one thread calculating the sections of the fractal, and each section is an interesting intermediate result. Mathematical models often benefit from the notion of successive refinement.

Image loading is another area where intermediate results are often important to the user: as parts of the image become available, they can be drawn on the screen so that the user sees them "scrolled" onto the screen. But remember: in the typical case, the Java program is loading the image over the network, which means that the thread reading the image will often block, so that there is no need to adjust any thread's priority. But if the Java program is calculating the image from some preloaded data set, lowering the priority of that thread is a good idea.

What if we had more than one CPU-intensive thread? In the case of the fractal, what if we'd set up a separate thread to calculate each section of the fractal? This is a programmatically elegant solution, but there's a danger here. When you have more than one CPU-intensive thread, you should lower the priority of each of the CPU-intensive threads. In that case, as long as each calculation thread is at a lower level than the applet thread, you get at least part of the behavior you want. The danger is that on platforms that, by default, support round-robin scheduling among threads of equal priority, the CPU-intensive threads compete for the CPU, and the individual calculation of each section takes longer than if the calculation of an individual section is allowed to run to completion. This means that the user sees the sections of the fractal (that is, the intermediate feedback) more slowly than in the case where there is a single calculation thread.

Other Thread-Scheduling Methods

There are other methods in Thread class that affect the scheduling of the currently running thread. As we'll see, these remaining methods are not always the most useful techniques with respect to Java scheduling. The reason for that is due to the combination of Java's strict priority-based scheduling mechanism with the possibility of the timer-based Java scheduling events. But we'll look at these methods, which have some specific uses, and examine the type of pitfalls they introduce into Java scheduling.

Using suspend() and resume()

There are two methods that can directly affect the state of a thread:

void suspend()
> Prevents a thread from running for an indefinite amount of time.

void resume()
> Allows a thread to run after being suspended.

The suspend() method moves a particular thread from the runnable state into the blocked state. In this case, the thread isn't blocked waiting for a particular resource, it's blocked waiting for some thread to resume() it. The resume() method moves the thread from the blocked state to the runnable state.

In previous sections, we posited the existence of four states a thread can have; actually, there is a separate suspended state that is different from the blocked state, even though there is no real conceptual difference between the suspended and blocked states. But strictly speaking, the suspend() method moves a thread to the suspended state from whatever state the thread was previously in—including blocked threads, which can be suspended just like any other thread. Similarly, the resume() method moves the thread from the suspended state to whatever state the thread was in before it was suspended—so a thread that has been resumed may still be blocked. But this is a subtle difference, and we'll persist in treating the blocked and suspended states as identical.

We could use these methods instead of the priority methods in the previous section to achieve the same effect of switching the currently runnable thread:

```
public class Fractal extends Applet implements Runnable {
    Thread t;

    public void init() {
        t = new Thread(this);
    }

    public void start() {
        t.start();
    }

    public void stop() {
        t.stop();
    }

    public void run() {
        while (sectionsToCalculate) {
            doCalc();
            repaint();
            t.suspend();
        }
    }

    public void paint(Graphics g) {
        // Draw the section
        t.resume();
    }
}
```

By suspending the calculation thread after each section is calculated, we give the applet thread an opportunity to become the currently running thread and to paint the new section of the fractal. There are two problems with this code, however. We might want our applet to do something else in addition to displaying the fractal: perhaps there are some controls on the applet that allow the user to change the parameters of the fractal calculation. If there were a checkbox on the applet that the user clicks on while the calculation thread is in the middle of the doCalc() method, the checkbox would not be able to repaint itself to show its new state until the calculation thread suspended itself. Nor would the action() method associated with the checkbox have an opportunity to run until the calculation thread suspended itself.

The second error comes about from a race condition and, hence, is more subtle. While the calculation thread is in the runnable state, the applet thread is normally in the blocked state; it's executing the read() method waiting for some sort of input to come from the windowing system. So the state of the threads looks like this:

```
PRIORITY 5:  Calculation -> NULL
   BLOCKED:  Applet -> NULL
```

When the repaint() method is called, the applet thread receives a repaint request and moves from the blocked state to the runnable state. At that point both the calculation and applet threads are in the runnable state, and the calculation thread remains the currently running thread:

```
PRIORITY 5:  Applet -> Calcuation -> NULL
   BLOCKED:  NULL
```

What happens now if, prior to the point at which the calculation thread suspends itself, a Java timer-based scheduling event occurs? This causes the applet thread to become the currently running thread, leaving the threads in this state:

```
PRIORITY 5:  Calculation -> Applet -> NULL
   BLOCKED:  NULL
```

The applet thread repaints the new section of the fractal and calls the resume() method on the calculation thread. Normally the resume() method moves the calculation thread from the blocked state to the runnable state, but the calculation thread is still in the runnable state: it has not yet been suspended, so the resume() method has no effect. Then the applet thread exits the paint() method, attempts to get the next event, and enters the blocked state. This causes the calculation thread to become the currently running thread:

```
PRIORITY 5:  Calculation -> NULL
   BLOCKED:  Applet -> NULL
```

The first thing the calculation thread does is suspend() itself so that both the applet and calculation threads are in the blocked state:

```
PRIORITY 5:  NULL
   BLOCKED:  Applet -> Calcuation -> NULL
```

All threads in the applet are now blocked. The applet appears to have frozen.[*]

This scenario happens because when the two threads are both in the runnable state at the same priority, the order of execution of those threads is undefined, and it's conceivable that one thread might interrupt another thread at any point in time. The suspend() and resume() methods affect a critical state of the thread; the same care must be taken with them as with any code that affects a shared variable.

In general, a good guideline to use with the suspend() and resume() methods is to have the same thread responsible for suspending and resuming other threads. Using this guideline, let's revise our fractal applet as follows:

```java
public class Fractal extends Applet implements Runnable {
    Thread t;

    public void start() {
        if (t == null) {
            t = new Thread(this);
            t.setPriority(Thread.currentThread().getPriority() - 1);
            t.start();
        }
        else t.resume();
    }

    public void stop() {
        t.suspend();
    }

    public void run() {
        // Do calculations, occassionally calling repaint()
    }

    public void paint(Graphics g) {
        // Paint the next section of the fractal
    }
}
```

This is the canonical use of the suspend() and resume() methods: they're often used to disable threads when the applet is no longer current. This is better than our first fractal example: in the first case when the user revisited the page with the fractal applet, the fractal calculation would have had to begin at its very

---

[*] If something else occurs to cause a paint() request, the applet resume()s the calculation thread, but you can't count on that.

beginning and redisplay all those results to the user as they were recalculated. Now, the applet can save the information of the fractal and simply pick up the calculation from the point the user interrupted it. And because only our higher priority thread is responsible for suspending and resuming the calculation thread, we've avoided the race condition shown in our second example.

Yielding Threads

A final method available for affecting which thread is the currently running thread is the use of the `yield()` method. The `yield()` method is useful because it allows threads that are of the same priority to allow another thread to run:

static void yield()

> Yields the current thread, allowing another thread of the same priority to be run by the Java virtual machine.

There are a few points worth noting about the `yield()` method. First, notice that it is a static method; the ramification of which is that the `yield()` method only ever affects the currently running thread. In the following code fragment

```
public class YieldApplet extends Applet implements Runnable {
    Thread t;
    public void init() {
        t = new Thread(this);
    }

    public void paint(Graphics g) {
        t.yield();
    }
}
```

when the applet thread executes the `paint()` method and calls the `yield()` method, it is the applet thread itself that yields, and not the calculation thread t, even though we used the object t to call the `yield()` method.

What actually happens when a thread yields? In terms of the state of the thread, nothing happens: the thread remains in the runnable state. But a Java scheduling event is created, so the Java virtual machine picks a thread to be the currently running thread, using the same rules it always has. Clearly, there are no threads that are higher in priority than the thread that has just yielded. So the new currently running thread is selected among all the threads that have the same priority as the thread that has just yielded. If there are no other threads in that group, the `yield()` method has no effect: the yielding thread is immediately selected again as the currently running thread.[*]

---

[*] Calling `yield()` has the same effect as calling `sleep(0)`.

If there are other threads in the priority group of the yielding thread, then one of those other threads becomes the currently running thread. So yielding is an appropriate technique provided you know there are multiple threads of the same priority.

Let's revisit our fractal example now and see how it looks when we use the yield() method instead of priority calls:

```
public class Fractal extends Applet implements Runnable {
    Thread t = null;

    public void start() {
        if (t == null) {
            t = new Thread(this);
            t.start();
        }
        else t.resume();
    }

    public void stop() {
        t.suspend();
    }

    public void run() {
        while (sectionsToCalculate) {
            doCalc();
            repaint();
            Thread.yield();
        }
    }

    public void paint(Graphics g) {
        // draw the next section
    }
}
```

Now when our calculation thread has results, it merely yields. The applet thread is in the runnable state; it was just moved to that state when the calculation thread called the repaint() method. So the Java virtual machine chooses the applet thread to be the currently running thread, the applet repaints itself, the applet thread blocks, and the calculation thread again becomes the currently running thread and calculates the next section of the fractal.

This example suffers from problems similar to those that plagued the suspend()/resume() example. First, because the applet thread is at the same priority as the calculation thread, the user is unable to interact with the applet until the calculation thread yields. And second, there is once again a race condition: if we're on a platform that automatically switches between threads of the same priority, then immediately after the calculation thread yields, a timer-based scheduling event may occur, so the calculation thread ends up interrupting the applet thread before the applet thread has completed painting. The good news in this case is that the program continues to execute, and the sections of the fractal get painted next time the calculation thread yields (or the next time the timer-based scheduling event occurs).

Comparison of Scheduling Mechanisms

We've now shown three mechanisms by which thread scheduling can be affected: adjusting thread priorities, suspending and resuming threads, and yielding threads. The question as to which mechanism to use tends to be somewhat subjective, since all methods have a similar effect on the threads.

Clearly from the example we used through these three sections, we prefer the priority-based methods to control thread scheduling. These methods offer the most flexibility to the Java developer.

We prefer to use the suspend() and resume() methods to control scheduling only on a global basis: when all the threads need to be stopped or started at once, as in the applet's start() and stop() methods. If you correctly synchronize calls to these methods, they control which threads run when, but doing so tends to be more complicated than using the priority calls. However, these calls do offer the ability to control absolutely whether a thread will run or not, which is something the priority calls cannot do.

We find the yield() method to be the least useful method. This may come as a surprise to thread programmers on systems where the yield() method is the most direct one to affect thread scheduling. But because of the indeterminate nature of scheduling among threads of the same priority on some Java platforms, the effect of the yield() method cannot be guaranteed: a thread that yields may immediately be rescheduled when a timer-based scheduling event occurs. On the other hand, if your threads yield() often enough, this rare race condition won't matter in the long run, and using the yield() method can be an effective way to schedule your threads.[*]

Daemon Threads

The last thing that we'll address in conjunction with thread scheduling is the issue of daemon threads. There are two types of threads in the Java system: daemon threads and user threads. The implication from these names is that daemon

---

[*] yield() is also the simplest of these methods to understand, which puts it in great favor with some developers.

threads are those threads created internally by the Java API and that user threads are those you create yourself, but this is not the case. Any thread can be a daemon thread or a user thread. All threads are created initially as user threads, so all the threads we've looked at so far have been user threads.

Some threads that are created by the virtual machine on your behalf are daemon threads. A daemon thread is identical to a user thread in almost all ways: it has a priority, it has the same methods, it can be stopped, started, suspended and resumed. In terms of scheduling, daemon threads are handled just like user threads: neither type of thread is scheduled in favor of the other. During the execution of your program, a daemon thread behaves just like a user thread.

The only time the Java virtual machine checks to see if particular threads are daemon threads is after a user thread has exited. When a user thread exits, the Java virtual machine checks to see if there are any remaining user threads left. If there are user threads remaining, then the Java virtual machine, using the rules we've discussed, schedules the next thread (user or daemon). If, however, there are only daemon threads remaining, then the Java virtual machine will exit, and the program will terminate. Daemon threads only live to serve user threads; if there are no more user threads, there is nothing to serve and no reason to continue.

The canonical daemon thread in the Java virtual machine is the garbage collection thread. The garbage collector runs from time to time and frees those Java objects that no longer have valid references, which is why the Java programmer doesn't need to worry about memory management. So the garbage collector is a useful thread. If we don't have any other threads running, however, there's nothing for the garbage collector to do: after all, garbage is not spontaneously created, at least not inside a Java program. So if the garbage collector is the only thread left running in the Java virtual machine, then clearly there's no more work for it to do, and the Java virtual machine can exit. Hence, the garbage collector is marked as a daemon thread.

There are two methods in the Thread class that deal with daemon threads:

void setDaemon(boolean on)
 Sets the thread to be a daemon thread (if on is true) or to be a user thread (if on is false).

boolean isDaemon()
 Returns true if the thread is a daemon thread and false if it is a user thread.

The `setDaemon()` method can be called only after the thread object has been created and before the thread has been started. While the thread is running, you cannot cause a user thread to become a daemon thread (or vice versa);

attempting to do so will generate an exception.* By default, a thread is a user thread if it was created by a user thread; it is a daemon thread if it was created by a daemon thread. The `setDaemon()` method is needed only if one thread creates another thread that should have a different daemon status.

Daemon threads become involved in scheduling because scheduling is the type of activity that's perfect for a background thread: if we write a thread to perform scheduling, that thread has useful work to do only while other (user) threads in the program are active. If there are no user threads to schedule, there is no reason for the scheduling thread to stick around.

Building a Thread Scheduler

The thread methods we've looked at so far are great when you have a fixed number of well-known threads and can analyze the behavior of the threads in advance. The priority-based scheduling methods also were most useful when there were intermediate results which the user might be interested in. But there are times when you have independent threads that need a round-robin timesliced behavior, regardless of the platform on which they're running. And there are times when it's convenient to create multiple threads, but you want to prevent the round-robin timesliced behavior you'd get on some platforms.

We'll look at the issues around developing a round-robin scheduler in this section and end by developing a fairly complete scheduler that is suitable for ensuring and preventing round-robin scheduling. We present this scheduler for two reasons:

1. There are limited times when such a scheduler is needed.

2. The development of such a scheduler illustrates the issues you need to consider when programming with many arbitrary threads.

Remember that at issue here is the behavior of a Java program that contains one or more CPU-intensive threads. A Java program could have hundreds of threads that may only periodically need access to the CPU and otherwise spend most of their life in the blocked state: in that case, there isn't likely to be much competition for the CPU, and each thread gets an opportunity to run whenever it has work to do. We only face the problem of CPU starvation when there is at least one CPU-intensive thread that may potentially prevent all other threads from running.

---

* To be completely correct, an exception is generated any time the thread `isAlive()` and the `set-Daemon()` method is called—even if `setDaemon(true)` is called on a thread that is already a daemon thread.

If we have only a single CPU-intensive thread, there is no need for a complicated scheduling mechanism: all we need to do is lower the priority of the CPU-intensive thread below the priority of the other threads in our Java program. This allows the other threads to run whenever they have work to do, while the CPU-intensive thread continues to process whenever the remaining threads are blocked. We'll build on this principle in our scheduler class: our CPU-intensive threads will all have a lower priority than threads that are mostly blocked.

We'll look at two schedulers in this section. The basic principle behind each scheduler is that each thread under its control is given a fixed amount of time during which it runs. When the specified time period elapses, another thread runs; this process proceeds indefinitely. This is the familiar thread-scheduling mechanism known as *round-robin scheduling*.

A Simple Round-Robin Scheduler

How do we go about creating a round-robin scheduler? Clearly, we need to begin with some sort of periodic timer; every time the timer goes off, we can make a different thread become the currently running thread. What do we need to do to make this happen?

The simplistic answer to this question is: nothing. That is, our simple scheduler is simply a high-priority timer that periodically wakes up only to go back to sleep immediately. This creates, in effect, a timer-based scheduling event: each time the timer thread wakes up, it becomes the currently running thread, which also adjusts the lists of threads at the priority of the previously running thread.

```
public class SimpleScheduler extends Thread {
    int timeslice;

    public SimpleScheduler(int t) {
        timeslice = t;
        setPriority(Thread.MAX_PRIORITY);
        setDaemon(true);
    }

    public void run() {
        while (true)
            try {
                sleep(timeslice);
            } catch (Exception e) {}
    }
}
```

We'll use this class in the example we started this chapter with, so that we can illustrate its behavior:

```
class TestThread extends Thread {
    String id;

    public TestThread(String s) {
        id = s;
    }
    public void run() {
        int i;
        for (i = 0; i < 10; i++) {
            doCalc(i);
            System.out.println(id);
        }
    }
}

public class Test {
    public static void main(String args[]) {
        new SimpleScheduler(100).start();
        TestThread t1, t2, t3;
        t1 = new TestThread("Thread 1");
        t1.start();
        t2 = new TestThread("Thread 2");
        t2.start();
        t3 = new TestThread("Thread 3");
        t3.start();
    }
}
```

In this program there are three threads (t1, t2, and t3) at the Java default priority of NORM_PRIORITY, and the SimpleScheduler thread that runs at a priority of MAX_PRIORITY. The SimpleScheduler thread is normally blocked, so the list of threads start out in this state:

```
PRIORITY 5:   t2 -> t3 -> t1 -> NULL
   BLOCKED:  SimpleScheduler -> NULL
```

At this point, t1 is the currently running thread, and we'll start to see output lines that say "Thread 1." Now when SimpleScheduler wakes up, it moves to the runnable state and, because it is the highest priority thread in the Java virtual machine, it becomes the currently running thread:

```
 PRIORITY 5:   t2 -> t3 -> t1 -> NULL
 PRIORITY 10:  SimpleScheduler -> NULL
```

SimpleScheduler immediately executes the sleep() method, moving it back to the blocked state; the Java virtual machine then selects the next thread in the list (t2) as the currently running thread and moves it to the end of the list:

```
PRIORITY 5:   t3 -> t1 -> t2 -> NULL
   BLOCKED:  SimpleScheduler -> NULL
```

As this continues, each thread in the list of threads at priority 5 becomes the currently running thread in turn.

There are some circumstances in which this simplistic scheduler doesn't work; those circumstances are discussed (and solved) in detail in the more complete scheduler shown next. But in those cases where you have threads that don't block and need to have a round-robin scheduling mechanism, this simple scheduler is quite adequate.

A More Complete Scheduler

Now we'll look into building a more complete scheduler that will schedule our threads in a round-robin fashion. We can also use it to avoid round-robin scheduling on platforms that have that as their default behavior.[*]

We'll start building this scheduler by establishing threads at three priority levels:

Level 6

> The scheduler itself is a separate thread running at level 6. This allows it to run in favor of the default threads created by the Java virtual machine and APIs and in favor of any threads the scheduler is controlling. This thread spends most of its time sleeping (i.e., blocked), so this thread doesn't usually become the currently running thread.

Level 4

> The scheduler selects one thread from all the threads it is controlling and assigns that thread a priority value of 4. Most of the time, this is the nonblocked thread with the highest priority in the Java virtual machine, so it is the currently running thread.

Level 2

> All remaining threads under control of our scheduler run at priority level 2. Since there is always a thread running at level 4, these threads never actually run at this priority; they remain at this priority until they are selected by our scheduler to have a priority level of 4, at which time they become the currently running thread.

The idea behind the scheduler is that the programmer assigns certain threads to be under control of the scheduler. The scheduler selects one and only one of these threads and assigns it a priority of 4, while the rest of the threads have a priority of 2. The priority 4 thread is the currently running thread; from time to time, the scheduler itself wakes up and selects a different thread as the single priority 4 thread.

---

[*] See the concluding section on scheduling fairness for a example of when you'd like to prevent timesliced behavior.

For all the threads in this scheduling system—the scheduler thread itself plus any threads the programmer designates to be controlled by our scheduler—it is clear that no CPU starvation will occur: the scheduler thread will always run when it needs to, and as long as that thread correctly adjusts the priorities of the remaining threads under its control, all other threads will get their opportunity to become the currently running thread.

In order to keep track of all the threads, we'll use the CircularList we developed in Chapter 5. This class gives us the queueing behavior we need to keep track of the threads under the control of our scheduler: we can add threads to the list with its insert() method, remove them with its delete() method, and, more important, go through the list by repeatedly calling its getNext() method.

Here's the first pass at our scheduler:

```java
public class CPUScheduler extends Thread {
    private int timeslice;        // # of millis thread should run
    private CircularList threads; // All the threads we're scheduling

    public CPUScheduler(int t) {
        threads = new CircularList();
        timeslice = t;
    }

    public void addThread(Thread t) {
        threads.insert(t);
        t.setPriority(2);
    }

    public void removeThread(Thread t) {
        t.setPriority(5);
        threads.delete(t);
    }

    public void run() {
        Thread current;
        setPriority(6);
        while (true) {
            current = (Thread) threads.getNext();
            if (current == null)
                return;
            current.setPriority(4);
            try {
                Thread.sleep(timeslice);
            } catch (InterruptedException ie) {};
            current.setPriority(2);
        }
    }
}
```

Although there are some necessary adjustments that we'll add to this scheduler throughout the rest of this chapter, this code is the essence of the scheduler.[*] There are two methods the programmer uses to interface with the scheduler: addThread(), which adds a thread object to the list of thread objects under control of the scheduler, and removeThread(), which removes a thread object from that list.[†]

Given this interface, we can use the CPUScheduler class in the ThreadTest class we introduced at the beginning of this section:

```java
class TestThread extends Thread {
    String id;
    public TestThread(String s) {
        id = s;
    }

    public void run() {
        int i;
        for (i = 0; i < 10; i++) {
            doCalc(i);
            System.out.println(id);
        }
    }
}

public class ThreadTest {
    public static void main(String args[]) {
        TestThread t1, t2, t3;
        CPUScheduler c = new CPUScheduler(100);
        t1 = new TestThread("Thread 1");
        c.addThread(t1);
        t2 = new TestThread("Thread 2");
        c.addThread(t2);
        t3 = new TestThread("Thread 3");
        c.addThread(t3);
        t1.start();
        t2.start();
        t3.start();
        c.start();
    }
}
```

---

[*] Many of these adjustments are required for the class to behave robustly; while the CPUScheduler code will run at this point, it won't necessarily behave correctly in many cases.

[†] There's a subtle error here, in that when the thread is removed from the scheduler, we assign it the default thread priority rather than the priority it had when it was added to the scheduler. The correct practice would be to save the thread's priority in the call to the addThread() method and then restore that priority in the removeThread() method; we'll leave that implementation to the reader.

When our program calls `c.start()`, the CPUScheduler's `run()` method gets called; it is this `run()` method that actually manipulates all the threads to create the timesliced, round-robin scheduling. At its base level, the logic for our scheduler is simple: it loops forever, going through all the threads in our circular list of threads and adjusts their priorities as it goes. In between, it sleeps for `timeslice` milliseconds. The thread `current` runs for that many milliseconds before the scheduler wakes up again and readjusts the thread's priority. When there are no threads left to schedule—which would happen if the programmer had called `removeThread()` on all the threads previously added—the CPUScheduler exits by returning from the `run()` method.

Let's examine how the four threads in our program—threads `t1`, `t2`, `t3`, and the CPUScheduler thread—will behave now. After we call the `c.start()` method, the threads in the program are in this state:

```
PRIORITY 2:   t1 -> t2 -> t3 -> NULL
PRIORITY 6:   CPUScheduler -> NULL
```

As the highest priority thread in the program, the CPUscheduler thread is the currently running thread. It starts executing the `run()` method, where the first thing it does is change the priority of thread `t1` to 4:

```
PRIORITY 2:   t2 -> t3 -> NULL
PRIORITY 4:   t1 -> NULL
PRIORITY 6:   CPUScheduler -> NULL
```

The CPUScheduler, still the currently running thread, now sleeps, placing it into the blocked state. This causes `t1` to become the currently running thread:

```
PRIORITY 2:   t2 -> t3 -> NULL
PRIORITY 4:   t1 -> NULL
   BLOCKED:   CPUScheduler -> NULL
```

When the CPUScheduler thread wakes up, it changes the priority of `t1` back to 2 and the priority of `t2` to 4:

```
PRIORITY 2:   t3 -> t1 -> NULL
PRIORITY 4:   t2 -> NULL
PRIORITY 6:   CPUScheduler -> NULL
```

And so the cycle continues.

Adjustment #1: Synchronizing data within the CPUScheduler

Now that we have the base logic of the CPUScheduler written correctly, we need to make sure the CPUScheduler class is itself thread-safe and that we haven't introduced any race conditions into the scheduler by having incorrectly synchronized data.

At first glance, there don't appear to be any variables that need synchronization: the only instance variable that needs to be protected is the variable threads, and all changes to the threads variable occur via methods of the CircularList class that are already synchronized. But what would happen if you called the removeThread() method and removed the thread that the CPUScheduler has marked as the current thread? It would be an error for the CPUScheduler to change the priority of this thread once it has been removed from the threads list, so the removeThread() method must somehow inform the CPUScheduler that the current thread has been removed.

This means that the variable current must become an instance variable so that both the run() and removeThread() methods can access it. We can then synchronize access to that variable. Here's the new CPUScheduler class:

```
public class CPUScheduler extends Thread {
    . . .
    private Thread current;
    public void removeThread(t) {
        t.setPriority(5);
        threads.delete(t);
        synchronized(this) {
            if (current == t)
                current = null;
        }
    }
    . . .
    public void run() {
        . . .
        try {
            Thread.sleep(timeslice);
        } catch (InterruptedException ie) {};
        synchronized(this) {
            if (current != null)
                current.setPriority(2);
        }
    }
}
```

Alternatively, we could make the run() and removeThread() methods synchronize themselves:

```
public synchronized void run() {
    . . .
}

public synchronized void removeThread(Thread t) {
    . . .
}
```

As we've seen, making the `run()` method synchronized is typically a bad idea, so we'll reject this idea for now, but we'll be revisiting this decision soon.

Adjustment #2: Making CPUScheduler thread-safe

We've synchronized all the variables of our CPUScheduler, but we're still not protected from threads that exit while they are under our control.

In particular, the `run()` method changes the priority of a thread, which is a valid operation only if a thread is in the runnable state. What happens if the thread that we've assigned to level 4 exits its `run()` method while our CPUScheduler is sleeping? When the CPUScheduler wakes up, it tries to set the priority of that thread, which is now in the exiting state, to 2—an operation that generates an exception. Similarly, if the thread that is running decides to call the `stop()` method of one of the priority 2 threads in the CPUScheduler's list, next time the CPUScheduler selected that thread and sets its priority, we'd get an exception.

So we need to place all the calls to the `setPriority()` method inside a `try/catch` clause in order to be alerted to these type of situations. This means we must modify our code everywhere we call the `setPriority()` method:

```
public void removeThread(Thread t) {
    try {
        t.setPriority(5);
    } catch(Exception e) {}
    threads.delete(t);
    synchronized(this) {
        if (current == t)
            current = null;
    }
}

public void run() {
    while (true) {
        ...
        try {
            current.setPriority(4);
        } catch (Exception e) {
            removeThread(current);
        }
        ...
        synchronized(this) {
            if (current != null)
                try {
                    current.setPriority(2);
```

```
            } catch (Exception e) {
                removeThread(current);
            }
        }
        ...
    }
}
```

The first `try` clause in the `run()` method protects us when the thread that was running at priority 4 has exited; the second clause protects us when a thread has been stopped from another thread. Note that in both cases, we need to remove the thread from the list of threads in which we're interested, which means that we must also use the catch clause in the `removeThread()` method.

Adjustment #3: More thread-safe modifications

We've made the methods of the CPUScheduler thread-safe, but what about the class itself? What if two threads try to create a CPUScheduler? This would be very confusing: we'd end up with two scheduling threads that would compete with each other to schedule other threads. So we need to allow only one instance of the class to be instantiated. We'll do this by creating a static variable in the class and testing it to make sure that an instance of the CPUScheduler class doesn't already exist. Because we can't make the constructor itself synchronized, we'll also need to introduce a synchronized method to access this static variable. Thus the constructor and related code for the class now looks like this:

```
public class CPUScheduler extends Thread {
    private static boolean initialized = false;
    private synchronized static boolean isInitialized() {
        if (initialized)
            return true;
        initialized = true;
        return false;
    }

    public CPUScheduler(int t) {
        if (isInitialized())
            throw new SecurityException("Already initialized");
        threads = new CircularList();
        timeslice = t;
    }
}
```

Adjustment #4: Devising an exit mechanism

If all the threads under its control exit, the CPUScheduler itself exits. In a program where the tasks are well-defined at the beginning of execution—like the

TestThread class we've looked at so far—that might be fine. But what if we wanted to add the CPUScheduler to our TCPServer? This is often a useful goal, since it allows multiple clients to receive intermediate results in a timesliced ("fair") manner.[*] But as presently written, the CPUScheduler wouldn't work for that case: as soon as no clients were connected to the TCPServer, the CPUScheduler would exit, and any further clients that connected to the server would not be timesliced.

What we need to do instead is make the CPUScheduler a daemon thread and adjust the logic of its run() method. This should make sense: the CPUScheduler is only useful when there are other threads in the program that it can schedule. In the TCPServer case, there will always be at least one other thread in the program: the listener thread of the TCPServer. That listener thread creates other threads for the CPUScheduler to manipulate as clients connect to the server. The implementation of our timesliced TCPServer to perform calculations looks like this:

```
import java.net.*;
import java.io.*;

public class CalcServer {
    public static void main(String args[]) {
        CalcRequest r = new CalcRequest();
        try {
            r.StartServer(3535);
        } catch (Exception e) {
            System.out.println("Unable to start server");
        }
    }
}


class CalcRequest extends TCPServer {
    CPUScheduler scheduler;
    CalcRequest() {
        scheduler = new CPUScheduler(100);
        scheduler.start();
    }

    public void run(Socket s) {
        scheduler.addThread(Thread.currentThread());
        doCalc(s);
    }
}
```

Every time the run() method of the CalcRequest class is called, it is called in a new thread, so we need to add that thread to the CPUScheduler that was created in the constructor of the class. As long as the CPUScheduler doesn't exit when

---

[*] We'll discuss the issue of fairness at the end of this chapter.

there are no threads to schedule (which now means simply that no client is currently connected), we'll have a timesliced calculation server. During an active session of our CalcServer, we'll have these threads:

One listener thread
> The thread that listens for connections and creates the client threads

Zero or more client threads
> These threads execute the calculation on behalf of a connected client

CPUScheduler thread
> The daemon thread performing the scheduling

We can gracefully shut down the CalcServer by stopping the listener thread; eventually the client threads complete their calculation and exit. When all the client threads have exited, only the daemon CPUScheduler thread remains in the program, and the program terminates.

We need to change the CPUScheduler so that instead of returning when there are no threads to be scheduled, it simply waits for more threads. Here's the entire code for the modified CPUScheduler class:[*]

```
public class CPUScheduler extends Thread {
    private CircularList threads;
    private Thread current;
    private int timeslice;
    private static boolean initialized = false;
    private boolean needThreads;

    private static synchronized boolean isInitialized() {
        if (initialized)
            return true;
        initialized = true;
        return false;
    }

    public CPUScheduler(int t) {
        if (isInitialized())
            throw new SecurityException("Already initialized");
        threads = new CircularList();
        timeslice = t;
        setDaemon(true);
    }

    public synchronized void addThread(Thread t) {
```

---

[*] We're showing the entire class here because the adjustments we'll make after this are not necessarily required for your program. So this complete scheduler is a useful implementation; it's simpler than the implementations to follow and is, in most cases, just as functional.

```
        t.setPriority(2);
        threads.insert(t);
        if (needThreads) {
            needThreads = false;
            notify();
        }
    }

    public void removeThread(Thread t) {
        threads.delete(t);
        synchronized(this) {
            if (t == current)
                current = null;
        }
    }

    public synchronized void run() {
        setPriority(6);
        while (true) {
            current = (Thread) threads.getNext();
            while (current == null) {
                needThreads = true;
                try {
                    wait();
                } catch (Exception e) {}
                current = (Thread) threads.getNext();
            }
            try {
                current.setPriority(4);
            } catch (Exception e) {
                removeThread(current);
                continue;
            }
            try {
                sleep(timeslice);
            } catch (InterruptedException ie) {};
            if (current != null) {
                try {
                    current.setPriority(2);
                } catch (Exception e) {
                    removeThread(current);
                }
            }
        }
    }
}
```

In the constructor, we've set the thread to be a daemon thread—the point of this adjustment. Note that we also changed the run() method so that when we try to retrieve a thread from the list, we loop until one is available. If no thread is in the list, we `wait()` until one is available, which requires that we add a flag to the `addThread()` method to signify whether or not it should `notify()` the CPU-Scheduler thread that a thread has been added.

Adjustment #5: Playing what-if games

The next two adjustments we'll make to the CPUScheduler are somewhat marginal, in the sense that in most cases, they make little difference in the overall scheduling of a program. The major impetus for presenting the next two adjustments is really to give you an idea of the complexities of low-level scheduling.

At this point, we already have a robust scheduler: we've synchronized all the internal state variables correctly, and we've made sure that external changes in the state of the threads we're manipulating won't cause an exception. But what about other changes in the state of the threads we're manipulating? What if one of those threads enters the blocked state instead of the exiting state we examined in adjustment #2?[*]

Let's see what would happen to our TestThread program if the currently running thread suddenly entered the blocked state. We'd start out with the threads in a state like this:

```
PRIORITY 2:  t3 -> t1 -> NULL
PRIORITY 4:  t2 -> NULL
   BLOCKED:  CPUScheduler -> NULL
```

Thread `t2` is the currently running thread, executing its calculations while the CPUScheduler is sleeping. If `t2` now enters the blocked state for some reason, we end up with threads in this state:

```
PRIORITY 2:  t3 -> t1 -> NULL
PRIORITY 4:  NULL
   BLOCKED:  t2 -> CPUScheduler -> NULL
```

This means that `t3` becomes the currently running thread, even though it's at priority 2. When the CPUScheduler wakes up, it resets the priority of `t2` to 2, sets the priority of `t3` to 4, and goes back to sleep, leaving our threads in this state:

```
PRIORITY 2:  t1 -> NULL
PRIORITY 4:  t3 -> NULL
   BLOCKED:  t2 -> CPUScheduler -> NULL
```

Everything is okay again, but at some point it will be `t2`'s turn to be priority 4. Since the CPUScheduler has no way of determining that `t2` is blocked, it sets the

---

[*] In the following discussion, we talk about what happens if a particular thread enters the blocked state, but the analysis is also true if the thread enters the exiting state.

priority of t2 to 4. The Java scheduler again selects one of the threads at priority 2 to be the currently running thread.

Our code was "correct": the threads involved all got some timeslice to run in. But what happened is that there was a short period of time during which the CPU-Scheduler slept, the priority 4 thread blocked, and a priority 2 thread became the currently running thread. In effect, this priority 2 thread "stole" some CPU time; it could do this because there was a time gap between when the priority 4 thread blocked and the priority 6 thread woke up.

It's probably not a crisis that this happened, since once the CPUScheduler woke up, we got back to the thread state we wanted. But we could have prevented this CPU stealing from happening if somehow we knew when the priority 4 thread had blocked.

It would be an intolerable burden (impossible in some cases) on the programmer if the thread somehow had to notify the CPUScheduler every time it was about to block; the scheduling should be transparent to the programmer (except for its initialization). So we need something else to indicate that the priority 4 thread has blocked: we need a priority 3 thread. The priority 3 thread becomes the currently running thread only when the priority 4 thread blocks. When the priority 3 thread is running, it knows that the priority 4 thread has blocked and should notify the priority 6 thread to go ahead and select another thread to be the priority 4 thread.

We'll call this priority 3 thread the ThreadNotifier thread, since its purpose is to notify the CPUScheduler thread that the priority 4 thread has blocked. Here's that class along with the modifications to the CPUScheduler class: *

```
class ThreadNotifier extends Thread {
    CPUScheduler c;

    public ThreadNotifier(CPUScheduler c) {
        setPriority(3);
        this.c = c;
    }

    public void run() {
        boolean done = false;
        while (!done) {
            c.wakeup();
        }
    }
}
```

---

* This is not the complete class; only enough of the class to illustrate the context of the changes is shown.

```
public class CPUScheduler implements Runnable {
    private ThreadNotifier notification;
    private Thread scheduler;

    public void startScheduler() {
        notification = new ThreadNotifier(this);
        notification.setDaemon(true);
        notification.start();
        scheduler = new Thread(this);
        scheduler.setDaemon(true);
        scheduler.start();
    }

    public void stopScheduler() {
        scheduler.stop();
        notification.stop();
    }

    public synchronized removeThread(Thread t) {
        threads.delete(t);
        if (current == t)
            current = null;
    }

    public synchronized void wakeup() {
        notify();
    }

    public synchronized void run() {
        Thread.currentThread().setPriority(6);
        while (true) {
            current = (Thread) threads.getNext();
            while (current == null) {
                needThreads = true;
                notification.suspend();
                try {
                    wait();
                } catch (Exception e) {}
                current = (Thread) threads.getNext();
            }
            notification.resume();
            try {
                current.setPriority(4);
            } catch (Exception e) {
                removeThread(current);
                continue;
            }
            try {
                wait(timeslice);
```

```
                    } catch (InterruptedException ie) {};
                    if (current != null) {
                        try {
                            current.setPriority(2);
                        } catch (Exception e) {
                            removeThread(current);
                        }
                    }
                }
            }
        }
```

This adjustment has caused quite a few changes to the code of our CPU-Scheduler. Let's look at the effect the thread notifier has on the threads scheduling: once all the threads in the program are initialized and the CPUScheduler has started, the threads will be in this state:

```
PRIORITY 2:   t2 -> t3 -> NULL
PRIORITY 3:   Notifier
PRIORITY 4:   t1 -> NULL
   BLOCKED:   CPUScheduler -> NULL
```

The CPUScheduler thread has entered the blocked state because it has executed the wait(timeslice) method. The t1 thread is the currently running thread, executing its doCalc() method, and the notifier thread is executing its run() method. Now when t1 blocks,

```
PRIORITY 2:   t2 -> t3 -> NULL
PRIORITY 3:   Notifier
PRIORITY 4:   NULL
   BLOCKED:   t1 -> CPUScheduler -> NULL
```

the notifier becomes the currently running thread. It executes the wakeup() method of the CPUScheduler class, waking up the CPUScheduler:

```
PRIORITY 2:   t2 -> t3 -> NULL
PRIORITY 3:   Notifier
PRIORITY 4:   NULL
PRIORITY 6:   CPUScheduler
   BLOCKED:   t1 -> NULL
```

The CPUScheduler assigns t1 a priority of 2, selects t2 from the threads list, assigns it a priority of 4, and then executes the wait() statement again, entering the blocked state. The priority 3 notifier thread enables us to detect when the priority 4 thread has blocked and allows the CPUScheduler to schedule another thread.

This is the only algorithmic change in the CPUScheduler; the other changes are necessary only to support this change. Since the CPUScheduler and the Thread-Notifier will use the wait and notify mechanism to communicate, we need to make the relevant methods synchronized, so that they hold the correct lock. Hence we provide the wakeup() method the ThreadNotifier calls after it grabs the CPU-Scheduler lock; we also modify the run() method so that it is synchronized and calls wait() with a timeout instead of sleep().* Since the run() method is now synchronized, we remove the synchronized blocks from it and make the removeThread() method synchronized.

Finally, we need to initialize the ThreadNotifier as well as start and stop it appropriately. Originally, the CPUScheduler class extended the Thread class and hence was initialized by calls to its start() and stop() methods. This was fine, since there was no other initialization that needed to be done. Now, however, we need to start and stop the ThreadNotifier whenever the CPUScheduler itself is started and stopped. Since we can't override the start() and stop() methods of the thread class, we have to provide new methods for this and change our class to implement the Runnable interface instead of extending the Thread class.

Adjustment #6: Further what-if games

The addition of the ThreadNotifier means that when the priority 4 thread blocks, we can immediately schedule another thread and thus keep a stricter account of the timeslice given to each thread; no priority 2 thread will be able to "steal" CPU cycles. But now we've created another problem: what happens if *all* the threads the CPUScheduler is controlling enter the blocked state? The way the CPUScheduler is currently written, the ThreadNotifier continually wakes up the CPUScheduler, which schedules a blocked thread and goes to sleep, thus allowing the ThreadNotifier to run again and wake up the CPUScheduler. Our CPUScheduler thrashes among all these threads, consuming 100 percent of the machine's CPU cycles while performing no useful work.

If the CPUScheduler is used only by careful programmers, this won't happen. We stated at the outset that the CPUScheduler was designed for threads that are CPU-intensive; it's not appropriate to use the CPUScheduler to schedule threads that are often going to block. In fact, if all the threads are going to block, they're not going to compete for the CPU and using the CPUScheduler becomes unnecessary.

But it's conceivable that we may have threads that are CPU-intensive even though they occasionally block, and that all the threads may end up blocked at the same time. So it would be nice in this case for our CPUScheduler not to thrash and consume all the available CPU cycles; instead, the CPUScheduler should itself block until there are unblocked threads to schedule.

---

* The differences between these two methods were discussed in Chapter 4.

Once again, there is no simple way to do this, since there is no way to interrogate a thread to find out if it is blocked. So the best that we can do is keep track of the state of the threads ourselves and when all the threads block, put the CPUScheduler to sleep for some period of time. When the CPUScheduler wakes up, it can attempt to run each thread again to see if there are some that are unblocked. Here's the new code to accomplish this task. Since this is the last adjustment we'll be making to this class, we'll show the entire code in this example:

```java
class CPUSchedulerNode {
    Thread thread;
    boolean blocked;

    CPUSchedulerNode(Thread t) {
        thread = t;
        blocked = false;
    }

    public boolean equals(Object o) {
        if (thread == o)
            return true;
        return false;
    }
}

class ThreadNotifier extends Thread {
    CPUScheduler c;

    public ThreadNotifier(CPUScheduler c) {
        setPriority(3);
        this.c = c;
    }
    public void run() {
        boolean done = false;
        while (!done) {
            c.wakeup();
        }
    }
}

public class CPUScheduler implements Runnable {
    private CircularList threads;
    private CPUSchedulerNode current;
    private int nThreads = 0;
    private ThreadNotifier notification;
    private Thread scheduler;
    private int timeslice;
    private static boolean initialized = false;
    private boolean needThreads = false;
```

```
private static synchronized boolean isInitialized() {
    if (initialized)
        return true;
    initialized = true;
    return false;
}

public CPUScheduler(int t) {
    if (isInitialized())
        throw new SecurityException("Already initialized");
    threads = new CircularList();
    timeslice = t;
    nThreads = 0;
}

public synchronized void addThread(Thread t) {
    CPUSchedulerNode n = new CPUSchedulerNode(t);
    t.setPriority(2);
    threads.insert(n);
    nThreads++;
    if (needThreads) {
        needThreads = false;
        notify();
    }
}

public synchronized void removeThread(Thread t) {
    Object n = threads.locate(t);
    threads.delete(n);
    if (t == current.thread)
        current = null;
    nThreads--;
}

public synchronized void wakeup() {
    notify();
}

public void startScheduler() {
    notification = new ThreadNotifier(this);
    notification.setDaemon(true);
    notification.start();
    scheduler = new Thread(this);
    scheduler.setDaemon(true);
    scheduler.start();
}

public void stopScheduler() {
    scheduler.stop();
```

```java
        notification.stop();
}

public synchronized void run() {
    long now, then;
    int nBlocked = 0;
    Thread.currentThread().setPriority(6);
    now = System.currentTimeMillis();
    while (true) {
        current = (CPUSchedulerNode) threads.getNext();
        while (current == null) {
            needThreads = true;
            try {
                wait();
            } catch (Exception e) {}
            current = (CPUSchedulerNode) threads.getNext();
        }
        try {
            current.thread.setPriority(4);
        } catch (Exception e) {
            removeThread(current.thread);
            continue;
        }
        then = now;
        if (nBlocked == nThreads)
            notification.suspend();
        else notification.resume();
        try {
            wait(timeslice);
        } catch (InterruptedException ie) {};
        now = System.currentTimeMillis();
        if (current != null) {
            try {
                current.thread.setPriority(2);
                if (now - then < timeslice) {
                    // Thread must have blocked
                    if (!current.blocked) {
                        current.blocked = true;
                        nBlocked++;
                    }
                }
                else {
                    if (current.blocked) {
                        current.blocked = false;
                        nBlocked--;
                    }
                }
```

```
                    } catch (Exception e) {
                        removeThread(current.thread);
                    }
                }
            }
        }
    }
```

Because we now need to keep track of the state of the threads under the CPUScheduler's control, we introduced the CPUSchedulerNode class to contain both the thread and the state of the thread. In the CPUScheduler class itself, instead of keeping a CircularList of threads, we now keep a CircularList of these CPUSchedulerNodes. In addition, we also need to keep track of the total number of threads in the CircularList and the number of those threads that are blocked; when the total number of threads is equal to the number of blocked threads, we know it's time to put the CPUScheduler temporarily to sleep in order to avoid needless thrashing.

The real change in logic, then, occurs in the run() method where we have the code.

```
        if (nBlocked == nThreads)
            notification.suspend();
        else notification.resume();
```

What this does is move the notification thread to the blocked state when all threads under control of the scheduler are also blocked. Note that we do not need to keep track of the state of the notification thread itself: this means that we will quite often resume() the notification thread when it hasn't actually been suspended. As we mentioned earlier, this is not an error.

The code to keep track of the number of blocked nodes (nBlocked) is part of the new run() method: when the scheduler thread wakes up, it checks to see how long it was waiting. If the difference between the time when it went to sleep and the current time is less than the timeslice, the scheduler thread concludes that the thread it scheduled has blocked; the scheduler thread increments nBlocked accordingly. Similarly, if the time difference is greater than or equal to the timeslice, the scheduler thread tests to see if the scheduled thread used to be considered a blocked thread, in which case it decrements nBlocked.

The methods of our CPUScheduler class need to be modified so that they operate in terms of CPUSchedulerNodes instead of threads and keep track of the number of threads under the CPUScheduler's control. This causes the changes to the addThread() and removeThread() methods to operate on objects of class CPUSchedulerNode.

There's a subtle change in logic here that is dictated by the addition of the CPUSchedulerNode class. The programmer who uses the CPUScheduler class knows only about threads, not about CPUSchedulerNodes, so the argument that gets passed to the removeThread() method is a thread, not a CPUSchedulerNode. In order to delete the thread from the CircularList, we need to search the list and find the node that contains the thread. The CircularList class contains a locate() method that finds an object based on the equals() method of the object it is storing; normally this compares object references and lets us locate only a CPUSchedulerNode. But we can define the CPUSchedulerNode class so that objects in the class are considered equal if they contain the same thread that explains the odd definition of the equals() method of the CPUSchedulerNode.

Round-Robin Scheduling and "Fairness"

Many developers are surprised to learn that equal-priority Java threads are not automatically timesliced by a round-robin scheduler. Part of this surprise stems from the tendency to think of threads within a program as equivalent in theory to processes in an operating system: it has long been ingrained in our psyches that a timesliced scheduler is the fairest mechanism to deal with multiple processes. And, in an interactive user environment, that's usually the case.

There are, however, occasions when a round-robin scheduler is not the fairest scheduling algorithm available and the programmer is required to make sure that no timeslicing of threads occurs.[*] Consider the case of our CalcServer class that accepts connections from multiple clients simultaneously and runs each client in a separate thread. This is an elegant server architecture, but the question of the best scheduling mechanism to employ with this architecture turns out to be a profound one.

Let's take the case of a CalcServer that performs some sort of complex, analytic calculation for each of the clients that connects to it; assume that the calculation requires some five seconds for each client. When five clients connect to the server at roughly the same time, the CalcServer starts five separate threads. If those threads are subject to timeslicing, it takes about 25 seconds for all threads to reach the end of their calculation, and because the CPU has been equitably shared, each thread reaches the end of its individual calculation at this 25-second mark. So each client receives an answer after 25 seconds.

If no timeslicing is in effect in our CalcServer, however, then we have a different case: the clients still all connect at the same time, but one client (somewhat arbi-

---

[*] Preventing timesliced scheduling can be achieved with the CPUScheduler class: simply create the CPUScheduler class with a timeslice of Integer.MAX_VALUE.

trarily) gets the opportunity to run its calculation to its conclusion; the first client gets its answer in just five seconds instead of 25 seconds. Then the second client's calculation begins; the second client gets its answer after 10 seconds have passed, and so on. Only the fifth client has to wait the entire 25 seconds for an answer.

Which of these scheduling modes is the "fairest?" The answer to that depends on what happens during the five seconds the server calculates on behalf of the client. If the server provides just a single answer to the client, clearly the nontimesliced version is "fairest": on average, each client has to wait 15 seconds for an answer versus 25 seconds for the timesliced version. If instead the server provides five answers to the client—one for every second of calculation—then the timesliced version is "fairest": each client has one answer after five seconds, whereas in the nontimesliced version, the fifth client won't have its first answer until 21 seconds have passed.

In other words, this is once again the "intermediate results" requirement: if inter-mediate results are important to us, a round-robin scheduler provides the fairest results to all the threads. But if all we care about is the final answer, a round-robin scheduler is not appropriate: in the best of cases, it doesn't provide any benefits, and in cases like our CalcServer calculator, it actually decreases throughput in the system.

This issue of fairness applies to any resource in a threaded system that is subject to contention; we'll see it again when we examine lock starvation in the next chapter.

Summary

Here are the methods of the Thread class that we introduced in this chapter:

void setPriority(int priority)
> Sets the priority of the given thread. If `priority` is outside the allowed range of thread priorities, an exception is thrown.

int getPriority()
> Retrieves the priority of the given thread.

void suspend()
> Prevents a thread from running for an indefinite amount of time.

void resume()
> Allows a thread to run after being suspended.

static void yield()
> Yields the current thread, allowing another thread of the same priority to be run by the Java virtual machine.

void setDaemon(boolean on)

> Sets the thread to be a daemon thread (if on is true) or to be a user thread (if on is false).

boolean isDaemon()

> Returns true if the thread is a daemon thread and false if it is a user thread.

We've spent a lot of time discussing the priority and scheduling of threads. Scheduling is one of the grey areas of Java programming because actual scheduling models are not defined by the Java specification. This means that scheduling behavior may vary from platform to platform. The reason for this is because of Java's quest for simplicity: since the scheduling model of a program rarely affects the ultimate outcome or usefulness of that program, Java leaves the added complexity of explicit scheduling to the developer in those cases where the scheduling is important.

Following this idea, we've presented several mechanisms to affect the scheduling of Java threads, from simple fixed-priority scheduling to a simple round-robin scheduler to a more complete (and hence more complicated) round-robin scheduler suitable for very demanding scheduling requirements. In your Java programs, you should try and use the simplest of these scheduling techniques that accomplishes your goal.

In future releases of Java, the area of scheduling is likely to change for two reasons: first, the Java specification may be amended to specify whether or not round-robin scheduling must be implemented by the Java virtual machine among threads of the same priority. Second, when the Java specification is enhanced to include support for truly simultaneous execution of threads on multiple processors, scheduling of Java threads will take on an added complexity. But the principles we've outlined here will carry you through these scheduling challenges as well as through the scheduling challenges of your current Java programs.

7

Advanced Synchronization Topics

In this chapter, we're going to look into some of the more advanced issues related to data synchronization. When you write a Java program that makes use of several threads, issues related to data synchronization are the most likely issues to create difficulties in the design of the program, and errors in data synchronization are often the most difficult to detect, since they depend on events happening in a specific order. Often an error in data synchronization can be masked in the code by timing dependencies. You may notice some sort of data corruption in a normal run of your program, but when you run the program in a debugger or add some debugging statements to the code, the timing of the program is completely changed, and the data corruption no longer occurs.

Synchronization Terms

Programmers with a background in a particular threading system generally tend to use terms specific to that system to refer to some of the concepts we discuss in this chapter, and programmers without a background in certain threading systems will not necessarily understand the terms we choose to use. So here's a comparison of particular terms you may be familiar with and how they relate to the terms in this chapter.

Condition variable

A condition variable is not actually a lock: it is a variable associated with a lock. Condition variables are often used in the context of data synchronization. Condition variables generally have an API that achieves the same functionality as Java's wait and notify mechanism; in that mechanism, the condition variable is actually the object the lock is protecting.

Critical section

A critical section is the same as a synchronized method or block. Critical sections do not nest like synchronized methods or blocks.

Event variables

Event variables are the same as condition variables.

Lock

This term refers to the access granted to a particular thread that has entered a synchronized method or a synchronized block. We say that a thread that has entered such a method or block has acquired the lock.[*]

Monitor

A generic synchronization term used inconsistently between threading systems. In some systems, a monitor is simply a lock; in others, a monitor is similar to the wait and notify mechanism.

Mutex

Another term for a lock. Mutexes do not nest like synchronized methods or blocks and generally can be used across processes at the operating-system level.

Reader-writer locks

A lock that can be acquired by multiple threads simultaneously as long as the threads agree to read only from the shared data or can be acquired by a single thread that wants to write to the shared data. Java has no reader-writer locks, but we'll develop a reader-writer lock class later in this chapter.

Semaphores

Semaphores are used inconsistently in computer systems. Many developers use semaphores to lock objects in the same way Java locks are used; this usage makes them equivalent to mutexes. A more sophisticated use of semaphores is to take advantage of the counter associated with them to nest acquisition to the critical section of the code; Java locks are exactly equivalent to semaphores in this usage. Semaphores are also used to gain access to resources other than code; the example of acquiring resources that we showed in the ResourceThrottle class in Chapter 4 implements this type of semaphore behavior.

Preventing Deadlock

Deadlock between threads competing for the same set of locks is the hardest problem to solve in any threaded program. It's a hard enough problem, in fact,

---

[*] As we discussed in Chapter 3, this lock is associated with either a particular instance of an object or a particular class.

that we will not solve it—or even attempt to solve it. What we'll try to offer instead is a good understanding of deadlock and some guidelines on how to prevent deadlock. Preventing deadlock is completely the responsibility of the Java developer—the Java virtual machine will not do deadlock prevention or deadlock detection on your behalf.

We'll look at deadlock in this chapter in conjunction with the following code that emulates how a kitchen might operate. When a cook wants to make cookies, she grabs the measuring cup to measure some ingredients into the bowl; when a cook wants to make an omelette, he grabs a bowl, beats some eggs, and then measures out the eggs for each individual omelette. This is the order a typical cook uses to make these items, and as long as we have only one cook, everything is fine with these procedures. If we have two cooks, however, and one wants to make cookies while one wants to make omelettes, we have a deadlock situation: the omelette maker needs the measuring cup to measure out the eggs that are in the mixing bowl; the cookie maker needs the bowl to put in the flour that is in the measuring cup.[*]

```java
public class Kitchen {
    static MeasuringCup theCup;
    static Bowl theBowl;

    public void makeCookie() {
        synchronized(theCup) {
            theCup.measureOut(1, theFlour);
            synchronized(theBowl) {
                theBowl.putIngredients(theCup);
                theBowl.mix();
            }
        }
    }

    public void makeOmelette() {
        synchronized(theBowl) {
            Eggs e[] = getBrokenEggs();
            theBowl.putIngredients(e);
            theBowl.mix();
            synchronized(theCup) {
                theCup.measureOut(theBowl);
            }
        }
    }
}
```

---

[*] Obviously, the code examples in this section are not complete examples. In addition to lacking all the methods and classes we refer to, we're missing some other useful methods as well. For example our class does not include a recipe for soup, since a multithreaded recipe would spoil the broth.

Like previous examples of deadlock we've seen, this example is simple, but more complicated conditions of deadlock don't involve anything other than the principles outlined in this example: they're harder to detect, but nothing more is involved than that two or more threads are attempting to acquire each other's locks.

What makes deadlock difficult to detect is that it could involve many classes that call each other's synchronized methods[*] in an order that isn't apparently obvious. Say we have twenty-six classes A to Z, and that the synchronized methods of class A call those of class B, those of class B call class C, and so on.   This leads us into the same sort of deadlock situation that we had between our `makeCookie()` and `makeOmelette()` methods, but it's unlikely that a programmer examining the source code would detect that deadlock.

Nonetheless, a close examination of the source code is the only option presently available to determine if deadlock is a possibility; Java virtual machines will not detect deadlock at run-time, and while it is possible to develop tools that examine the source code to detect potential deadlock situations, no such tools exist yet for Java.

The simplest way to avoid deadlock is to follow the rule that says a synchronized method should never call a synchronized method. That's a good rule, often advocated, but it's not the ideal rule for two reasons:

- It's impractical: many useful Java methods are synchronized, and you'll want to call them from your synchronized method. As an example, we've called the `addElement()` method of Java's Vector class from several of our synchronized methods.

- It's overkill: if the synchronized method you're going to call does not in turn call another synchronized method, there's no way that deadlock can occur (which is why we always got away with calling the `addElement()` method from a synchronized method; the `addElement()` method makes no further synchronization calls). Generically, the synchronized method can call other synchronized methods in ways we'll explore later.

Nonetheless, if you can manage to obey this rule, there will be no deadlock in your program.

Another often-used technique to avoid deadlock is to lock some higher-order object that is related to the many lower-order objects we'll need to use: in our

---

* For purposes of this discussion, a synchronized block is the same as a synchronized method.

example, that means locking the kitchen instead of locking the individual utensils as we use them.[*] This makes our methods synchronized as follows:

```
public class Kitchen {
    public synchronized void makeCookie() { ... }
    public synchronized void makeOmelette() { ... }
}
```

The problem with this technique is that it often leads to situations where the locking granularity is not ideal. By synchronizing the methods of the kitchen class, we are essentially preventing more than one cook from using the kitchen at a time; the purpose of having multiple threads is to allow more than one cook to use the kitchen.

If we've done our program design correctly, there was probably a reason why we attempted to acquire multiple locks rather than a single global lock. Solving deadlock issues by violating this design becomes somewhat counterproductive.

The most practical rule to avoid deadlock is to make sure that locks are always acquired in the same order. In the case of our deadlock example, this would mean to make sure that the mixing bowl lock is always acquired before the measuring cup lock (or vice versa, as long as we're consistent). This implies the need for a lock hierarchy among classes. The lock hierarchy is unrelated to the Java class hierarchy: it is a hierarchy of objects rather than of classes. Furthermore, the hierarchy of the objects is unrelated to the hierarchy of the classes: the MeasuringCup and Bowl classes are probably sibling classes in the class hierarchy, but in the lock hierarchy, we must place one object above the other. The lock hierarchy is a queue rather than a tree: each object in the hierarchy must have one and only one parent object (as in the Java class hierarchy), but it must have one and only one descendant as well.

If you're developing a complex program in Java, it's a good idea to develop a lock hierarchy when you develop your class hierarchy; sample hierarchies are shown in Figure 7-1. But since there is no mechanism to enforce the lock hierarchy, it's up to your good programming practices to make sure that the lock hierarchy is followed.

We can use this rule to prevent deadlock in our kitchen by requiring that all methods acquire the bowl before the measuring cup even if they intend to use the measuring cup first. We'd rewrite the `makeCookie()` method like this:

---

[*] There are many variations on that technique. We could create a BusyFlag for the measuring cup and bowl combination and just acquire that lock whenever we needed one or the other utensil. We also could make it a programmatic rule that to use either the measuring cup or mixing bowl, you must acquire the lock only for the mixing bowl. All these variations suffer from the lock-granularity problem that follows.

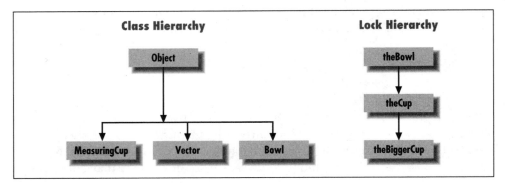

Figure 7-1. Class and lock hierarchies

```
public void makeCookie() {
    synchronized(theBowl) {
        synchronized(theCup) {
            theCup.measureOut(1, theFlour);
            theBowl.putIngredients(theCup);
            theBowl.mix();
        }
    }
}
```

Following this lock-acquisition hierarchy is the best way to guarantee that dead-lock will not occur in your Java program when you use the standard synchronization techniques of the Java language.

What about the BusyFlag class that we've developed; could that be useful in preventing dead-lock? The answer is yes, to a point. Using the BusyFlag class adds a certain complexity to a Java program, and it introduces the possibility of a new kind of deadlock that standard Java synchronization techniques don't allow. But these classes also allow us to build more complicated deadlock recovery into our program, which may be useful in certain circumstances.

The feature in the BusyFlag class that helps us avoid deadlock is the try-GetBusyFlag() method. In standard Java synchronization calls, there is no such concept as a test-and-set acquisition of a lock: standard Java threads attempt to acquire the lock and block only until the lock is acquired. The BusyFlag class allows us to see if we can acquire the lock and also attempt some sort of recovery if the flag is busy.

Let's rewrite our kitchen example to use the BusyFlag:

```
public class Kitchen {
    static MeasuringCup theCup;
    static Bowl theBowl;
    static BusyFlag theCupFlag, theBowlFlag;
```

```
    public void makeCookie() {
        theCupFlag.getBusyFlag();
        theCup.measureOut(1, theFlour);
        theBowlFlag.getBusyFlag();
        theBowl.putIngredients(theCup);
        theBowl.mix();
        theBowlFlag.freeBusyFlag();
        theCupFlag.freeBusyFlag();
    }

    public void makeOmelette() {
        theBowlFlag.getBusyFlag();
        Eggs e[] = getBrokenEggs();
        theBowl.putIngredients(e);
        theBowl.mix();
        theCupFlag.getBusyFlag();
        theCup.measureOut(theBowl);
        theCupFlag.freeBusyFlag();
        theBowlFlag.freeBusyFlag();
    }
}
```

So far we've just substituted the BusyFlag class for Java's standard synchronized blocks with the effect that we can still have deadlock. But we could go further and rewrite the makeCookie() method like this:

```
public void makeCookie() {
    theCupFlag.getBusyFlag();
    theCup.measureOut(1, theFlour);
    if (theBowlFlag.tryGetBusyFlag()) {
        theBowl.putIngredients(theCup);
        theBowl.mix();
        theBowlFlag.freeBusyFlag();
    }
    else {
        // ... do something else ...
    }
    theCupFlag.freeBusyFlag();
}
```

Here we've prevented deadlock by testing to see if the bowl's BusyFlag is free as we grab it. If the flag is free, we'll grab the lock and continue to make our cookies. Even if, at this point, another cook thread comes along to make an omelette, we won't have deadlock, as that thread blocks until we've released the locks for both the bowl and the cup.

Whether or not we've achieved anything by preventing deadlock depends on what logic we could put into the else clause of the makeCookie() method. Perhaps there is another bowl we could use in the else clause, but that doesn't do us any good: what if that bowl is being used by a cook thread executing the make-Trifle() method? The logic in the else statement must do one of two things: it must do either something that requires no utensils to be locked, or something that allows the measuring cup's BusyFlag to be released. If we have a square of waxed paper available, we could put the flour onto the waxed paper and then wait for the bowl:

```
public class makeCookie() {
    theCupFlag.getBusyFlag();
    theCup.measureOut(1, theFlour);
    if (theBowlFlag.tryGetBusyFlag()) {
        theBowl.putIngredients(theCup);
        theBowl.mix();
        theBowlFlag.freeBusyFlag();
        theCupFlag.freeBusyFlag();
    }
    else {
        WaxedPaper thePaper = new WaxedPaper();
        thePaper.emptyOnto(theCup);
        theCupFlag.freeBusyFlag();
        theBowlFlag.getBusyFlag();
        theBowl.putIngredients(thePaper);
        theBowl.mix();
        theBowlFlag.freeBusyFlag();
    }
}
```

This type of logic would not have been possible with the synchronized keyword since we cannot release the lock at will. To use Java's synchronized keyword, we would always have had to use waxed paper:

```
public class makeCookie() {
    WaxedPaper thePaper = new WaxedPaper();
    synchronized(theCup) {
        theCup.measureOut(1, theFlour);
        thePaper.emptyOnto(theCup);
    }

    synchronized(theBowl) {
        theBowl.putIngredients(thePaper);
        theBowl.mix();
    }
}
```

The code using the synchronized keyword is certainly cleaner, easier to understand, and easier to maintain. But in a world where waxed paper is a rare commodity, the BusyFlag code has the advantage of not using scarce resources unless it is necessary to do so.

Using the BusyFlag is also more complex compared to the technique using the lock hierarchy. But here again, there is an advantage to the BusyFlag code: there is a larger degree of parallelism in the BusyFlag example than in the ordered lock acquisition example. In the BusyFlag example, one cook thread could be measuring the flour at the same time another cook thread is whisking the eggs for the omelette, whereas in the ordered lock acquisition example, the omelette maker must wait to whisk the eggs until the cookie maker has released both utensils.

You must decide whether these types of benefits outweigh the added complexity of the code when you design your Java program. If you start by creating a lock hierarchy, you'll have simpler code at the possible expense of the loss of some parallelism. We think that it's easier to write the simpler code first, and address the parallelism problems if they become a performance bottleneck.

Another Type of Deadlock

In our last example of the kitchen with the BusyFlag, we introduced the possibility of another type of deadlock that could not have occurred had we used only Java's synchronized keyword. At issue is what happens if a thread should die unexpectedly when it is holding a lock.

Let's simplify our example somewhat by changing class so that it has only a single synchronized method. The class definition would look something like this:

```
public class Kitchen {
    public synchronized void makeCookie() { ... }
}
```

Now we have two cook threads, one that is executing the makeCookie() method and another that is blocked attempting to enter the makeCookie() method. Under normal circumstances, the first thread completes the makeCookie() method and exits the method, at which time the second thread has the opportunity to enter the makeCookie() method and make its own cookies.

What happens instead if the first thread encounters a run-time exception and terminates? Under many threading systems, this leads to a type of deadlock, because the thread that terminates does not automatically release the locks it held. Under those systems, the second thread would wait forever trying to make its batch of cookies because it can't acquire the lock. In Java, however, locks are always given up when the thread leaves the scope of the synchronized block, even if it leaves that scope due to an exception. So in Java, this type of deadlock never occurs.

But if we use the BusyFlag class instead of Java's synchronized keyword, we've introduced the possibility of this type of deadlock. In this case, our methods look like this:

```
public void makeCookie() {
    flag.getBusyFlag();
    // ... do some work ...
    flag.freeBusyFlag();
}
```

If in the process of doing some work we encounter a run-time exception, the Busy-Flag will never be freed. This means that our second cook thread would never be able to make its batch of cookies.[*]

There is a way around this: we can use Java's `finally` clause to make sure the BusyFlag is freed no matter what happens during the execution of our method. To use the BusyFlag so that it has the same lock semantics as the synchronized keyword, you need to do something like this:

```
public void makeCookie() {
    try {
        flag.getBusyFlag();
        // ... do some work ...
    } finally {
        flag.freeBusyFlag();
    }
}
```

Now our BusyFlag behaves the same as if we'd used the synchronized keyword. Clearly in the example we've used in this chapter, we can always arrange our `try`/`finally` clauses so that the locks are released even when an exception is encountered. But in other examples we've seen, this is not always possible. One of the techniques that is possible with the BusyFlag class is the ability to release the lock in a method other than the one in which the lock was acquired. If you use that technique, you have to be aware that this new type of deadlock is still possible.

By the way, the fact that Java's synchronized keyword does not allow this type of deadlock is not necessarily a good thing. When a thread encounters a run-time exception while it is holding a lock, there's the possibility—indeed, the expectation—that it will leave the data it was manipulating in an inconsistent state. If another thread is then able to acquire the lock, it may encounter this inconsistent data and proceed erroneously. In our example, if the first thread was in the middle of making chocolate-chip cookies when the run-time exception occurred, it would have left a bunch of ingredients in the bowl. Under normal circumstances, the `makeCookie()` method would have cleaned out the bowl, but when the exception occurred, that didn't happen. So now our second thread comes

---

[*] Note that this logic applies only to run-time exceptions, since Java requires you to catch all other types of exceptions. Often a run-time exception is a catastrophic error that you can't recover from anyway, so it may not matter if you didn't release the BusyFlag, but we wouldn't make that assumption.

along attempting to make oatmeal-raisin cookies; the end result is chocolate-chip-oatmeal-raisin cookies.*

This is a hard problem to solve completely. In many cases, it's better to use the BusyFlag and risk deadlock if a thread exits unexpectedly than to allow a second thread to use that inconsistent data. Consider a stock trading system where a thread is in the process of updating the current price information when it encounters the run-time exception: if another thread accesses the incorrect current price and a trade is made on the wrong price, the exposure of the firm executing that trade could be in the millions of dollars. In cases like this, it's really better to use some sort of back-end database that has transactional integrity built into it so that you're protected against an unexpected thread termination.†

Lock Starvation

Whenever multiple threads compete for a scare resource, there's a danger of starvation. Earlier we discussed this concept in the context of CPU starvation; with a bad choice of scheduling options, some threads never had the opportunity to become the currently running thread and suffered from CPU starvation.

A similar situation is theoretically possible when it comes to locks granted by the synchronized keyword. Lock starvation occurs when a particular thread attempts to acquire a lock and never succeeds because another thread is already holding the lock. Clearly, this can occur on a simple basis if one thread acquires the lock and never releases it: all other threads that attempt to acquire the lock will never succeed and will starve. But lock starvation can be more subtle than that: if there are six threads competing for the same lock, it's possible that each of five threads will hold the lock for only 20 percent of the time, thus starving out the sixth thread.

Like CPU starvation, lock starvation is not something most threaded Java programs need to consider. If our Java program is producing a result in a finite period of time, then eventually all threads in the program will acquire the lock, if only because all the other threads in the program have exited. But also like CPU starvation, lock starvation includes the question of fairness: there are certain times when we want to make sure that threads acquire locks in a reasonable order, so that one thread won't necessarily have to wait for all other threads to exit before it has its chance to acquire a lock.

---

* We could put the method that cleans the bowl into a `finally` clause to solve this problem, but what if that is the method that throws the exception?

† The logic to solve this problem is standard in every database package that implements a two-phase commit. You could write such logic into your Java program directly, but it's difficult to get right.

Consider the case of two threads that are competing for a lock. Assume that thread A acquires the object lock on a fairly periodic basis as shown in Figure 7-2.

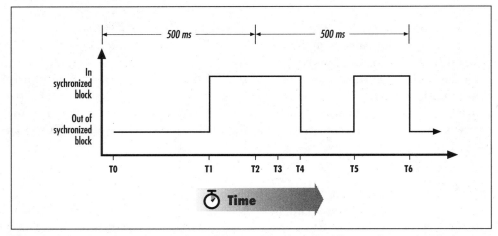

Figure 7-2. Call graph of synchronized methods; thread A repeatedly calls a synchronized method

Also assume that the two threads are operating under a timeslicing scheduler that creates a scheduling event every 500 milliseconds. Here's what happens at the various points on the graph.

T0

> At time T0, both thread A and thread B are in the runnable state, and thread A is the currently running thread.

T1

> Thread A is still the currently running thread, and it acquires the object lock when it enters the synchronized block.

T2

> A scheduling event occurs due to the timeslicing mechanism; this causes thread B to become the currently running thread.

T3

> Very soon after becoming the currently running thread, thread B attempts to enter the synchronized block. This causes thread B to enter the blocked state, which in turn causes a scheduling event so that thread A becomes the currently running thread. Thread A continues executing in the synchronized block.

T4

> Thread A exits the synchronized block. This causes thread B to enter the runnable state but does not cause a scheduling event, so thread A continues to be the currently running thread.

T5

> Thread A once again enters the synchronized block and acquires the lock. Thread B remains in the runnable state.

T6

> Thread B once again becomes the currently running thread. It immediately tries to enter the synchronized block, but the lock for the synchronized block is once again held by thread A, so thread B immediately enters the blocked state. Thread A is left to become the currently running thread again, and we are now at the same state we were in at time T3.

It's possible for this cycle to continue forever, so that even though thread B is often in the runnable state, it can never acquire the lock and actually do useful work.

Clearly this example is a pathological case: the round-robin scheduling events have to occur only during those time periods when thread A holds the lock for the synchronized block. With two threads, that's extremely unlikely and generally indicates that thread A is holding the lock almost continuously. With several threads, however, it's not out of the question that one thread may find that every time it is scheduled, another thread already holds the lock the first wants.

The common pitfall that creates lock starvation is to implement code similar to the following:

```
public class MyThread extends Thread {
    public void run() {
        while (true) {
            synchronized(someObject) {
                // ... do some calculations ...
            }
        }
    }
}

public class Test {
    public static void main(String args[]) {
        MyThread t1, t2;
        t1 = new MyThread();
        t2 = new MyThread();
        t1.start();
        t2.start();
    }
}
```

At first glance, we might expect this code to work just fine, thinking that when thread `t1` exits the synchronized block, thread `t2` then immediately gets the lock on `someObject` and the two threads continue alternating the acquisition of the lock. But as we've seen, that is not the case: unless the round-robin scheduling event occurs during the short interval between the end of the synchronized block (when the lock is released) and the beginning of the next iteration of the loop (when the lock is reacquired), thread t2 will never acquire the someObject lock and will never become the currently running thread.[*]

There are two points to take away from this:

Acquisition of locks does not queue
>   When a thread attempts to acquire a lock, it does not check to see if another thread is already attempting to acquire the lock (or, more precisely, if another thread has tried to acquire the lock and blocked because it was already held). In pseudo-code, the process looks like this:

```
while (lock is held)
    wait for a while
acquire lock
```

>   For threads of equal priority, there's nothing in this process that prevents a lock from being granted to one thread even if another thread is waiting.

Releasing a lock does not create a scheduling event
>   When a lock is released, any threads that were blocked waiting for that lock are moved from the blocked state into the runnable state. However, no actual scheduling event occurs, so none of the threads that have just moved into the runnable state become the currently running thread; the thread that has just released the lock remains the currently running thread (again, assuming that all threads had the same priority).

Nonetheless, lock starvation remains, as might be guessed from our example, something that occurs only in rare circumstances. In fact, each of the following circumstances must be present for lock starvation to occur:

Multiple threads are competing for the same lock
>   This lock becomes the scarce resource for which some threads may starve.

>   There must be an period of time during which there is not enough CPU time to accommodate all the threads.

>   Either at least two threads must always be in the runnable state during this time period, or a thread that holds the lock enters the blocked state while it still holds the lock (This is generally a bad thing).

>   If there is adequate CPU time to satisfy all threads (and no thread blocks while holding the lock), then a thread that wants to acquire the lock must at some

---

[*] Adding a call to the yield() method will solve this simple case, but it is not a general solution.

point actually acquire the lock, if only because it's the only thread in the runnable state.

The results that occur during this period of contention must be interesting to us

If, for example, we're calculating a big matrix, there's probably a point in time at the beginning of our calculation during which multiple threads are competing for the same lock and the CPU. But since all we care about is the final result of this calculation, it doesn't matter to us that some threads are temporarily starved for the lock: we'll still get the final answer in the same amount of time.

As in the case of CPU starvation, we're only concerned about lock starvation if there's a period of time during which it matters that the lock be given out fairly.

These threads must all have the same priority

In the example we discussed above, if thread B has a higher priority than thread A, then consider what would happen at time T4. When thread B moves from the blocked state to the runnable state because thread A has released the lock, a priority-based scheduling event occurs, and thread B becomes the currently running thread.

Of course, if thread A has a higher priority than thread B, thread B would still never get the opportunity to become the currently running thread, but in that case, thread B would be subject to CPU starvation rather than lock starvation.

These threads must be under control of a round-robin scheduler

If the equal-priority threads are not under control of a round-robin scheduler, they are again subject to CPU starvation rather than lock starvation. Note also that this round-robin scheduler must not adjust the priorities of the threads, or the previous rule might be violated. Threads that are under control of the SimpleScheduler in Chapter 6 are subject to lock starvation.

All of the properties of lock starvation stem from the fact that a thread that attempts to acquire a lock checks only to see if another thread already holds the lock, and not if another thread is already waiting for the lock. So if we're in one of those rare situations where lock starvation can occur, we need to develop a lock that has a queue associated with it so that the lock is given out fairly to every thread that wants to acquire the lock.

This is a simple class to write: we can use the Java Vector class to implement the queue, and then we need only write methods to allow classes to acquire and release the lock. The `acquire()` method places requests on the queue, and the `release()` method notifies the next thread on the queue that the lock is now available.

Our QueuedLock class then looks like this:

```
import java.util.*;

public class QueuedLock {
    private Vector waiters;
    private Thread current = null;

    public QueuedLock() {
        waiters = new Vector();
    }
    public synchronized void acquire() {
        Thread me = Thread.currentThread();
        waiters.addElement(me);
        while ((Thread) waiters.elementAt(0) != me)
            try {
                wait();
            } catch (Exception e) {}
        current = me;
    }

    public synchronized void release() {
        if (Thread.currentThread() != current)
            throw new IllegalArgumentException("QueuedLock not held");
        waiters.removeElementAt(0);
        notifyAll();
    }
}
```

This is a complete, albeit simplistic, implementation of a QueuedLock class. When a thread attempts to acquire a lock, it enters the acquire() method and puts itself into the waiters vector. It then waits until it is the first element in the waiters vector. Similarly, when a thread releases the lock, it removes itself from the waiters vector and notifies the other threads waiting on the vector that they should check to see if they are now first in line.

This implementation is particularly inefficient, in that it relies on the noti-fyAll() method to wake up the threads waiting to acquire the lock. If there are thirty threads waiting for the lock, all thirty threads will be wakened, even though only one thread will acquire the lock and the other twenty-nine threads will just call the wait() method again. So you only want to use this technique in those special cases when you know that lock starvation will be a problem.[*]

---

[*] We could develop a more efficient implementation by using the targeted notification technique we discussed in Chapter 4. We leave that as an exercise for the reader.

To use the QueuedLock class, instead of making our methods synchronized, we must explicitly call the acquire() and release() methods just as we did when we implemented the BusyFlag class:

```
public class DBAccess {
    private QueuedLock lock;

    public DBAccess() {
        lock = new QueuedLock();
    }
    public Object read() {
        Object o;
        try {
            lock.acquire();
            o = someMethodThatReturnsData();
            return o;
        } finally {
            lock.release();
        }
    }

    public void write(Object o) {
        try {
            lock.acquire();
            someMethodThatSendsData(o);
        } finally {
            lock.release();
        }
    }
}
```

There are a few more niceties we could add to the QueuedLock class in order to make it more useful. First, we want the QueuedLock class to have the same semantics as Java's synchronized methods (except for the queuing part that we're adding); this means that calls to acquire the lock should nest. The other nice thing we'd like our QueuedLock class to include is the ability to test if the lock can be acquired. As in the case of the BusyFlag class, the tryAcquire() method checks to see if the lock is held. If it is held, tryAcquire() returns false, otherwise it grabs the lock and returns true.

Taking this all into account, our new class look like this:

```
import java.util.Vector;

public class QueuedLock {
    private Thread current = null;
    private int nAcquires;
    private Vector waiters;
```

```
public QueuedLock() {
    waiters = new Vector();
}
public synchronized void acquire() {
    Thread me = Thread.currentThread();
    if (me == current) {
        nAcquires++;
        return;
    }
    waiters.addElement(me);
    while ((Thread) waiters.elementAt(0) != me) {
        try {
            wait();
        } catch (Exception e) {}
    }
    current = me;
    nAcquires = 0;
}

public synchronized void release() {
    if (Thread.currentThread() != current)
        throw new IllegalArgumentException("QueuedLock not held");
    if (nAcquires == 0) {
        waiters.removeElementAt(0);
        notifyAll();
    }
    else nAcquires--;
}

public synchronized boolean tryAcquire() {
    if (waiters.size() != 0 && current != Thread.currentThread())
        return false;
    acquire();
    return true;
}
}
```

That concludes our look into the QueuedLock class and the basics of our discussion about lock starvation. In the next section, we'll see a more complicated case of lock starvation and develop another useful locking class to solve it.

Reader-Writer Locks

Sometimes you need to read information from an object in an operation that might take a fairly long period of time. You'll need to lock the object so that the information you read is consistent, but you don't necessarily need to prevent another thread from also reading data from the object at the same time: as long as all the threads are only reading the data, there's no reason why they couldn't read the data in parallel, since this doesn't affect the data each thread is reading.

In fact, the only reason we need data locking in the first place is when the data is being changed: when the data is being written. The change to the data introduces the possibility that a thread reading the data sees the data in an inconsistent state. And until now, we've been content to have a lock that allowed only a single thread to access that data whether the thread is reading or writing the data, based on the theory that the lock is only held for a short period of time.

But if the lock needs to be held for a long period of time, it makes sense to consider the possibility of allowing multiple threads to read the data simultaneously so that these threads don't need to compete against each other to acquire the lock. Of course, we must still only allow a single thread to write the data, and we must make sure that none of the threads that were reading the data are still active while our single writer thread is changing the internal state of the data.

Consider the case of a binary tree that contains some sort of information that is designed to be searched quite often by multiple threads. Depending on the amount of information contained in the binary tree, searching for a particular entry may require a long period of time. The interface for such a binary tree might look like this:

```
public class BTree {
    public synchronized boolean find(Object o) {
        // Perform time-consuming search, returning the object if
        // found or null if the object is not found
    }

    public synchronized void insert(Object o) {
        // Perform a time-consuming insert
    }
}
```

The problem here is that if two threads call the find() method at the same time, one of them blocks while it waits to acquire the lock; this thread remains blocked for a long time while the first thread continues to perform its search. If these two threads are operating in a timesliced environment, they won't be able to timeslice since they're competing for the same single lock. But if this binary tree is part of a server that is to be accessed by multiple clients, we'd really like for the threads calling the find() method to timeslice in order to achieve the fairness goal of our server.

This is where the reader-writer lock comes in. If we have a lock that allows multiple threads to read a data structure simultaneously, we could use an interface that looks like this:

```
public class BTree {
    RWLock lock;
    public boolean find(Object o) {
        try {
            lock.lockRead();
            // Perform time-consuming search, returning the object
            // if found or null if the object is not found
            return answer;
        } finally {
            lock.unlock();
        }
    }

    public void insert(Object o) {
        try {
            lock.lockWrite();
            // Perform a time-consuming insert
        } finally {
            lock.unlock();
        }
    }
}
```

We now have the capability of allowing multiple threads to read the B-tree simultaneously, even though the B-tree can still be updated by only a single thread.

The bad news is that the Java API does not provide anything like reader-writer
locks, but the good news is that writing your own reader-writer lock is not difficult.
We'll now look at a simple implementation of a reader-writer lock.

```
class RWNode {
    static final int READER = 0;
    static final int WRITER = 1;
    Thread t;
    int state;
    int nAcquires;
    RWNode(Thread t, int state) {
        this.t = t;
        this.state = state;
        nAcquires = 0;
    }
}

public class RWLock {
    private Vector waiters;

    private int firstWriter() {
        Enumeration e;
        int index;
        for (index = 0, e = waiters.elements();
```

```
                                   e.hasMoreElements(); index++) {
            RWNode node = (RWNode) e.nextElement();
            if (node.state == RWNode.WRITER)
                return index;
        }
        return Integer.MAX_VALUE;
    }

    private int getIndex(Thread t) {
        Enumeration e;
        int index;
        for (index = 0, e = waiters.elements();
                        e.hasMoreElements(); index++) {
            RWNode node = (RWNode) e.nextElement();
            if (node.t == t)
                return index;
        }
        return -1;
    }

    public RWLock() {
        waiters = new Vector();
    }

    public synchronized void lockRead() {
        RWNode node;
        Thread me = Thread.currentThread();
        int index = getIndex(me);
        if (index == -1) {
            node = new RWNode(me, RWNode.READER);
            waiters.addElement(node);
        }
        else node = (RWNode) waiters.elementAt(index);
        while (getIndex(me) > firstWriter()) {
            try {
                wait();
            } catch (Exception e) {}
        }
        node.nAcquires++;
    }
    public synchronized void lockWrite() {
        RWNode node;
        Thread me = Thread.currentThread();
        int index = getIndex(me);
        if (index == -1) {
            node = new RWNode(me, RWNode.WRITER);
            waiters.addElement(node);
        }
        else {
```

```
            node = (RWNode) waiters.elementAt(index);
            if (node.state == RWNode.READER)
                throw new IllegalArgumentException("Upgrade lock");
            node.state = RWNode.WRITER;
        }
        while (getIndex(me) != 0) {
            try {
                wait();
            } catch (Exception e) {}
        }
        node.nAcquires++;
    }

    public synchronized void unlock() {
        RWNode node;
        Thread me = Thread.currentThread();
        int index;
        index = getIndex(me);
        if (index  > firstWriter())
            throw new IllegalArgumentException("Lock not held");
        node = (RWNode) waiters.elementAt(index);
        node.nAcquires--;
        if (node.nAcquires == 0)
            waiters.removeElementAt(index);
        notifyAll();
    }
}
```

The interface to the reader-writer lock is very simple: there's a method lock-
Read() to acquire the read lock, a method lockWrite() to acquire the write
lock, and a method unlock() to release the lock (only a single unlock()
method is required for reasons we'll explore in a moment). Just as in our Queued-
Lock class, threads that are attempting to acquire the lock are held in the
waiters Vector until they are "first" in line for the lock, but the definition of first
in line has changed somewhat.

A Reader-Writer Lock Is a Single Lock

You might be tempted to think of the reader-writer lock as two separate but related locks: a lock to read and a lock to write. One reason you might be led to
think this is because of our vocabulary: we consistently refer to a reader lock
and a writer lock as if there were two separate locks involved in this process.
On a logical level, that's true, and we'll continue to use that vocabulary, even
though we're actually implementing a single lock.

Because we need to keep track of how each thread wants to acquire the lock—whether they want to acquire the read lock or the write lock—we need to create a class to encapsulate the information of the thread that made the request and the type of request it made. This is the RWNode class; our `waiters` queue now holds elements of type RWNode instead of Thread as it did in the QueuedLock class.

The acquisition of the read lock is the same as the logic of the QueuedLock class except for the new definition of *first in line*. First in line for the read lock means that no other node in the `waiters` queue ahead of us wants to acquire the write lock. If the only nodes in the `waiters` queue that are ahead of us want only to acquire the read lock, then we can go ahead and acquire the lock. Otherwise, we must `wait()` until we are first in line.

The acquisition of the write lock is stricter: we must be in position 0 for the lock in order to acquire it, just as was required in our QueuedLock class.

The logic to keep track of the number of times a particular thread has acquired a lock has undergone a slight change. In the QueuedLock class, we were able to keep track of this number as a single instance variable. Since the read lock can be acquired by multiple threads simultaneously, we can no longer use a simple instance variable; we must associate the `nAcquires` count with each particular thread. This explains the new logic in both acquisition methods that checks to see if there is already a node associated with the calling thread.

Our reader-writer lock class does not have the notion of "upgrading" a lock; that is, if you hold the reader lock, you cannot acquire the writer lock. You must explicitly release the reader lock before you attempt to acquire the writer lock, or you will receive an IllegalArgumentException.[*]

Finally, our reader-writer lock class contains some helper methods to search the `waiters` queue for the first node in the queue that represents a thread attempting to acquire the write lock (`firstWriter()`) and to find the index in the queue of the node associated with the calling thread (`getIndex()`).[†]

Figure 7-3 shows the state of the `waiters` queue through several attempts at lock acquisition. Threads that have acquired the lock have a white background while threads that are waiting to acquire the lock have a shaded background; each box

---

[*] If an upgrade feature were provided, the class would also have to release the reader lock before acquiring the writer lock. A true upgrade is not possible.

[†] We can't use the Vector class' `indexOf()` method for this purpose, because we'd have to pass the `indexOf()` method an object of type RWNode, but all we have is a thread. In Chapter 6, we had a similar problem with the CircularList class that we solved by overriding the `equals()` method of the CPUSchedulerNode class, but that technique won't work in this case due to some implementation details of the Vector class.

notes whether the thread in question is attempting to acquire the read or the write lock.

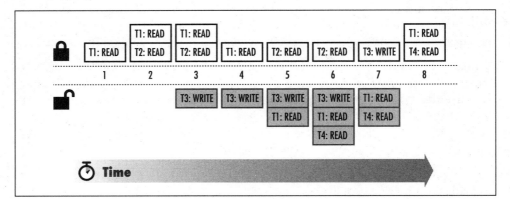

Figure 7-3. Reader-writer lock queue

At point 1, thread T1 has acquired the read lock. Since it is the only thread in the `waiters` queue, the `getIndex()` method returns 0 while the `firstWriter()` method returns `MAX_VALUE`. Since the index was less than the firstWriter, the lock is granted. At point 2, thread T2 has requested (and been granted) the read lock based on the same logic. Here's a point at which two threads have the read lock simultaneously.

At point 3, thread T3 attempts to acquire the write lock. Because the index of T3 in the queue is 2, it cannot grab the lock and instead executes the `wait()` method inside the `lockWrite()` method. Then at point 4, thread T1 releases the read lock. The `unlock()` method calls `notifyAll()` which wakes up T3, but because T3's index in the queue is now 1, it again executes the `wait()` method.

At point 5, thread T1 again attempts to acquire the read lock, but this time, because its index in the queue (2) is greater than the index of the first writer (1), it does not immediately get the lock and instead executes the `wait()` method inside the `lockRead()` method. We might be tempted at this point to allow T1 to acquire the read lock since T2 already has the read lock, and we generally allow multiple simultaneous acquisitions of the read lock. But if we implement that logic, we will starve the threads attempting to acquire the write lock: we could have multiple threads acquiring the read lock, and even though they might individually give up the lock frequently, one of them could always prevent a thread from acquiring the write lock. That's the rationale for always putting the requesting thread into the `waiters` queue and then testing its index against other threads in the queue, as happens again at point 6.

At point 7, thread T2 releases the read lock, notifying all other threads that the lock is free. Because T3 is a writer lock with an index of 0, the `lockWrite()`

method gives it the lock while the other threads in the `lockRead()` method `wait()`.

Finally, at point 8, thread T3 releases the lock. This time when the two remaining threads are notified that the lock is free, they are both able to acquire it, as their indices are less than `MAX_VALUE` (the integer returned when there are no threads attempting to acquire the write lock). Once again we have multiple threads that have simultaneous access to the read lock. This is also a case where the `notifyAll()` method makes it easy to wake up multiple threads at once.

Summary

Java's strong integration of locks into the language and API are very useful for programming with Java's threads. Nonetheless, despite their strength, Java's locking mechanisms are not suitable for every type of synchronization you might need for more complex Java programs. Fortunately, the built-in synchronization techniques provide good building blocks to create the more complicated, more intelligent locks you need in special situations.

Like other parts of Java, its built-in locking mechanism is designed to be simple in order to reduce errors in your Java programs. And, like other parts of Java, this simplicity is enough to carry you through all but the more complex programming situations. You should use the built-in techniques unless you really need the more complex behavior of the mechanisms described in this chapter.

8

Thread Groups

In this chapter, we're going to discuss Java's ThreadGroup class, which, as the name implies, is a class that handles a group of threads. Thread groups are useful for two reasons: they allow you to manipulate many threads by calling a single method, and they provide the basis that Java's security mechanism uses to interact with threads. The actual use of thread groups is really limited to writers of Java applications: within an applet, virtually no operations on thread groups are possible, due to those security mechanisms that we'll explore.

Thread Group Concepts

Say that you're writing a server using the TCPServer class we developed in Chapter 5. Each client that connects to the server runs as a separate thread; now say that for each client, the server is going to create many other threads: perhaps a timer thread, a separate thread to read data coming from the client, another to write data to the client, maybe some threads for a calculation algorithm. Well, you get the idea: the server has a lot of threads it needs to manage.

Now a particular client connected to the server terminates abnormally. You have to terminate all the threads for that client at this point, and you'd like an easier way to do it than to put in many calls to the stop() method. This is where the ThreadGroup class comes into play. Thread groups allow you to modify many threads with one call—making it easier to control your threads and making it less likely that you'll forget one. With a thread group, you can stop (among other things) all the threads in the group at once without the logic of keeping track of those threads.

Although we haven't yet mentioned thread groups, they've been around all along: all threads in the Java virtual machine belong to a thread group. Every thread you create automatically belongs to a default thread group the Java virtual machine sets up on your behalf. So all the threads that we've looked at so far belong to this existing thread group.[*]

Thread groups are more than just arbitrary groupings of threads, however; they are related to each other as well. Every thread group has a parent thread group (with the obvious exception of the first thread group), so the groups exist in a tree hierarchy. The root of this tree is known as the *system thread group*.

You can create your own thread groups as well; each thread group is the child of an existing thread group. In the TCPServer example we discussed earlier, the thread hierarchy might appear as shown in Figure 8-1.

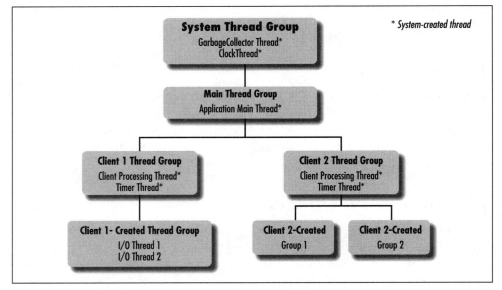

Figure 8-1. A thread group hierarchy

We'll end up with at least one thread group for each connected client; note that the thread groups have the option of creating other thread groups underneath them. Also note that the threads themselves are interspersed among the groups in the entire hierarchy: a thread group contains threads as well as (possibly) other thread groups.

---

[*] In Appendix C, we'll list all the thread groups and threads of a typical program.

Creating Thread Groups

There are two constructors that create new thread groups:

ThreadGroup(String name)
> Creates a thread group with the given name.

ThreadGroup(ThreadGroup parent, String name)
> Creates a thread group that descends from the given parent and has the given name.

In the case of the first constructor, the new thread group is a child of the current thread's thread group; in the second case, the new thread group is inserted into the thread group hierarchy with the given thread group as its parent.[*] Only Java applications are allowed to ᴄreate thread groups; Java applets can work only with the thread group of which they are a member.[†]

Each of these constructors creates an empty thread group—a thread group with no threads. There is no method to move a thread into a particular group; a thread is placed into a group only when the thread object is created. As this restriction implies, there are some additional constructors[‡] for the thread class that specifies the thread group to which the thread should belong:

Thread(ThreadGroup group, String name)
> Constructs a new thread that belongs to the given thread group and has the given name.

Thread(ThreadGroup group, Runnable target)
> Constructs a new thread that belongs to the given thread group and runs the given target object.

Thread(ThreadGroup group, Runnable target, String name)
> Constructs a new thread that belongs to the given thread group that runs the given target object and has the given name.

In the constructors we learned about in Chapter 2, the thread becomes a member of the same thread group to which the current thread belongs.

Similarly, there is no method by which a thread can be deleted from a thread group: a thread is a member of its thread group for the duration of the its life. However, when the thread terminates, it is removed automatically from the thread group.

---

[*] Though it's probably bad design to do so, by default a thread group can be inserted anywhere into a Java application's thread group hierarchy.

[†] It's a little more complicated than that, as we'll discuss in the section on security.

[‡] Note that there is no constructor that takes just a ThreadGroup as a parameter, which seems to be an oversight.

We can use these constructors to modify the TCPServer class so that each client is placed in a separate thread group as well as being run in a separate thread. Doing so is simple: we need only create the thread group immediately before creating the client thread, so that when the client thread is started, it is a member of the new thread group.

```java
import java.net.*;
import java.io.*;

public class TCPServer implements Cloneable, Runnable {
    Thread runner = null;
    ServerSocket server = null;
    Socket data = null;
    ThreadGroup group = null;
    int groupNo = 0;

    public synchronized void StartServer(int port) throws IOException {
        if (runner == null) {
            server = new ServerSocket(port);
            runner = new Thread(this);
            runner.start();
        }
    }

    public synchronized void StopServer() {
        if (server != null) runner.stop();
    }

    public void run() {
        if (server != null) {
            while (true) {
                try {
                    Socket datasocket = server.accept();
                    TCPServer newSocket = (TCPServer) clone();

                    newSocket.server = null;
                    newSocket.data = datasocket;
                    newSocket.group =
                        new ThreadGroup("Client Group " + groupNo++);
                    newSocket.runner =
                        new Thread(newSocket.group, newSocket);
                    newSocket.runner.start();
                } catch (Exception e) {}
            }
        } else {
            run(data);
        }
    }
```

```
            public void run(Socket data) {
            }
    }
```

Remember that the TCPServer is subclassed in order to provide functionality for the client; in the next section, we'll look at how establishing this thread group makes the code that handles the client easier to program.

Manipulating Thread Groups

Now that we have a thread group, it's time to investigate the methods available for manipulating the thread group. As we mentioned at the outset, one reason we're interested in the thread group is to change the state of its threads easily. To that end, there are three methods in the thread group class that allow us to do just that.

void suspend()
> Suspends all threads that descend from this thread group.

void resume()
> Resumes all threads that descend from this thread group.

void stop()
> Stops all threads that descend from this thread group.

These methods all function in the same way as their counterparts in the Thread class, except that these methods affect all threads in the thread group as well as all threads that are contained in the thread groups that descend from this group. In other words, these methods operate recursively on all groups that descend from the specified group. In the case of our TCPServer thread group hierarchy, this means that if, for example, we suspended the Client1 thread group, we suspend all threads in that group as well as the I/O threads in the Client1-created thread group.[*]

We can use these calls to save some programming when we create the subclass of our TCPServer. In our ServerHandler subclass, we left out the processing that is performed on behalf of the client. This time, we'll assume that the server reads a set of commands from the client and runs each command in a separate thread; this allows the client to send commands asynchronously, without waiting for the server to finish the previous commands. By placing all these threads in one group, we're able to modify all the threads running on behalf of the client in one call via the thread-group mechanism.

---

[*] We know you're anxious to try it yourself, but yes, if you suspend the system thread group in a Java application, every thread in the virtual machine will be suspended, effectively hanging the virtual machine. The same is not true of Java applets due to security restrictions we discuss later.

In this example, we're using this mechanism to handle the case where the client closes the connection: with one call, we can stop all threads running on behalf of this client. We'll also assume for this example that the client might send messages asking us to suspend and resume calculations on its behalf.

We're also going to set up another thread group to which we'll add all the client threads that we create. The end result of this will be that we'll have these thread groups:

- The thread group of the TCPServer, containing the thread that is listening for client requests.

- The thread group of the client, containing the thread that is communicating with the client. This is the thread that is running in our server handler.

- The calculation thread group of the client, containing all the threads that are performing calculations on behalf of the client. This is the thread group we create in the code below.

This is a useful technique: it's better to have a thread outside of the thread group actually manipulate the thread group. This is not an absolute requirement: you could, for example, suspend() the thread group to which you belong. But in order for the thread group to continue, a thread outside of the group has to resume() the thread group, and we feel it's a better design to have the same thread responsible for suspending and resuming a group of threads.[*]

Here's our modified ServerHandler class with this additional thread group logic:

```
import java.net.*;
import java.io.*;

class CalculateThread extends Thread {
    OutputStream os;
    CalculateThread(ThreadGroup tg, OutputStream os) {
        super(tg, "Client Calculate Thread");
        this.os = os;
    }
    public void run() {
        // do the calculation, sending results to the OutputStream os
    }
}

public class ServerHandler extends TCPServer {
    public static final int SUSPEND = 0;
    public static final int RESUME = 1;
```

---

[*] That's one reason why this class is of slight benefit to applet writers: you can suspend all the threads in your applet group, but nothing else will be around to resume those threads.

```java
    public static final int CALCUALTE = 2;
    ThreadGroup tg;

    private int getCommand(InputStream is) {
        // read the command data
    }

    public void run(Socket data) {
        tg = new ThreadGroup("Client Thread Group");
        try {
            InputStream is = data.getInputStream();
            OutputStream os = data.getOutputStream();
            while (true) {
                switch(getCommand(is)) {
                    case SUSPEND:
                        tg.suspend();
                        break;
                    case RESUME:
                        tg.resume();
                        break;
                    case CALCULATE:
                        new CalculateThread(tg, os).start();
                        break;
                }
            }
        } catch (Exception e) {
            tg.stop();
        }
    }
}

public class MyServer {
    public static void main(String args[]) throws Exception {
        TCPServer serv = new ServerHandler();
        serv.startServer(300, 5);
    }
}
```

Note the interesting syntax used in the CALCULATE case of the switch statement: we're creating a new CalculateThread object, but we're not explicitly saving the object reference anywhere. We mentioned earlier that the thread object in this case is held internally so that it won't be garbage-collected; the thread group is the location where it is stored.

You've also probably noticed that these calls are not entirely symmetrical: there are suspend() and resume() methods, but there is no start() method to match the stop() method. This is a feature of the API: the threads can only be started from the thread object and not from the thread group object.

Miscellaneous Thread Group Methods

The thread group methods we've seen so far are the most useful ones in day-to-day programming. But there are some other thread group methods that prove useful in certain circumstances.

Finding Thread Groups

There are often times when you'd like to call one of the thread group methods but don't necessarily have a thread group object. The thread class has a method that returns a reference to the thread group of a thread object:

ThreadGroup getThreadGroup()
> Returns the ThreadGroup reference of a thread.

You can also retrieve the parent thread group of a thread group with the `getParent()` method of the ThreadGroup class:

ThreadGroup getParent()
> Returns the ThreadGroup reference of the parent of a thread group.

Finally, you can test whether a particular thread group is an ancestor of another thread group with the `parentOf()` method:

boolean parentOf(ThreadGroup g)
> Returns true if the group g is an ancestor of a thread group.

Note that the `parentOf()` method is badly named; it returns true if the group g is the same as the calling thread group, or the parent of the thread group, or the grandparent, on up the thread group hierarchy.

Enumerating Thread Groups

The next set of methods we'll explore allows you to retrieve a list of all threads in a thread group. Enumeration of threads is really a province of the ThreadGroup class: although the Thread class also contains methods that enumerate threads, those methods simply call their counterpart methods of the ThreadGroup class.

There are two basic methods in the ThreadGroup class that return a list of threads:

int enumerate(Thread list[])
> Fills in the `list` array with a reference to all threads in this thread group and all groups that descend from this thread group.

int enumerate(Thread list[], boolean recurse)

> Fills in the `list` array with a reference to all threads in this thread group and, if `recurse` is true, all groups that descend from this thread group.

These calls fill in the input parameter `list` with a thread reference for each "appropriate" thread and return the count of threads that were inserted into the array. The appropriateness of the thread depends on the `recurse` parameter: if `recurse` is true, all threads of the given thread group are returned as well as all threads that are in thread groups that descend from the current thread group.[*] Not surprisingly, calling `enumerate` with `recurse` set to false returns only those threads that are actually a member of the current thread group.

Since arrays in Java are a fixed size, the size of the parameter `list` must be determined before the `enumerate()` method is called (or you may not get a complete list). In order to know the correct size for the `list` array, use the `active-Count()` method:

int activeCount()

> Returns the number of active threads in this and all descending thread groups.

There is no recursion option available with this method; the `activeCount()` method always returns the count of all threads in the current and in all descending thread groups.

The following code fragment shows how to use these methods to display the threads in the current thread group. Changing the parameter in the `enumerate()` method displays the threads in this and all descending groups.

```
ThreadGroup tg = Thread.currentThread().getThreadGroup();
int n = tg.activeCount();
Thread list[] = new Thread[n];
int count = tg.enumerate(list, false);
System.out.println("Threads in thread group " + tg);
for (int i = 0; i < count; i++)
    System.out.println(list[i]);
```

You can also request an enumeration of ThreadGroup objects rather than Thread objects via the `enumerate()` method with these signatures:

int enumerate(ThreadGroup list[])

> Retrieves all thread group references that are immediate descendants of the given thread group and all descendants of the current thread group.

---

[*] Calling the `enumerate()` method with `recurse` set to true on the system thread group returns all the threads in the virtual machine.

int enumerate(ThreadGroup list[], boolean recurse)
> Retrieves all thread group references that are immediate descendants of the given thread group and, if `recurse` is true, of all descendants of the current thread group.

These methods are conceptually equivalent to the methods that we've just discussed. In order to determine the size of the `list` parameter, use the `active-GroupCount()` method:

int activeGroupCount()
> Returns the number of thread group descendants (at any level) of the given thread group.

Recall that the Thread class also had an `enumerate()` method. The Thread class's `enumerate()` method always searches recursively; it is really shorthand for:

```
Thread.currentThread().getThreadGroup().enumerate(list, true);
```

Similarly, the Thread class' `activeCount()` method is really shorthand for:

```
Thread.currentThread().getThreadGroup().activeCount();
```

Thread Group Priority Calls

Java thread groups carry with them the notion of a maximum priority. This maximum priority interacts with the priority methods of the Thread class: the priority of a thread cannot be set higher than the maximum priority of the thread group to which it belongs. By default, the maximum priority of a thread group is the same as the maximum priority of its parent thread group. As you might have guessed, the maximum priority of the system thread group is 10 (`Thread.MAX_PRIORITY`). The maximum priority of the applet thread group—the group to which all threads in an applet belong—is only 6.

There are two methods that handle a thread group's priority:

void setMaxPriority(int priority)
> Sets the maximum priority for the thread group.

int getMaxPriority()
> Retrieves the maximum priority for the thread group.

In the reference version of the JDK 1.0.2, the maximum priority of a thread group is enforced silently: if the thread group to which your thread belongs has a maximum priority of 6, and you attempt to raise your thread's priority to 8, your thread is silently given a priority of 6. In other versions of the JDK, if you attempt to set an individual thread's priority higher than the maximum priority of the thread group, a SecurityException will be thrown.

Once the maximum priority of a thread group has been lowered, it cannot be raised.

These values are only checked when a thread's priority is actually changed. Thus, if you have a thread group with a maximum priority of 10 that contains a thread with a priority of 8, changing the thread group's maximum priority to 6 doesn't affect that thread: it continues to have a priority of 8 until that thread's setPriority() method is called. However, the priority of any nested thread groups is changed immediately: any thread groups that are contained within the target thread group will have their priority lowered to the requested value. This change is propagated recursively throughout the thread group hierarchy.

Destroying Thread Groups

A thread group can be destroyed with the destroy() method:

void destroy()
> Cleans up the thread group and removes it from the thread group hierarchy.

The destroy() method is of limited use: it can only be called if there are no threads presently in the thread group. And the destroy() method operates recursively, so it destroys not only the target thread group but all thread groups that descend from the target thread group. If any of these thread groups have active threads within them, the destroy() method generates an IllegalThread-StateException. If you want to destroy a thread group, it's a good idea to call the thread group's stop() method before calling its destroy() method.

Daemon Thread Groups

The ThreadGroup class has the notion of a daemon thread group, which is similar to the notion of a daemon thread. The two are unrelated, however: daemon threads can belong to non-daemon thread groups, and a daemon thread group can contain non-daemon threads. The benefit of a daemon thread group is that it is destroyed automatically once all the threads it contains have exited and all the groups that it contains have been destroyed. Unlike a thread, a thread group's daemon status can be changed at any time:

void setDaemon(boolean on)
> Changes the daemon status of the thread group.

boolean isDaemon()
> Returns true if the thread group is a daemon group.

We should stress that a daemon thread group is destroyed only if all threads in the group have actually exited: if there are only daemon threads in a daemon thread group, the daemon thread group is not destroyed unless the daemon threads it contains are stopped first. This is because daemon threads serve user threads throughout the virtual machine, not just the user threads of a particular thread group.

Of course, the benefit of daemon threads in the first place is that the programmer never bothers to stop them explicitly. Thus, while the concept of a daemon thread group that automatically exits when it contains only daemon threads may be attractive, it does not work that way.

Thread Groups, Threads, and Security

The various restrictions on applets that we've mentioned in this chapter are a product of Java's security mechanism. There are security mechanisms at several points in Java: in the language itself, in the virtual machine, and built into the Java API. As far as threads are concerned, only the security mechanisms of the API come into consideration, and we'll examine how those mechanisms affect both threads and thread groups in this section.

Java's thread security is enforced by the SecurityManager class; security policies in a Java program are established when an instance of this class is instantiated and installed in the virtual machine. When certain operations are attempted on threads or thread groups, the API consults the security manager to determine if those operations are permitted. In a Java application, there is no security manager unless you write and install one yourself; this is the reason that all the operations that we've discussed are legal in Java applications. In a Java applet, there typically is a security manager in place that enforces particular restrictions.

There is one method in the SecurityManager class that handles security policies for the Thread class and one that handles security policies for the ThreadGroup class. These methods have the same name but a different signature:

void checkAccess(Thread t)
> Checks if the current thread is allowed to modify the state of the thread `t`.

void checkAccess(ThreadGroup tg)
> Checks if the current thread group is allowed to modify the state of the thread group `tg`.

Like all methods in the SecurityManager class, these methods throw an object of type SecurityException if they determine that a violation of the security policy could occur. As an example, here's the code the `stop()` method of the Thread class implements (this is actually a conflation of code contained in the Thread class):

```
public void stop() {
```

Browsers and Security Managers

When you write a Java applet, you're not given the opportunity to do anything with the security manager: the security manager is instantiated and installed by the browser itself and, once installed, the security manager cannot be changed.

But the Java specification does not specify what policies the security manager should enforce. Instead, the security policies at this level are a product of the particular browser. Different browsers may implement different levels of security: for example, the Netscape browser does not permit Java applets to read any files from the user's local disk, but Sun's HotJava browser allows the user to specify a list of directories in which the applet can read files.

The policies that various browsers take with respect to thread operations are somewhat unclear. In most cases, developers of browsers are following the lead of Sun and implementing the same thread-security mechanisms Sun implements. Sun has announced its intention to change the security model it uses for threads in its 1.1 release of Java, and while it's anticipated that most browsers will follow Sun's lead on this, it's possible that different browsers may implement the security policies differently.

```
        SecurityManager s = System.getSecurityManager();
        if (s != null)
            s.checkAccess(this);    // this is Thread.currentThread();
        stop0(new ThreadDeath());
    }
```

This is the canonical behavior for thread security: the checkAccess() method is called, which generates a run-time exception if thread policy is violated by the operation. Assuming that no exception is thrown, an internal method is called that actually performs the logic of the method.

Because there is only one method in the SecurityManager class that's available to the Thread class and only one available to the ThreadGroup class, thread security policies are an all-or-nothing proposition. If you determine that a particular policy applies to prevent some threads from stopping other threads, that policy must also apply in order to prevent those same threads from setting the priority of other threads.

Table 8-1 lists the methods in the Thread class that call the security manager to determine if an operation is legal. The basic design of the applet policy is that each applet is given its own thread group. Within an applet, threads can manipulate other threads only if both threads are members of the applet's thread group. If you have multiple applets on a page, each is given its own applet group, and the

---

Security and the checkAccess() Method

Both the Thread and ThreadGroup classes have an internal method named `checkAccess()`; this method, by default, calls the Security Manager's `checkAccess()` method passing either the thread or the thread group object.

The `checkAccess()` method within the Thread and ThreadGroup classes is public, so you can call it directly from any thread or thread group object if you want to check what security policy is in place.

The `checkAccess()` method within the ThreadGroup class is final; it may not be overridden. In some releases of the JDK, the `checkAccess()` method within the Thread class is not final, meaning that you could override it and effectively change the security policy for threads. You should not expect this feature to exist.

---

applet groups are separate from each other so that threads in one applet cannot affect threads in another applet.

Table 8-1. Thread Methods Affected by the Security Manager

Thread Method	Default Applet Policy
Thread(ThreadGroup tg, String name), Thread(ThreadGroup tg, Runnable o), Thread(ThreadGroup tg, Runnable o, String name)	Applets can create threads only as members of the applet's thread group
stop()	Only if in the same applet group
suspend()	Only if in the same applet group
resume()	Only if in the same applet group
setPriority(int priority)	Only if in the same applet group
setName(String s)	Only if in the same applet group
setDaemon(boolean on)	Only if in the same applet group

Table 8-2 lists the methods in the ThreadGroup class that are affected by the security manager. Again, the basic design is that an applet works within a separate thread group and can affect only its own particular thread group.

Table 8-2. ThreadGroup Methods Affected by the Security Manager

Thread Group Method	Default Applet Policy
`ThreadGroup(ThreadGroup parent,` `              String name)`	Applets cannot create thread groups
`setDaemon(boolean on)`	Can't set the applet thread group to daemon[a]
`setMaxPriority(int priority)`	Can lower the maximum priority only of the applet thread group
`getParent()`	No restrictions in 1.0.2[b]
`stop()`	Can stop only the applet thread group
`suspend()`	Can suspend only the applet thread group
`resume()`	Can resume only the applet thread group
`destroy()`	Can't destroy the applet thread group[c]

[a] This is not a security policy as much as the policy regarding setting groups to be daemons.

[b] This may change in later versions of JDK; see the next section.

[c] This is a logistic problem rather than a security problem; in order to destroy the applet thread group, all applet threads have to be stopped, and there is no thread left to destroy the applet thread group.

A Caution About Applet Thread Security

If you've ever worked with threads and thread groups in an applet with early versions of Java, some of the security restrictions we've mentioned here may seem, well, wrong. What we've actually described in this section is a security policy for applets that does not yet exist in any browser or in the reference JDK from Sun.

The policies of Sun's 1.0.2 release of the JDK, subsequently adopted by browser developers, are actually more lenient in their thread security than what has been described here. Those policies allow applets to see each other's threads and to know about the threads in the system thread group. Unfortunately, this allowed some applet developers to take advantage of this feature to write some applets that engaged in antisocial behavior. This behavior was not exactly a security violation in the spirit of Java's security policies: it didn't allow the applet to access any private information on the machine, nor install a virus, nor corrupt information on the machine.

Nonetheless, the antisocial behavior allowed by the 1.0.2 thread security policies can be extremely annoying and confusing:[*] imagine having the applet on your

---

[*] It was also extremely useful; for example, it allowed programmers to write thread monitoring applets that monitored the state of all threads in the browser. With the new stricter security measures imposed on applets, these types of applets can no longer be written; if you want a thread monitor, you'll need to use a browser that includes a thread monitor as part of the browser (Sun's HotJava browser has this feature).

current page suddenly stop working because another applet (possibly on another page) called the `stop()` method on all the threads of your applet. It's very difficult for most users to figure out why this has happened; it most often looks like a bug in the current applet rather than an attack by some other applet. So the decision has been made that, beginning with Sun's 1.1 release of the JDK, the stricter thread security model we've described here will be the default applet security model.

So, if you're developing applets and wonder what they will and won't be able to do in the future, we recommend following the guidelines that we've outlined in this section. If you follow the security policies of the 1.0.2 JDK and corresponding browsers, you'll need to change your applets when the new security policies are implemented anyway.

The easiest way to keep out of trouble with your applets is to ignore the existence of the ThreadGroup class altogether: if you stick to the calls available in the Thread class, you'll always be safe, as those calls only affect threads to which your applet has access.* As we said at the outset of this chapter, the ThreadGroup class, which forms the basis of the thread security mechanism, is useful only to Java application developers.

Summary

Here are the methods of the ThreadGroup class we introduced in this chapter:

ThreadGroup(String name)
> Creates a thread group with the given name.

ThreadGroup(ThreadGroup parent, String name)
> Creates a thread group that descends from the given parent and has the given name.

void suspend()
> Suspends all threads that descend from this thread group.

void resume()
> Resumes all threads that descend from this thread group.

void stop()
> Stops all threads that descend from this thread group.

void destroy()
> Cleans up the thread group and removes it from the thread group hierarchy.

---

* In the case of the `enumerate()` method, you may see a difference in the threads that are returned due to an organizational change in the thread hierarchy. This organizational change will be an artifact of the new security policy.

ThreadGroup getParent()

>   Returns the ThreadGroup reference of the parent of a thread group.

boolean parentOf(ThreadGroup g)

>   Returns true if the group g is an ancestor of a thread group.

int enumerate(Thread list[])

>   Fills in the `list` array with a reference to all threads in this thread group and all groups that descend from this thread group.

int enumerate(Thread list[], boolean recurse)

>   Fills in the `list` array with a reference to all threads in this thread group and, if `recurse` is true, all groups that descend from this thread group.

int activeCount()

>   Returns the number of active threads in this and all descending thread groups.

int enumerate(ThreadGroup list[])

>   Retrieves all thread group references that are immediate descendants of the given thread group and all descendants of the current thread group.

int enumerate(ThreadGroup list[], boolean recurse)

>   Retrieves all thread group references that are immediate descendants of the given thread group and, if `recurse` is true, of all descendants of the current thread group.

int activeGroupCount()

>   Returns the number of thread group descendants (at any level) of the given thread group.

void setMaxPriority(int priority)

>   Sets the maximum priority for the thread group.

int getMaxPriority()

>   Retrieves the maximum priority for the thread group.

void setDaemon(boolean on)

>   Changes the daemon status of the thread group.

boolean isDaemon()

>   Returns true if the thread group is a daemon group.

In addition, we introduced these new methods of the Thread class:

Thread(ThreadGroup group, String name)

>   Constructs a new thread that belongs to the given thread group and has the given name.

Thread(ThreadGroup group, Runnable target)
> Constructs a new thread that belongs to the given thread group and runs the given target object.

Thread(ThreadGroup group, Runnable target, String name)
> Constructs a new thread that belongs to the given thread group that runs the given target object and has the given name.

ThreadGroup getThreadGroup()
> Returns the ThreadGroup reference of a thread.

Finally, we introduced these methods of the SecurityManager class that operate on threads:

void checkAccess(Thread t)
> Checks if the current thread is allowed to modify the state of the thread t.

void checkAccess(ThreadGroup tg)
> Checks if the current thread group is allowed to modify the state of the thread group tg.

In this chapter, we filled in the final piece of Java's thread mechanism: a way to group threads together and operate on all threads within the group.

Like the other topics in the last few chapters, the ThreadGroup class is not one that is needed by the majority of programs; it's a special-use class for cases in which you need the additional control over groups of threads. The ThreadGroup class is the last of the special-use mechanisms you need in order to complete your understanding of using threads in Java. While we present some informative miscellaneous topics in the appendixes, the information we've presented in the body of this book should allow you to write productive and, if need be, very complex threaded programs in Java.

A

Miscellaneous Topics

Throughout this book, we examine the various parts of the threading system. This examination is based on various examples and issues that commonly occur during program development. However, there are certain issues that fall through the cracks. This is caused by the fact that either the issue or topic is really obscure, or that the implementation is too immature to use at this time. These are the topics we examine in this appendix.

Thread Interruption

Throughout our examples, we noticed that many of the methods in the Java API throw an InterruptedException object.[*] The tasks of these methods all relate to waiting for an event. An InterruptedException is thrown when the method returns before the event occurs.

What is the cause of this interruption? While we have looked at InterruptedExceptions, we have not looked at just exactly what throws these exceptions. The intent of the InterruptedException is to provide a general mechanism that allows one thread to interrupt another. This is not yet fully implemented.

There is a method developers can use that allows one thread to interrupt another. This method is as follows:

void interrupt()
> Sends an interruption to the specified thread. This is a method of the Thread class, and currently simply sets a Boolean flag indicating that an interruption has been requested.

---

[*] See Appendix B for a complete list.

static boolean interrupted()

> Returns a Boolean that indicates whether the current thread has been interrupted. This is a static method of the Thread class and may be called through the class specifier. Currently, this method simply returns the flag that is set by the `interrupt()` method.

boolean isInterrupted()

> Returns a Boolean that indicates whether the specified thread has been interrupted. This is a method of the Thread class and currently simply returns the Boolean flag that is set by the `interrupt()` method.

This actually seems to be a good way to send information from one thread to another. Why has this mechanism not been mentioned up to now? The major reason is that at the time of this writing, the mechanism has not been fully implemented. While it is possible to set the interruption flag and get the interruption flag, no method actually throws the InterruptedException or resets the flag.[*] The act of setting the Boolean flag does not actually cause a thread to be interrupted, it merely reports that it was interrupted: calling the `interrupt()` method on a thread that is sleeping will not wake up the thread.

This means that this mechanism is presently nothing more than a way to send a Boolean from one thread to another. The goal of this mechanism is to wake up a thread from any blocked state, which makes it more general than the wait and notify mechanism once it is actually implemented.

Thread Stack Information

The Thread class provides these methods to supply the programmer with stack information of a thread:

int countStackFrames()

> Returns the number of stack frames in the specified thread. The thread must be suspended in order for this method to work. This is a method of the Thread class and does not count the frames that are from native methods. Since the thread must be suspended, it is not possible to obtain the count for the current thread directly.[†]

---

[*] Until JDK 1.0.2, these methods did even less: all three of these methods simply used to throw a NoSuch-MethodError condition.

[†] You would have to have another thread that `suspend()`s, counts, and `resume()`s the currently running thread in order to count the current thread's frames.

static void dumpStack()

Prints the stack trace of the current thread to `System.err`. This is a static method of the Thread class and may be accessed with the Thread specifier. Only the stack trace of the currently running thread may be obtained.

Interestingly, we would conclude from these two methods that we can both count the number of stack frames and actually print the stack frames out. However, these two methods cannot be used together. Since the thread needs to be suspended in order to count the stack frames, it is not possible to count the frames of the current thread while the `dumpStack()`* method can only print the stack information of the current thread.

General Thread Information

In order to print thread information, use the following methods:

String toString()

Returns a string that describes the object. Originally a method of the Object class, it is overridden by the Thread class to provide the name of the thread, the priority of the thread, and the name of the thread group to which the thread belongs.

String toString()

Returns a string that describes the object. Originally a method of the Object class, it is overridden by the ThreadGroup class to provide the name of the thread group, and the maximum priority of the group.

The `toString()` method is overridden by the thread classes to allow a sensible conversion of the object into a string. Hence, the following code

```
Thread t = new TimerThread(this, 500);
System.out.println(t);
```

yields the following output:

```
Thread[TimerThread-500,6,group applet-TimerApplet]
```

void list()

Prints the current layout of the thread group hierarchy starting with the specified thread group. This is a method of the ThreadGroup class and simply prints the information to `System.out`. This method operates recursively on the thread group.

---

* The information printed by the `dumpStack()` method is the same information provided by the `printStackTrace()` method of the Throwable class. The `dumpStack()` method is just a convenience method; it actually instantiates an Exception object and calls the `printStackTrace()` method.

The information that is printed by the list() method is the information returned by the toString() methods. A sample list() of an applet may be as follows:

```
java.lang.ThreadGroup[name=system,maxpri=10]
    Thread[clock handler,11,system]
    Thread[Idle thread,0,system]
    Thread[Async Garbage Collector,1,system]
    Thread[Finalizer thread,1,system]
    java.lang.ThreadGroup[name=main,maxpri=10]
        Thread[main,5,main]
        Thread[AWT-Input,5,main]
        Thread[AWT-Motif,5,main]
        Thread[Screen Updater,4,main]
        AppletThreadGroup[name=group applet-Ticker,maxpri=6]
            Thread[thread applet-Ticker,6,group applet-Ticker]
            Thread[SUNW stock reader,5,group applet-Ticker]
            Thread[APPL stock reader,5,group applet-Ticker]
            Thread[NINI stock reader,5,group applet-Ticker]
            Thread[JRA stock reader,5,group applet-Ticker]
            Thread[ticker timer thread,4,group applet-Ticker]
```

Default Exception Handler

We examined the start() method to the extent of saying that "the start() method indirectly calls the run() method," but let's examine what happens. The start() method does start another thread of control, but the run() method is not the "main" routine for this new thread. There are other bookkeeping details that must be taken care of first. The thread must be set up in the Java virtual machine before the run() method can execute. This process is shown in Figure A-1.

All exceptions conditions are handled by code outside of the run() method before the thread terminates. It is this exception handling we examine here.

Why is this exception handler interesting to us? The default exception handler is a Java method; it can be overridden. This means that it is possible for an application to write a "new" default exception handler.[*] This method looks like this:

void uncaughtException(Thread t, Throwable o)

The default exception handler method. Called as a final handler to take care of any exceptions not caught by the thread in the run() method. This is a method of the ThreadGroup class.

---

[*] Whether overriding the exception handler is useful is debatable, which is why this study is in an appendix.

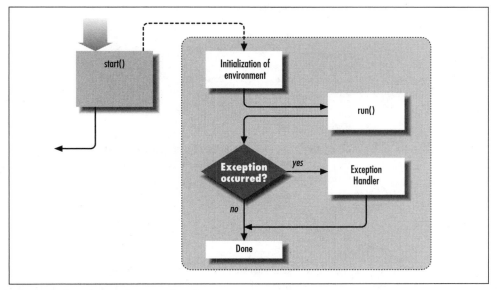

Figure A-1. Flowchart of the main thread

The default exception handler is a method of the ThreadGroup class. It is called only when an exception is thrown from the run() method. The thread is technically completed when the run() method finished, even though the exception handler is still running in the thread. But just what is done by the default exception handler?

Practically nothing. The only task accomplished by the default exception handler is to print out the stack trace recorded by the Throwable object. This is the stack trace of the thread that threw the object in the first place. (The only exception to this is if the throwable object is a ThreadDeath object, in which case nothing happens. We'll discuss that situation next.)

Let's return to the banking example in Chapter 3. We know that any uncaught exception in our ATM system is unacceptable, so we must handle every exception. But certain problems, like the ATM running out of money, may be encountered in more than one location in our algorithm. Handling the "out of money" condition in the default exception handler may be the best solution.

Let's examine a possible implementation of our default exception handler:

```
public class ATMOutOfMoneyException extends RuntimeException {
    public ATMOutOfMoneyException() {
        super();
    }
```

```
        public ATMOutOfMoneyException(String s) {
            super(s);
        }
    }

    public class ATMThreadGroup extends ThreadGroup {
        public ATMThreadGroup(String name) {
            super(name);
        }

        public void uncaughtException(Thread t, Throwable e) {
            if (e instanceof ATMOutOfMoneyException) {
                AlertAdminstrator(e);
            } else {
                super.uncaughtException(t, e);
            }
        }
    }
}
```

You can implement a default exception handler by overriding the uncaught-
Exception() method. This requires that you subclass the ThreadGroup class,
instantiate an instance of that subclass, and create all your threads so that they
belong to that instance. The method is passed an instance of the Thread class that
threw the object, along with the actual object that was thrown. In our case, we are
only concerned with the "out of money" condition. Every other object that is
thrown is passed to the original default handler.

The ThreadDeath Class

The ThreadDeath class is a special Throwable class that is used to stop a thread.
This class extends the Error class and hence should not be caught by the
program.[*]

How does throwing an object actually stop a thread? As we mentioned, the thread
cleans up after itself when the run() method completes. Of course, there are two
ways for the run() method to complete: it can complete on its own by simply
returning, or it can throw or fail to catch an exception.[†]

By default, if the run() method throws an exception, the thread prints an error
message, along with the stack trace of the exception. However, a special case is
made for the ThreadDeath object. If a ThreadDeath object is thrown from the
run() method, the uncaughtException() method simply returns.

---

[*] In theory, there is no reason to catch and handle any Throwable object that is not an object of the Exception class.

[†] When we use the term "exception" here, we mean any throwable object.

Is it possible to catch the ThreadDeath object? It is possible to catch any Throwable object; however, it is not advisable to use this technique to prevent the death of the thread. After all, if we did not want a thread to die, why did we `stop()` the thread in the first place? And what about threads that expect the thread to die when it stops? If you catch ThreadDeath, a thread that is attempting to `join()` that thread will still wait for the thread to die.

We could use this technique to handle cleanup conditions when the thread has stopped. In this case, we would "catch" the ThreadDeath object, execute the cleanup code, and then "re-throw" the object. However, even in this case, it is hard to justify catching the ThreadDeath object; we can accomplish the same thing by using the `finally` clause.* But as an example, let's modify the TimerThread from Chapter 2 to send a final `repaint()` request when the TimerThread is stopped; this final request is made only when the thread is stopped.

```java
import java.awt.*;

public class TimerThread extends Thread {
    Component comp;        // Component that need repainting
    int timediff;          // Time between repaints of the component

    public TimerThread(Component comp, int timediff) {
        this.comp = comp;
        this.timediff = timediff;
    }

    public void run() {
        while (true) {
            try {
                comp.repaint();
                sleep(timediff);
            } catch (Exception e) {
            } catch (ThreadDeath td) {
                comp.repaint();
                throw td;
            }
        }
    }
}
```

---

* But the `finally` clause is *always* executed, and you may conceivably only want the code to be executed if the thread is stopped.

In this new version of the TimerThread class, we have added an extra "catch" block. The object we are catching is a ThreadDeath object, and in this block we request one last `repaint()`, and re-throw the ThreadDeath object [*]

Inheriting from the ThreadDeath Class

The ThreadDeath object is used in conjunction with a new `stop()` method:

void stop(Throwable o)
>   Terminates an already running thread. The thread is stopped by throwing the specified object.

The `stop()` method is overloaded with a signature that allows the developer to unwind the stack with any Throwable object. Up until now, there was little reason to `stop()` the thread with any other object but a ThreadDeath object. But we can now override the default exception handler; if we wanted a thread to die due to a particular reason and handle the special reason, we might create a new Throwable type and handler as follows:

```
public class ATMThreadDeath extends ThreadDeath {
    public int reason;
    public ATMThreadDeath(int reason) {
        this.reason = reason;
    }
}

public class ATMThreadGroup extends ThreadGroup {
    public ATMThreadGroup(String name) {
        super(name);
    }

    public void uncaughtException(Thread t, Throwable e) {
        if (e instanceof ATMThreadDeath) {
            HandleSpecialExit(e);
        }
        super.uncaughtException(t, e);
    }
}
```

Assuming that there are special exit-handling conditions that need to be taken care of, we can create a new version of the ThreadDeath class that contains the reason for the death. Given this new version of the ThreadDeath class, we can then create a special handler to take care of the exit conditions. Of course, we must now use the other `stop()` method to send our ATMThreadDeath object:

---

[*] We could have also continued the loop and not rethrown the object. Of course, that would be a bad idea.

```
runner.stop(new ATMThreadDeath(3));
```

Can we use the stop() method to deliver a generic exception to another thread? It will work, but it is not advisable.[*] There are many reasons against doing so. Depending on the exception and when the stop() method is called, we might throw an exception that violates the semantics of the throws keyword. The compiler requires that you handle exceptions it knows will be thrown, but the complier will not, in this case, know about the generic exception you are causing the other thread to throw. If you execute this code:

```
runner.stop(new IOException());
```

the runner thread may be executing code that is not prepared to handle an IOException. This is confusing at best.

We could list more reasons against using this technique, but that will not stop certain developers from using this technique as a signal delivery system.[†] Simply put, stop() was not designed as a signal delivery system, and using it as such may yield unexpected or platform-specific results.

More on Thread Destruction

There is actually a very important reason for the thread stop() method to destroy a thread by throwing an exception. This has to do with the synchronization locks. By using the exception mechanism to exit the run() method, we cause the run() method to exit prematurely and, hence, allow the thread to terminate. We could also have killed the thread using the destroy() method, which in turn, terminates the execution of the run() method. The difference is the way the run() method exits: the first case allows the run() method to terminate, and hence kill the thread. The second mechanism kills the threads, which terminates the run() method.

By allowing the run() method to terminate, the stack for the thread is allowed to unwind. This means that the finally clauses are all allowed to execute as the stack is unwound. This allows a better state to exist in the program when the thread terminates; it also allows synchronization locks to be released as the stack is unwound. Because of these benefits, the thread is always allowed to unwind, rather than to just terminate.

However, in order to be complete in our discussion, we'll examine the destroy() method, which allows the thread to be destroyed without unwinding the stack. This method is a last resort.

---

[*] Actually, the stop() method does mark the thread as being stopped, but does not actually stop the thread. So, it just so happens to work, but this may be implementation-specific.

[†] Or from using the exception system as a callback mechanism.

void destroy()

> Destroys a thread immediately. This method of the Thread class does not perform any cleanup code, and any locks that are locked prior to this method call will remain locked.

Why would you want not to clean up after a thread? There should be no case where you do not want to clean up after a thread. However, there may be cases where the cleanup code may not work. For example, with the wait and notify mechanism, it may not be possible to immediately unwind the stack due to an unavailable lock: a thread that is stopped while it is executing the `wait()` method may not terminate for quite a while.[*] This waiting period to unwind may not be acceptable.

However, we should regard this as a bug in the program and fix the code rather than leave possibly unreleased locks. For the time being, this is irrelevant: the call to the `destroy()` method throws a NoSuchMethodError in the current implementation.

---

* If the thread deadlocks while trying to reacquire the lock, the thread never exits.

B

Exceptions and Errors

So far we have discussed the Thread class and its related classes with little attention to error conditions. One of the reasons for this is the lack of actual error conditions, because the threading system does not depend on external hardware or have a complex interaction structure. Classes that deal with the disk or network have to handle all possible error conditions that exist due to the failure of the hardware. Databases or the windowing system need an error system, which allows the programmer to better control the interaction between application, data structures, and user.

But what is necessary to deal with threading? Threading is a processor resource. Starting another thread means simply setting up data structures that allow the processor to run code and configure the processor to switch between the different threads. Threading may involve the operating system;[*] it may involve more than one processor. But in any case, the only hardware involved is the processor(s) and possibly additional memory. The synchronization system also only involves memory: there is not much that can go wrong when there is little hardware involved. We can get processor or memory errors, but these errors generally affect the entire virtual machine and not an individual thread.

The only errors that we need to be concerned with, then, are programmer errors. It is possible for the programmer to accidentally configure the threads incorrectly or to use threads or the synchronization mechanism incorrectly.

---

[*] Java threads are known as *user-level* threads and do not require the operating system to switch between them; different implementations may use the operating system to perform this task, but it is not required.

How are error conditions reported? As with any other classes provided with the Java system, the thread classes use the concept of "throwing" exceptions and errors.[*] Let's examine some of the exceptions and errors that are thrown from the threading system.

InterruptedException

The InterruptedException is probably the most common exception condition we have encountered in this book.[†] It indicates the method has returned earlier than expected. While we have chosen to catch and ignore these exceptions in our examples, we didn't have to: depending on the program, it may be possible to handle the exception condition. (The solution may be as simple as calling the method again.)

Let's examine the interrupted exception conditions that we have encountered in this book:

The join() method

> The Thread class provides the `join()` method, which allows a thread to wait for another thread to finish or be terminated (see Chapter 2). If this exception is thrown, it simply means that the other thread may not have completed. The `join()` method is also overloaded with two other method signatures that allow the program to specify a timeout. If the exception is thrown with these methods, it means that neither the termination of the other thread nor the timeout condition has been satisfied.

The sleep() method

> The Thread class provides the `sleep()` method, which allows a thread to wait a specified time period (see Chapter 2). When this exception is thrown, it simply means that the `sleep()` method has not slept for the specified amount of time.

The wait() method

> The Object class provides the `wait()` method, which allows a thread to wait for a notification condition (see Chapter 3). When this exception is thrown, it means that the `wait()` method has not received the notification. The `wait()` method is also overloaded with two other method signatures that allow the program to specify a timeout. If the exception is thrown with these methods, it means that neither the notification nor the timeout condition has been satisfied.

---

* We assume that the concept of exceptions and errors is understood by the reader, at least at the basic level.

† Although the actual throwing of this exception is not completely implemented at the time of this writing.

The waitForAll() method

The MediaTracker class provides the `waitForAll()` method, which allows a thread to wait for the completion of an image load from the server (see Appendix C). When this exception is thrown, it means that the `wait-ForAll()` method has not waited for all registered images to be loaded. The MediaTracker class also provides the `waitForID()` method, which allows the thread to wait for a particular image. While we have not used this method in our examples, it can also throw this exception condition.

NoSuchMethodError

The NoSuchMethodError probably should not be an Error, but an Exception. When the Thread class was designed, certain methods were not immediately supported. To avoid changing the interface to the Thread class, most of the methods were simply configured to throw this error condition. As more functionality is added, fewer of these methods will throw the NoSuchMethodError. As of this writing, the only method that throws this error object is the `destroy()` method of the Thread class (see Appendix A).

Exceptions or Errors

What is the difference between an Error and an Exception? As far as the virtual machine is concerned, there is little difference between the two: they are simply objects that are thrown to report a condition. It is possible to catch an Error object just as an Exception object is caught. In practice however, the usage of the two types of conditions are different.

Error conditions are faults in the Java virtual machine. In general, they are a sign of a problem that cannot be solved by the program. This can be caused by an out-of-memory condition, stack overflow, or problem in loading or resolving the classes in the program. The reason they are separated is to allow a "catch-all" of general exceptions. A program may catch all Exception conditions by catching the Exception object, but a program should have little reason to catch an Error object.

RuntimeException

The RuntimeException is not thrown directly by any of the methods in the thread classes; it is simply a base class that specifies a special group of exceptions.

Runtime exceptions are considered so basic that it may be considered too tedious to check for every possible run-time exception that may be thrown.[*]

All of the following exceptions are run-time exceptions.

IllegalThreadStateException

The IllegalThreadStateException is thrown by the thread classes when the thread is not in a state where it is possible to fulfill the request. This is caused by an illegal request made by the program and generally indicates a bug in the program. The following are the possible cases in the thread system where the IllegalThreadStateException is thrown.

The start() method

> The Thread class provides the start() method, which starts a new thread (see Chapter 2). As mentioned, a thread should be started only once. However, if a program decides to call the start() method of an already running thread, the IllegalThreadStateException is thrown.

The setDaemon() method

> The Thread class provides the setDaemon() method, which specifies whether the thread is a daemon thread (see Chapter 6). As mentioned, the daemon status of a thread must be set before the thread is started. If the setDaemon() method is called when the thread is already running, the IllegalThreadStateException is thrown.

The countStackFrames() method

> The Thread class provides the countStackFrames() method, which determines how deep in the call stack the thread is currently executing (see Appendix A). A thread should be suspended in order for this count to take place. If the thread is not suspended when this method is called, the IllegalThreadStateException is thrown.

The destroy() method

> The ThreadGroup class provides the destroy() method to allow the thread group to be destroyed (see Chapter 8). A ThreadGroup instance can only be destroyed when the group does not contains any threads, or contains any groups that contain threads. If the destroy() method is called on a group that contains threads or is already destroyed, the IllegalThreadStateException is thrown.

---

[*] Another reason is because these exceptions are generally bugs in the program.

The Thread constructors

The Thread class contains certain constructors that allow the thread to be placed into a specific thread group (see Chapter 8). The thread group that is passed to these constructors must not have been destroyed; if the constructor is passed a thread group that has been destroyed, the IllegalThreadStateException is thrown.

IllegalArgumentException

It is possible to call methods of the thread classes with incorrect parameters. When this is done, an IllegalArgumentException is thrown. Only one method related to the thread classes throws the exception:

The setPriority() method

The Thread class provides the `setPriority()` method, which controls the priority assigned to the thread (see Chapter 6). The priority that is assigned must fall between the system minimum and minimum priority. If the priority requested is not within this range, an IllegalArgumentException is thrown.[*]

The IllegalThreadStateException is actually a subclass of the IllegalArgumentException class; if you attempt to catch objects of type IllegalArgumentException, you will also catch objects of type IllegalThreadStateException.

IllegalMonitorStateException

The IllegalMonitorStateException is thrown by the Thread system when an operation is made with a synchronization lock and the state of the lock is not valid for the operation to take place. Currently, the only operation that involves synchronization locks is the wait and notify mechanism.[†]

The wait() method

The Object class provides the `wait()` method, which allows a thread to `wait()` for a notification condition (see Chapter 3). The `wait()` method must be called while the synchronization lock for the object is held. The `wait()` method is also overloaded with two other method signatures, which allows the program to specify a timeout. If any of these methods is called without owning the synchronization lock, the IllegalMonitorStateException is thrown.

---

[*] The `setPriority()` method can also throw a SecurityException; see below.

[†] Grabbing and releasing lock operations do not throw exceptions because they are not method calls.

The notify() method

> The Object class provides the `notify()` method, which allows a thread to send a notification signal to any threads waiting (see Chapter 3). The `notify()` method must be called while the synchronization lock for the object is held. The thread class also provides the `notifyAll()` method, which wakes up all the waiting threads. If either of these methods is called without owning the synchronization lock, the IllegalMonitorStateException is thrown.

NullPointerException

The thread classes throw this exception in the following cases:

The stop() method

> The thread class provides a version of the `stop()` method, which allows the user to specify the object used to stop the thread (see Appendix A). Normally, programs do not use this method, however, if the program does use this method and passes a null object to stop a thread, the NullPointerException is thrown.

The ThreadGroup constructor

> The ThreadGroup class provides a version of its constructor, which allows the application to specify the parent group (see Chapter 8). If null is specified for the parent group, the NullPointerException is thrown.

In addition, the NullPointerException can be thrown by the Java virtual machine itself while it is executing code within the thread classes.

SecurityException

Most methods of the Thread and ThreadGroup class can throw a SecurityException. The SecurityException can be thrown by the following methods:

The checkAccess() method

> The Thread class provides the `checkAccess()` method, which simply calls the security manager to determine if the thread can be accessed by the current thread group (see Chapter 8). A SecurityException is thrown if access is not permitted. For a complete list of methods that call the `checkAccess()` method and their restrictions, see Table 8-1.

The checkAccess() method

> The ThreadGroup class provides the `checkAccess()` method, which simply calls the security manager to determine if the thread group can be accessed by the current thread group (see Chapter 8). A SecurityException is thrown if

access is not permitted. For a complete list of methods that call the checkAc-cess() method and their restrictions, see Table 8-2.

The setPriority() method

The Thread class provides the setPriority() method, which sets the sched-uling priority of the thread (see Chapter 8). The priority requested must be less than the maximum priority of the thread group to which the thread belongs. If the priority is greater than this maximum priority, a SecurityExcep-tion is thrown.

Arbitrary Exceptions

Arbitrary run-time exceptions may be thrown by:

The run() method

The run() method of the thread class executes user-specific code and, hence, can throw any run-time exception the user code does not catch. Excep-tions that the run() method throws are caught by in the manner we describe in Appendix A.

C

Threading Within the Java API

Unlike many other programming environments where a threading system is provided as an interface for its applications, the Java environment is integrated with its threading system. Java applets themselves run in their own threads. Separate threads are used to download and to play audio files, as well as to download graphic images. All of these cases are supported by classes and constructs that are integrated into the language and handle all the details of synchronizing and communicating between the threads.

In this appendix, we'll give the details of all the threads that are created under the covers of the Java API and the Java virtual machine. As always, the details given here are specific to the 1.0.2 release of the reference platform of Java. Vendors who release versions of Java are free to change the details of the implementation as long as they don't change the functionality: a Java implementation must have a garbage collector, but it may not be implemented with the threads that we'll describe in this appendix.*

Threads Within a Minimal Java Application

As we know, when a Java application begins execution, a default thread executes the `main()` method. It turns out to be more complicated than that: there are at least two thread groups the Java virtual machine creates, as well as a number of other daemon threads in those groups. These thread groups are known as the

---

* In particular, Netscape chooses a different implementation for the threads in the system group that we're about to describe, though they do implement all the other threads in this appendix.

system thread group and the main thread group. The system thread group is the topmost thread group in the Java virtual machine; here's how these threads appear:

System thread group

The system thread group contains four daemon threads that provide some of the required functionality of the virtual machine:

Clock handler

The clock handler multiplexes internal timer events within the virtual machine. For developers, it is primarily of interest because it handles time-outs created by calls to the `sleep()` and `repaint(int)` methods. We'll look at this in more detail when we look behind the scenes of a Java applet.

Idle thread

The idle thread is a low priority thread; in fact, because it is internal to the virtual machine, it can bypass the normal constraints on threads and run at priority 0. Thus, the idle thread lives up to its name and will only be run when every other thread in the virtual machine is blocked. The primary use of the idle thread is to let the garbage collector know that it is a good time to scan for unreferenced objects.

Garbage collector

The garbage collector scans the objects within the virtual machine, tests if they are still in use, and frees them if they are not. The garbage collector sleeps for one second; when it awakens, it checks to see if the idle thread has run. If the idle thread has run, the garbage collector assumes that the system is idle and begins to scan memory; if the idle thread has not run, the garbage collector goes back to sleep for one second.

The garbage collector runs at priority 1, so it usually runs only when no other threads in the system are active. However, the finalizer thread also runs at priority 1,[*] so when the garbage collector wakes up, there may be other nonblocked threads. This is why the garbage collector and the idle thread collaborate: so that the garbage collector can know when the system was truly idle.

Finalizer thread

The finalizer thread calls the `finalize()` method on objects that the garbage collector has freed. It runs at priority 1.

---

[*] As could an arbitrary thread created by the developer.

Main group
> *Main thread*
>> The main thread group contains a single thread: the default thread of the application that executes starting at the `main()` method.

Recall that thread groups are organized in a tree hierarchy; the system thread group is the parent of the main thread group.

Threads Within a GUI Application

When a Java application creates a window and other user-interface objects, other threads are created to handle some of the details of the windowing system. These threads are added to the main thread group, so that the main thread group ends up with the following threads:

Main thread
AWT-Input
> Handles the input from the underlying window system and then makes the necessary calls to the AWT event-handling methods.

AWT-Toolkit
> Handles the events from the underlying window system and feeds them to the appropriate AWT methods. This thread is platform-specific and is usually named AWT-Motif (for UNIX platforms), AWT-Windows, etc. Some platforms use two threads for these events.

ScreenUpdater
> Handles the calls to the `repaint()` method. When a program calls the `repaint()` method, this thread is notified and can call the `update()` methods of all the affected components.

Threads Within a Java Applet

All the threads that we've discussed so far exist in a Java applet as well as a stand-alone application. When a browser is about to run an applet, it creates a new thread group for that applet; this new thread group is a child of the main thread group. Then, inside the applet thread group, the browser creates a new thread; this new thread is responsible for running the applet.[*]

---

[*] The organization of these threads within their thread groups is likely to change with Java's 1.1 security model that we discussed in Chapter 8.

Repaint Threads

Within the applet API, there are other places where threads exist, usually unknown to the developer. We'll look at some examples where these threads come into play. Let's start by looking at this applet:

```java
import java.applet.Applet;
import java.awt.*;

public class CountDown extends Applet {
    int count;
    Font f = new Font("courier", Font.BOLD, 24);

    public void init() {
        count = 10;
    }

    public void paint(Graphics g) {
        g.setFont(f);
        if (count == 0) {
            g.drawString("boom!!", 10, 20);
            count = 10;
        } else {
            g.drawString(new Integer(count--).toString(), 10, 20);
        }
        repaint(1000);  // Request paint again 1 second later
    }
}
```

In this example, we're looking at a simple applet that does a countdown from 10 and explodes with a boom upon reaching zero. The last method called by the paint() method is the repaint() method; this posts a request to the system to call the paint() method again in one second. A graphical representation of this appears in Figure C-1.

Clearly, there must be some thread behind the scene here: if the thread executing the repaint() method blocks for one second, the applet itself freezes for that one second. In the diagram, that means that the calls to the mouseDown() and mouseDrag() methods are delayed for one second. That's precisely why we need a threaded system: to help the applet avoid freezing for a period of time like this.

This is where the clock handler thread comes in: the repaint() method asks the clock handler thread to sleep for one second, and then the clock handler thread arranges for the update() method to be called. This means that the clock handler thread must coordinate with the screen updater thread; this latter thread calls the update() method when the clock handler thread tells it to. Meanwhile

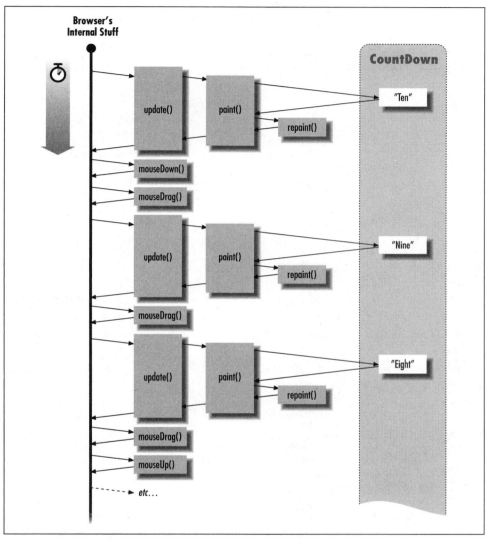

Figure C-1. Thread of control for the CountDown applet

the applet thread can continue to execute: it returns from the paint() method and handles the next event from the window system.

Playing Audio

To play an audio file located back at the server, we simply call the play() method that is part of the Applet class; a modification of our last countdown applet to use an audio countdown is as follows:

```java
import java.applet.Applet;
import java.awt.*;

public class CountDown extends Applet {
    int count;

    public void init() {
        count = 10;
    }

    public void paint(Graphics g) {
        if (count == 0) {
            play(getCodeBase(), "boom.au");
            count = 10;
        } else {
            play(getCodeBase(), new Integer(count--).toString()+".au");
        }
        repaint(1000);  // Request paint again 1 second later
    }
}
```

In this applet, the count is played as audio instead of being displayed in the panel space provided by the applet. If you've used the play() method before, you're probably aware that the portion of the play() method that loads the data from the network does not run in a separate thread: calling the play() method can introduce a serious delay in the applet during which it is unresponsive to user input or unable to repaint itself.

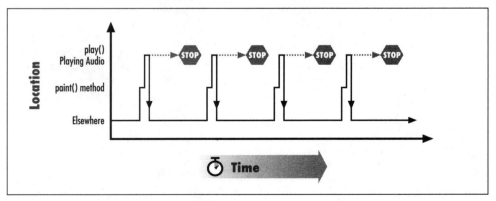

Figure C-2. Threads of the AudioCountDown applet

However, sending the data to the audio device is performed in a separate thread, as shown in Figure C-2. This means that while the audio is actually being sent to the speaker device, the applet is able to perform other tasks. The audio player thread runs at a priority of 10: when you write data to the audio device, the write() method blocks while the audio is playing. Since this thread spends almost all of its time blocked, it makes sense that it be at such a high priority thread; the applet is then able to perform other tasks (like animation) while the audio is playing, if not while it is loading.

This separate thread to play audio is also used by the AudioClip interface.

Displaying Images

A simple applet to draw an image would look like this:

```
import java.applet.Applet;
import java.awt.*;

public class Animate extends Applet {
    Image picture;
    public void init() {
        picture = getImage(getCodeBase(), "1.jpg");
    }

    public void paint(Graphics g) {
        g.drawImage(picture, 0, 0, this);
    }
}
```

At first glance, displaying an image is very similar to playing an audio clip: a call to the getImage() method returns an object representation of the image that is then drawn to the applet space with a call to the drawImage() method. However, the getImage() method is actually asynchronous: it uses a separate thread to load the image data and immediately returns. This means that when it is time for the drawImage() method to draw the image, the image data may not be available. Some type of communication must exist between the applet thread and the image-loading thread so that when it is available, the image may be displayed in full.

Two simple solutions would be for the drawImage() method to wait until the image is loaded so that it can be drawn, or for the drawImage() method to draw only what is available. Neither of these solutions is perfect. If the drawImage() method waits until the image is loaded before drawing, it defeats some of the purpose of having a separate thread loading the image in the first place; if the drawImage() method does not draw the full image, it will not complete the request made by the applet.

Obviously, the image-loading thread must have some way of communicating with the applet thread; this communication is achieved by the fourth parameter passed to the drawImage() method. This fourth parameter is an ImageObserver, which is simply a reference that allows the image-loading thread some access to the applet thread.[*] Let's walk through the each piece of the communication mechanism to examine how it works:

A thread is first started by the applet thread (via the getImage() method call)

This new thread, which we call the image thread, simply loads the image. This loading uses a system of producers and consumers. The simplest definition of these entities is that the producer sends the data that is loaded across the network to any consumer that wants the data. There is only one thread in this step: the image thread; the consumer is just callback code executed by the image thread from the producer code to store the data.

When the drawImage() method is called, it simply draws the data that has been delivered to the consumer

Obviously, not all the data may be available, so the applet thread needs some way to process this future data when it arrives. So the `drawImage()` method registers the fourth parameter, an observer, with the consumer. The consumer not only processes the data it receives from the producer, it also informs every observer that has been registered with it. In other words, the `drawImage()` method draws whatever image data is available and provides a mechanism to be informed when more data arrives. It does not wait to draw the entire image, nor does it draw the rest of the image when it arrives.

The applet repaint()s itself when more data arrives

The Component class is the class that implements the observer. As an observer, the Component class does not know what to do with the image when more data arrives; it simply assumes that its subclasses will know how to handle the data, and it also assumes that the image data has to do with the drawable part of the Component. So, when the Component class observes that new data has arrived from the image object, it calls its `repaint()` method and assumes that the newly loaded image data will be painted.

This entire process is shown in Figure C-3. In our example, the `paint()` method calls the `drawImage()` method, which draws the available image and registers the applet that's to be informed when more data arrives. When more data arrives, the applet `repaint()`s, which starts the cycle all over again. This continues until all the data is loaded, and there is no longer a reason for the consumer to notify the observer to `repaint()` the image.[†]

---

[*] The applet thread can access the image-loading thread via the image object itself.

[†] The complexity of this interface is not caused by the threading system; Java could have provided a simpler interface that still had all the threading benefits this interface has. The reason there is a need for producers and consumers is to isolate the image format from the I/O and the drawing mechanisms: by having an interface that separates producers and consumers, it is possible to create new producers and consumers to handle different image sources, formats, and destinations without changing code throughout the system.

The ImageObserver Interface

ImageObserver is actually an interface that defines only one method. This method, imageUpdate(), takes many parameters, which includes x, y, width, and height information, a flag that determines what data is now available, and the Image itself. The Image object calls the ImageObserver to report on the state of the loading of the image. This is of course, done from the image-loading thread.

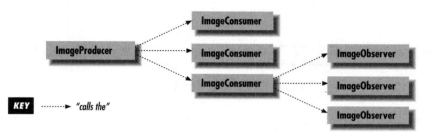

There can be many ImageObserver classes registered with the ImageConsumer that reads from the ImageProducer. When the producer receives data in the image-loading thread, it calls all the consumers to pass the data along. The consumer that is registered by the getImage() method call not only stores the data, but calls all the observers to inform them of that fact.

The ImageObserver can use these calls to determine when width and height information is available, or when a certain region of an image is available. It is the job of the ImageObserver to take appropriate action based on these reports.

Multiplexing Image Loading

In the previous section, we said that when an image is loaded, it is loaded in an image-loading thread. As it happens, there are four image-loading threads available to an applet. The four threads attempt to strike a reasonable balance for applets that load many images in parallel.

The reason that image loading is done in a separate thread stems from the fact that the data is being read over a socket, and there will probably be periods during which the thread that is reading the image data will block, waiting for that data. If we have two image-loading threads, the two images can load faster: data for one image can be processed in one thread while another thread is waiting for data for the second image. It's still possible that these two threads may be blocked at the same time, so if a third image thread were available, it could process data while the two threads were blocked.

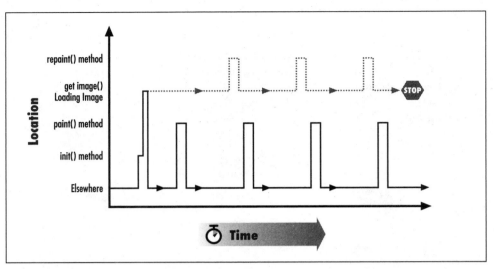

Figure C-3. Graphical representation of the drawImage() system

Conceivably, this argument could apply no matter how many image-loading threads are available. On the other hand, there is no advantage to having more threads than needed: consider what might happen if we set up twenty threads to load twenty different images. In that case, we'd probably always have at least two threads that have data to process and are competing for the CPU. It would be slightly more efficient to create exactly the number of threads that we need such that only one thread at a time has data to process. This would save the amount of time necessary to create the extra threads and also save the memory required to store the thread objects.[*]

The Java API has determined that four threads generally gives the best mix between having too few threads and too many threads. These four image-loading threads are created when the first image is retrieved, and they run at a high priority of 8 (since they spend most of their time blocked).

---

[*] Threads can usually be thought of as lightweight entities: they are inexpensive to create and don't require a lot of memory. So this optimization is a slight one.

All the Threads Together

Table C-1 summarizes the threads that are running in any application or applet. We've discussed most of them in this appendix.

Table C-1. Threads Within the Java Virtual Machine

Thread Group	Thread Name	Description
System		
	Clock handler	Merges all `sleep()` and `wait(timeout)` requests into a queue and processes that queue
	Idle thread	Bookkeeping thread for garbage collection
	Garbage collector	Frees unreferenced objects
	Finalizer thread	Sets up the `finalize()` method on freed objects
Main		
	Main	Executes the `main()` method of applications (or the setup methods of a browser)
AppletViewer[a]		
	AWT-Input	Handles input from the native windowing system
	AWT-Toolkit (e.g., AWT-Motif)	Handles events from the native windowing system. Some platforms implement this as multiple threads
	Screen updater	Merges `repaint()` requests and generates `paint()` calls
	Image fetcher	Four separate threads load images from the network
	Audio player	Plays audio output
AppletName[b]		
	AppletName	Applet thread that calls `start()`, `stop()`, etc.

[a] When a program is being run as a Java application, this thread group will not exist, and its threads will belong to the main thread group.

[b] The group and its thread are not present in Java applications.

In an applet that uses images and audio, there are some 16 threads (depending on the platform) all performing separate tasks, and that's before you even begin to add your own threads. Clearly, the success of Java is dependent on the success of Java's threading model.

D

Thread Debugging

Under the best of circumstances, debugging a threaded program poses a new set of problems for a developer. While Java remains a leading-edge technology, those problems become yet more difficult due to the lack of mature, robust tools available to assist your debugging efforts. This is a situation that is likely to change quickly—so quickly that it has definitely changed since we've written this book, and probably also since you've obtained it. In addition, while the standard JDK release comes with a simple debugger (*jdb*), vendors of integrated Java development environments will release their own debuggers.[*] These debuggers will be more powerful than *jdb*, have graphical interfaces that provide a nicer interface than *jdb*, and may implement features that aren't available in *jdb*. These debuggers will also be vendor-specific, so their operation will vary.

Therefore, information on Java thread debugging is incomplete and likely to change. What we'll do in this appendix is to give you an overview of the thread-specific commands of *jdb* and a look into a debugging problem that is specific to threaded programs.

Introduction to jdb

We'll start with a sample *jdb* session that will give you an idea of the thread-related facilities available within *jdb* (on the theory that whatever debugger you end up running will have similar facilities). This example also illustrates the new situations in which you'll find yourself when you're debugging a threaded program. We'll assume you're familiar with the basic facilities of *jdb* or other debuggers: setting breakpoints, examining variables, etc.

---

[*] The *jdb* debugger is also built into the appletviewer that comes with Sun Microsystem's JDK; when you run `appletviewer -debug` you're actually running *jdb*.

The program below is what we're going to run in the debugger. This program is based on the ubiquitous ticker that displays scrolling stock data or news headlines or other text on pages throughout the Web. In ticker programs, there are typically two threads: one thread reads data from a network server (e.g., a server sending out stock quotes) and places this data into a buffer. The second thread wakes up every second, grabs the next character out of the buffer, and puts it onto the screen, scrolling the previous data as it does so.

We'll simplify this program a little: the thread that normally reads the data via a socket instead just puts arbitrary characters into the buffer, and the thread that normally scrolls data on the screen instead just prints out data to System.out.

```java
public class Stock extends Applet implements Runnable {
    StringBuffer buffer;
    Thread t;

    public void init() {
        buffer = new StringBuffer();
    }

    public void start() {
        t = new Thread(this);
        t.setPriority(6);
        t.start();
    }

    public void stop() {
        t.stop();
        t = null;
    }

    public void paint(Graphics g) {
        char c = getNextCharacter();
        System.out.println(c);
        repaint(1000);
    }

    private char getNextCharacter() {
        int len = buffer.length();
        if (len == 0)
            return '.';
        char c[] = new char[len];
        buffer.getChars(0, len, c, 0);
        buffer = new StringBuffer(new String(c, 1, len - 1));
        return c[0];
    }

    public void run() {
```

```
                char c = 'a';
                while (true) {
                    try {
                        Thread.sleep(500);
                        buffer.append(c++);
                        if (c == '{')
                            c = 'a';
                    } catch (Exception e) {}
                }
            }
        }
```

Hopefully, you've already been able to spot an error in the program (especially if you read Chapter 2 where we introduced the topic of race conditions): if you run the program, you'll get lines of output starting with the letter "a," then "b," and so on through "z" at which point the output cycles through again. Eventually,[*] however, the output skips one or more characters, and you see something like:

```
c
d
f
g
```

Something is wrong, so we'll put this program into the debugger and see if we can figure out just what. After we load the program into the debugger and execute the run command in the debugger, we notice the first difference between *jdb* and debuggers targeted to single-threaded languages: we're able to give certain commands to the debugger while the program is executing.

Upon reflection, this is not such a surprising concept: *jdb* is written in Java, and so *jdb* is itself a threaded program. That means it's set up so that it has an input thread separate from the threads running the program. The *jdb* input thread can read and process commands while the other (program) threads are still running (making *jdb* an advertisement for the power behind threads).[†] So the first thing to keep in mind when you're interacting with *jdb* is that your program may still be running even as you give commands.

Thread Commands

Since we're speaking of threads, the first *jdb* command that we'll look at lists all the threads in the program:

---

[*] Like all bugs involving race conditions, the "eventually" here may require a lot of patience depending on the luck of the timing on your machine.

[†] The debugger included with many integrated development environments is not written in Java and may or may not have this feature.

threads

Lists all the threads in the program.

Here's the list of threads in the Stock program shown above:

```
Group sun.applet.AppletViewer.main:
  1. (sun.awt.motif.InputThread)0xee30e5d8 AWT-Input      running
  2. (java.lang.Thread)0xee30e600          AWT-Motif      cond. waiting
  3. (sun.awt.ScreenUpdater)0xee30e970      Screen Updater running
Group group applet-Stock:
  4. (java.lang.Thread)0xee30e248 thread applet-Stock cond. waiting
  5. (java.lang.Thread)0xee30fd60 Thread-5           cond. waiting
```

Notice that the threads are separated by the thread group to which they belong; the applet we're debugging shows the two threads we expect. The first column in this output—the number—is referred to as the thread id and is used in many of the commands we're about to show. The final column of the thread shows its current state: running, suspended, or blocked (indicated by cond. waiting). So our two applet threads are both blocked, which makes sense, as both are sleeping.[*]

The threads are listed beginning with the current thread group. This current thread group is a notion of *jdb* itself; *jdb* allows you to set any thread group to be the current thread group. Setting the current thread group has no effect on the operation of your program; it's just a bookkeeping notion for *jdb*.

Just as *jdb* has the notion of the current thread group, it has the notion of the current thread. The current thread is the one used by commands that print the stack (the where command), and to provide a thread context for commands (like the dump command) that require a context. The current thread is set by the thread command:

thread id

Makes the thread identified by number the current thread.

To examine the stack and variables of the thread that is producing data, you'd execute the command

```
thread 5
```

This automatically makes the thread group that contains thread 5 the current thread group.

ThreadGroup Commands

The threads printed by the threads command are only those threads that belong to the current thread group and groups that descend from the current thread

---

[*] We might happen to catch these threads in the runnable state.

group. By default (and in the last example), the current thread group is the applet's main thread group, which contains the thread group in which our particular applet is running. You can list all the thread groups in the debugger with the `threadgroup` command:

threadgroups

Lists all the thread groups in the debugger.

In our case, we'd see these thread groups:

```
1. (java.lang.ThreadGroup)0xee3000b8 system
2. (java.lang.ThreadGroup)0xee300aa8 main
3. (java.lang.ThreadGroup)0xee30bf00 sun.applet.AppletViewer.main
4. (sun.applet.AppletThreadGroup)0xee30e260 group applet-Stock
```

The system thread group contains threads to handle garbage collection, the *jdb* input thread, and so on. If you want to change the current thread group, you can use the `threadgroup` command:

threadgroup name

Makes the named thread group the current thread group.

So that if we execute the command `threadgroup system`, the system thread group becomes the current thread group. Then if we execute the `threads` command, we'll see all the threads in the debugger:[*]

```
Group system:
 1. (java.lang.Thread)0xee3001f8 clock handler      cond. waiting
 2. (java.lang.Thread)0xee3002a0 Idle thread        running
 3. (java.lang.Thread)0xee300318 Garbage Collector  suspended
 4. (java.lang.Thread)0xee300370 Finalizer thread   suspended
 5. (java.lang.Thread)0xee300a18 Debugger agent     running
 6. (sun.tools.debug.BreakpointHandler)0xee30a8d8
                          Breakpoint handler      cond. waiting
Group main:
 7. (java.lang.Thread)0xee3000a0 main suspended
Group sun.applet.AppletViewer.main:
 8. (sun.awt.motif.InputThread)0xee30e5d8 AWT-Input      suspended
 9. (java.lang.Thread)0xee30e600           AWT-Motif      suspended
10. (sun.awt.ScreenUpdater)0xee30e970      Screen Updater suspended
Group group applet-Stock:
11. (java.lang.Thread)0xee30e248 thread applet-Stock suspended
12. (java.lang.Thread)0xee30fd60 Thread-5            suspended
```

---

[*] While *jdb* presently allows you to see all the threads in the program, this may no longer be the case when the default security model for thread groups changes in the 1.1 release of the JDK.

Commands to Manipulate Thread States

In most cases, you probably don't want your program to be running while you're actually giving commands in *jdb*, and there are certain commands that cannot be given while the program is running. So the next two *jdb* commands we'll look at allow you to control all the threads:

suspend
> Suspends all program threads.

resume
> Resumes all program threads.

These two commands affect all the nonsystem threads in the debugger: essentially, all the threads in the applet thread group and the main thread group. Threads shown above in the system thread group cannot be suspended or resumed from the debugger.

These suspend and resume commands are also executed implicitly when the debugger hits a breakpoint. When the debugger hits a breakpoint, all threads are implicitly suspended. When you execute a continue, step, or next statement, all threads are implicitly resumed. If you execute a step command, the threads are implicitly resumed and then implicitly suspended when the statement that you're stepping over has executed.

The suspend and resume commands can also affect single threads, if desired, by giving a thread id to the command:

```
suspend 5
```

This suspends the thread that is producing data for our Stock applet.

A Debugging Session Using jdb

With this background, let's continue our debugging session by setting a breakpoint in the getNextCharacter() method to see if we can figure out why we sometimes drop characters. When we first hit the breakpoint, we'll examine the local variable length in the getNextCharacter() method as well as the buffer object to see if they're in sync:[*]

```
Breakpoint hit: Stock.getNextCharacter (Stock:28)
AWT-Motif[1] print len
len = 1
AWT-Motif[1] dump buffer
this.buffer = (java.lang.StringBuffer)0xee312738 {
```

---

[*] In this section, input commands are highlighted in bold; all other text is printed by *jdb* itself.

```
        private char value[] = "a"
        private int count = 1
        private boolean shared = false
}
```

So far, so good. If we now execute a next statement, we'll test if len == 0 (which we already know is false), but then what happens if we print out our variables again? We'll get the following:

```
AWT-Motif[1] next
AWT-Motif[1]
Breakpoint hit: Stock.getNextCharacter (Stock:29)
AWT-Motif[1] print len
len = 1
AWT-Motif[1] dump buffer
this.buffer = (java.lang.StringBuffer)0xee3149b0 {
        private char value[] = "ab"
        private int count = 2
        private boolean shared = false
}
```

What has happened here? Our len variable is still 1, but the length of the buffer has increased to 2. When we executed the next statement, *all* threads were resumed. This means that the data-producing thread also had an opportunity to run, and since the data-producing thread has a higher priority than our printing thread, it interrupted the printing thread and added a new variable to the buffer. Then the data-producing thread went back to sleep, and the printing thread then became the currently running thread, executed the next statement, and returned control to the debugger.

There's good news, and there's bad news here: the good news is that we've pretty clearly found our bug: we need to synchronize access to the buffer variable, or we can get interrupted at a critical point in the getNextCharacter() method and introduce an error. The bad news is that we've shown an example of the hardest problem that's involved in debugging a threaded program: there are all sorts of external events and timing events that can affect the behavior of the program.

Timing and Threaded Programs

That's really the crux of the issue in debugging threaded programs: threaded programs contain the type of bugs caused by logic errors that you're used to finding in single-threaded programs with the aid of a debugger, and *jdb* (and other debuggers) still help to find those errors. But threaded programs also contain errors caused by incorrect synchronization, race conditions, and deadlock, and *jdb* may or may not help find those errors. In the example we just looked at, *jdb* actually helped us find the synchronization error because it caused the synchronization error to occur much sooner than it occurred when we ran the program under appletviewer or in a browser.

We skewed this example so that we'd see the problem immediately by setting the priority of the data-producing thread to be higher than the printing thread. If we had kept the threads at the same priority, we would have had the same error when we ran in a browser, but it would have been harder to see under *jdb* because the data thread would not have interrupted us when we executed the next statement.

As an example of how *jdb* can actually hinder finding a bug caused by a race condition, let's revisit the banking example we first saw in Chapter 3. We've modified our original class so that it looks like this:

```
public class Teller {
    public boolean withdraw(double amt, Account acct) {
        Pin pin;
        pin = requestPin(acct);
        acct.validate(pin);
        if (amt < acct.balance) {
            //Point of potential interruption
            acct.balance -= amt;
            dispense(amt);
        }
    }
}
```

Recall that if the account is held jointly, a race condition occurs if a thread operating on behalf of one holder of the account interrupts another thread operating on behalf of another holder of the account exactly at the point indicated by the comment. You might see this problem when you actually run the program, but if you run the program under *jdb*, you might never see the problem. This is because *jdb*—or any debugger—executes the Java program at a different rate than does the standard Java virtual machine. As a result, it's a common problem to observe race conditions in a running program that are impossible to catch when the program is run under control of a debugger.[*] In Figure D-1, we see an example of how this could happen: on the left-hand side, we're assuming that the two holders of the account are running in separate threads and that each thread is given a timeslice sufficient to execute three statements.[†] When the same code is run under *jdb*, it tends to execute slower, perhaps such that each thread can run only two statements in its timeslice before being interrupted, as is shown on the right-

---

[*] While the debugger may hide some race conditions, the reverse is also true: the new speed of execution may exacerbate a race condition by bringing about the correct set of thread timings that causes it to occur.

[†] In the real world, it would take considerably longer to execute the statement requestPin() than to execute the statement if amt < balance, but pretend for now that they require the same amount of time.

hand side of Figure D-1. So the standard execution environment is going to produce an error even when the *jdb* execution environment is not.

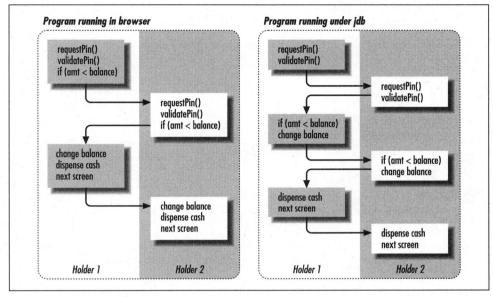

Figure D-1. Execution order differences

Race conditions are most easily diagnosed by a source-code analyzer tool: the same tool that helps to detect deadlock once such a tool becomes available. In the meantime, if you find an error situation that occurs under the virtual machine that you can't reproduce when running under the control of a debugger, you must insert code into your program to try and determine what's going wrong when. Most often, this means sticking a bunch of `print()` and `println()` methods into your code to print out helpful information.

As debugging tools become more sophisticated, better support for dealing with these threaded issues will also become available.[*] Until then, your own ingenuity and old-fashioned debugging techniques will have to suffice.

---

[*] "Back when we started to program, we didn't have those newfangled, fancy GUI symbolic debuggers. We were lucky even to have a `printf()` routine to call. Usually we had to debug in octal." "You had octal?"

Index

About the Authors

Scott Oaks is a lead tactical engineer at Sun Microsystems, where he has worked since 1987. While at Sun, he has specialized on many disparate technologies, from the SunOS kernel to network programming and RPCs to the X Window System to threading. Since early 1995, he has primarily focused on Java and bringing Java technology to end users; he writes a monthly column on Java solutions for *The Java Report*. Around the Internet, Scott is best known as the author of *olvwm*, the OPEN LOOK window manager.

Scott holds a Bachelor of Science in mathematics and computer science from the University of Denver and a Master of Science in computer science from Brown University. Prior to joining Sun, he worked in the research division of Bear, Stearns.

In his other life, Scott enjoys music (he plays flute and piccolo with community groups in New York), cooking, theater, and traveling with his husband, James.

Henry Wong is a tactical engineer at Sun Microsystems, where he has worked since 1989. Originally hired as a consultant to help customers with special device drivers, kernel modifications, and DOS interoperability products, Henry has also worked on Solaris ports, performance tuning projects, and multithreaded design and implementations for benchmarks and demos. Since early 1995, Henry has been involved in developing Java prototypes, and supporting customers who are using Java.

Prior to joining Sun, Henry earned a Bachelor of Science degree in chemical engineering from The Cooper Union in 1987. He joined a small software company in 1986 working on SCSI device drivers, image and audio data compression, and graphics tools used for a medical information system.

When not in front of a computer, Henry is an instrument-rated private pilot, who also likes to dabble in archery, cooking, and traveling to different places with his wife, Nini.

Colophon

Our look is the result of reader comments, our own experimentation, and feedback from distribution channels. Distinctive covers complement our distinctive approach to technical topics, breathing personality and life into potentially dry subjects.

The top image on the cover of *Java Threads* is from the CMCD PhotoCD Collection. It was manipulated by Edie Freedman using Adobe Photoshop 3.0 and Adobe

Gallery Effects filters. The cover layout was produced with Quark XPress 3.3 using the Bodoni Black font from URW Software.

The inside layout was designed by Nancy Priest. Text was in FrameMaker 5.0 by Mike Sierra. The heading font is Bodoni BT; the text font is New Baskerville. The illustrations that appear in the book were created in Macromedia Freehand 5.0 by Chris Reilley.

Exploring Java

By Patrick Niemeyer & Joshua Peck
1st Edition May 1996
426 pages, ISBN 1-56592-184-4

The first book in our new Java documentation series, *Exploring Java* introduces the basics of Java, the object-oriented programming language for networked applications. This book shows you how to get up to speed writing Java applets and other applications, including networking programs, content and protocol handlers, and security managers.

Java in a Nutshell

By David Flanagan
1st Edition February 1996
460 pages, ISBN 1-56592-183-6

Java in a Nutshell is a complete quick-reference guide to Java, the hot new programming language from Sun Microsystems. This comprehensive volume contains descriptions of all of the classes in the Java 1.0 API, with a definitive listing of all methods and variables. It also contains an accelerated introduction to Java for C and C++ programmers who want to learn the language fast.

Java in a Nutshell introduces the Java programming language and contains many practical examples that show programmers how to write Java applications and applets. It is also an indispensable quick reference designed to wait faithfully by the side of every Java programmer's keyboard. It puts all the information Java programmers need right at their fingertips.

Java Virtual Machine

By Troy Downing & Jon Meyer
1st Edition Winter 1997
380 pages (est.), ISBN 1-56592-194-1

This book is a comprehensive programming guide for the Java Virtual Machine (JVM). It gives readers a strong overview and reference of the JVM so that they may create their own implementations of the JVM or write their own compilers that create Java object code.

Java Language Reference

By Mark Grand
1st Edition Fall 1996
360 pages (est.), ISBN 1-56592-204-2

The *Java Language Reference* will be an indispensable tool for every Java programmer. Part of O'Reilly's new series on the Java language, this edition describes Java Version 1.0.2. It covers the syntax (presented in easy-to-understand railroad diagrams), object-oriented programming, exception handling, multithreaded programming, and differences between Java and C/C++.

Java Fundamental Classes Reference

By Mark Grand
1st Edition Winter 1997
330 pages (est.), ISBN 1-56592-241-7

The *Java Fundamental Classes Reference* provides complete reference documentation for the Java fundamental classes. These classes contain architecture-independent methods that serve as Java's gateway to the real world and provide access to resources such as the network, the windowing system, and the host filesystem.

Java AWT Reference

By John Zukowski
1st Edition Winter 1997
400 pages (est.), ISBN 1-56592-240-9

The *Java AWT Reference* provides complete reference documentation on the Abstract Windowing Toolkit (AWT), a large collection of classes for building graphical user interfaces in Java. Part of O'Reilly's new Java documentation series, this edition describes Version 1.0.2 of the Java Developer's Kit. The *Java AWT Reference* includes easy-to-use reference material on every AWT class and provides lots of sample code to help you learn by example.

For information: **800-998-9938**, 707-829-0515; **info@ora.com; http://www.ora.com/**
To order: **800-889-8969** (credit card orders only); **order@ora.com**

Developing Web Content

Building Your Own WebSite

By Susan B. Peck & Stephen Arrants
1st Edition July 1996
514 pages, ISBN 1-56592-232-8

This is a hands-on reference for Windows® 95 and Windows NT™ desktop users who want to host their own site on the Web or on a corporate intranet. This step-by-step guide will have you creating live Web pages in minutes. You'll also learn how to connect your web to information in other Windows applications, such as word processing documents and databases. Packed with examples and tutorials on every aspect of Web management. Includes highly acclaimed WebSite™ 1.1—all the software you need for Web publishing.

Web Client Programming with Perl

By Clinton Wong
1st Edition Fall 1996
250 pages (est.), ISBN 1-56592-214-X

Web Client Programming with Perl teaches you how to extend scripting skills to the Web. This book teaches you the basics of how browsers communicate with servers and how to write your own customized Web clients to automate common tasks. It is intended for those who are motivated to develop software that offers a more flexible and dynamic response than a standard Web browser.

JavaScript: The Definitive Guide

By David Flanagan
1st Edition Winter 1997
700 pages (est.), ISBN 1-56592-234-4

This definitive reference guide to JavaScript, the HTML extension that gives Web pages programming language capabilities, covers JavaScript as it is used in Netscape 3.0 and 2.0 and in Microsoft Internet Explorer 2.0. Learn how JavaScript really works (and when it doesn't). Use JavaScript to control Web browser behavior, add dynamically created text to Web pages, interact with users through HTML forms, and even control and interact with Java applets and Navigator plug-ins.

HTML: The Definitive Guide

By Chuck Musciano & Bill Kennedy
1st Edition April 1996
410 pages, ISBN 1-56592-175-5

A complete guide to creating documents on the World Wide Web. This book describes basic syntax and semantics and goes on to show you how to create beautiful, informative Web documents you'll be proud to display. The HTML 2.0 standard and Netscape extensions are fully explained.

Designing for the Web: Getting Started in a New Medium

By Jennifer Niederst with Edie Freedman
1st Edition April 1996
180 pages, ISBN 1-56592-165-8

Designing for the Web gives you the basics you need to hit the ground running. Although geared toward designers, it covers information and techniques useful to anyone who wants to put graphics online. It explains how to work with HTML documents from a designer's point of view, outlines special problems with presenting information online, and walks through incorporating images into Web pages, with emphasis on resolution and improving efficiency.

WebMaster in a Nutshell

By Stephen Spainhour & Valerie Quercia
1st Edition October 1996
378 pages, ISBN 1-56592-229-8

Web content providers and administrators have many sources of information, both in print and online. *WebMaster in a Nutshell* pulls it all together into one slim volume—for easy desktop access. This quick-reference covers HTML, CGI, Perl, HTTP, server configuration, and tools for Web administration.

*For information: **800-998-9938**, 707-829-0515; **info@ora.com; http://www.ora.com/***
*To order: **800-889-8969** (credit card orders only); **order@ora.com***

World Wide Web Journal

Fourth International World Wide Web Conference Proceedings

*A publication of O'Reilly & Associates
and the World Wide Web Consortium (W3C)*
Winter 1995/96
748 pages, ISBN 1-56592-169-0

The *World Wide Web Journal* provides timely, in-depth coverage of the W3C's technological developments, such as protocols for security, replication and caching, HTML and SGML, and content labeling. It also explores the broader issues of the Web with Web luminaries and articles on controversial legal issues such as censorship and intellectual property rights. Whether you follow Web developments for strategic planning, application programming, or Web page authoring and designing, you'll find the in-depth information you need here.

The *World Wide Web Journal* is published quarterly. This issue contains 57 refereed technical papers presented at the Fourth International World Wide Web Conference, held December 1995 in Boston, Massachusetts. It also includes the two best papers from regional conferences.

Key Specifications of the World Wide Web

*A publication of O'Reilly & Associates
and the World Wide Web Consortium (W3C)*
Spring 1996
356 pages, ISBN 1-56592-190-9

The key specifications that describe the architecture of the World Wide Web and how it works are maintained online at the World Wide Web Consortium. This issue of the *World Wide Web Journal* collects these key papers in a single volume as an important reference for the Webmaster, application programmer, or technical manager.

In this valuable reference, you'll find the definitive specifications for the core technologies in the Web: Hypertext Markup Language (HTML), Hypertext Transfer Protocol (HTTP), and Uniform Resource Locators (URLs), plus the emerging standards for portable graphics (PNG), content selection (PICS), and style sheets (CSS).

The Web After Five Years

*A publication of O'Reilly & Associates
and the World Wide Web Consortium (W3C)*
Summer 1996
226 pages, ISBN 1-56592-210-7

As the Web explodes across the technology scene, it's increasingly difficult to keep track of myriad new protocols, standards, and applications. The *World Wide Web Journal* is your direct connection to the work of the World Wide Web Consortium (W3C) as it helps members understand the forces behind current developments and leads the way to further innovation.

This issue is a reflection on the web after five years. In an interview with Tim Berners-Lee, the inventor of the Web and Director of the W3C, we learn that the Web was built to be an interactive, intercreative, two-way medium from the beginning. At the opposite scale, as a mass medium, are urgent questions about the Web's size, character, and users. These issues are addressed in selections from the MIT/W3C Workshop on Web Demographics and Internet Survey Methodology, along with commerce-related papers selected from the Fifth International World Wide Web Conference, which took place from May 6–10 in Paris.

Building an Industrial Strength Web

*A publication of O'Reilly & Associates
and the World Wide Web Consortium (W3C)*
Fall 1996
244 pages, ISBN 1-56592-211-5

Issue 4 focuses on the infrastructure needed to create and maintain an "Industrial Strength Web," from network protocols to application design. Included are the first standard versions of core Web protocols: HTTP/1.1, Digest Authentication, State Management (Cookies), and PICS. This issue also provides guides to the specs, highlighting new features, papers explaining modifications to 1.1 (sticky and compressed headers), extensibility, support for collaborative authoring, and using distributed objects.

Perl

Programming Perl, 2nd Edition

By Larry Wall, Tom Christiansen & Randal L. Schwartz
2nd Edition September 1996
676 pages, ISBN 1-56592-149-6

Programming Perl, second edition, is the authoritative guide to Perl version 5, the scripting utility that has established itself as the programming tool of choice for the World Wide Web, UNIX system administration, and a vast range of other applications. Version 5 of Perl includes object-oriented programming facilities. The book is coauthored by Larry Wall, the creator of Perl.

Perl is a language for easily manipulating text, files, and processes. It provides a more concise and readable way to do many jobs that were formerly accomplished (with difficulty) by programming with C or one of the shells. Perl is likely to be available wherever you choose to work. And if it isn't, you can get it and install it easily and free of charge.

This heavily revised second edition of *Programming Perl* contains a full explanation of the features in Perl version 5.003. It covers version 5.003 syntax, functions, library modules, references, debugging, and object-oriented programming.

Learning Perl

By Randal L. Schwartz, Foreword by Larry Wall
1st Edition November 1993
274 pages, ISBN 1-56592-042-2

Learning Perl is ideal for system administrators, programmers, and anyone else wanting a down-to-earth introduction to this useful language. Written by a Perl trainer, its aim is to make a competent, hands-on Perl programmer out of the reader as quickly as possible. The book takes a tutorial approach and includes hundreds of short code examples, along with some lengthy ones. The relatively inexperienced programmer will find *Learning Perl* easily accessible.

Each chapter of the book includes practical programming ~~rcises. Solutions are presented for all exercises.

~~~ detailed guide to advanced
~~illy's companion book,

CGI Programming on the World Wide Web

By Shishir Gundavaram
1st Edition March 1996
450 pages, ISBN 1-56592-168-2

The World Wide Web is more than a place to put up clever documents and pretty pictures. With a little study and practice, you can offer interactive queries and serve instant information from databases, worked up into colorful graphics. That is what the Common Gateway Interface (CGI) offers.

This book offers a comprehensive explanation of CGI and related techniques for people who hold on to the dream of providing their own information servers on the Web. Gundavaram starts at the beginning, explaining the value of CGI and how it works, then moves swiftly into the subtle details of programming. For most of the examples, the book uses the most common platform (UNIX) and the most popular language (Perl) used for CGI programming today. However, it also introduces the essentials of making CGI work with other platforms and languages.

Perl 5 Desktop Reference

By Johan Vromans
1st Edition February 1996
39 pages, ISBN 1-56592-187-9

This booklet gives you quick, well-organized access to the vast array of features in Perl version 5. Perl is a language for easily manipulating text, files, and processes.

Having first established itself as the UNIX programming tool of choice, Perl is now becoming the World Wide Web programming tool of choice. This guide provides a complete overview of the language, from variables to input and output, from flow control to regular expressions, from functions to document formats—all packed into a convenient, carry-around booklet.

Perl 5 Desktop Reference is the perfect companion to *Learning Perl*, a carefully paced tutorial course by Randal L. Schwartz, and *Programming Perl*, the complete, authoritative reference work coauthored by Perl developer Larry Wall, Tom Christiansen, and Randal L. Schwartz.

-9938, 707-829-0515; **info@ora.com; http://www.ora.com/**
89-8969 *(credit card orders only);* **order@ora.com**

Stay in touch with O'REILLY™

Visit Our Award-Winning World Wide Web Site

http://www.ora.com/

VOTED

"Top 100 Sites on the Web" —*PC Magazine*
"Top 5% Websites" —*Point Communications*
"3-Star site" —*The McKinley Group*

Our Web site contains a library of comprehensive product information (including book excerpts and tables of contents), downloadable software, background articles, interviews with technology leaders, links to relevant sites, book cover art, and more. File us in your Bookmarks or Hotlist!

Join Our Two Email Mailing Lists

LIST #1 NEW PRODUCT RELEASES: To receive automatic email with brief descriptions of all new O'Reilly products as they are released, send email to: listproc@online.ora.com and put the following information in the first line of your message (NOT in the Subject: field, which is ignored): **subscribe ora-news "Your Name" of "Your Organization"** (for example: **subscribe ora-news Kris Webber of Fine Enterprises)**

List #2 O'REILLY EVENTS: If you'd also like us to send information about trade show events, special promotions, and other O'Reilly events, send email to: **listproc@online.ora.com** and put the following information in the first line of your message (NOT in the Subject: field, which is ignored): **subscribe ora-events "Your Name" of "Your Organization"**

Visit Our Gopher Site

- Connect your Gopher to **gopher.ora.com**, or
- Point your Web browser to **gopher://gopher.ora.com/**, or
- telnet to **gopher.ora.com** (login: **gopher**)

Get Example Files from Our Books Via FTP

There are two ways to access an archive of example files from our books:

REGULAR FTP — ftp to: **ftp.ora.com** (login: **anonymous**—use your email address as the password) or point your Web browser to: **ftp://ftp.ora.com/**

FTPMAIL — Send an email message to: **ftpmail@online.ora.com** (write "help" in the message body)

Contact Us Via Email

order@ora.com — To place a book or software order online. Good for North American and international customers.

subscriptions@ora.com — To place an order for any of our newsletters or periodicals.

software@ora.com — For general questions and product information about our software.
- Check out O'Reilly Software Online at **http://software.ora.com/** for software and technical support information.
- Registered O'Reilly software users send your questions to **website-support@ora.com**

books@ora.com — General questions about any of our books.

cs@ora.com — For answers to problems regarding your order or our products.

booktech@ora.com — For book content technical questions or corrections.

proposals@ora.com — To submit new book or software proposals to our editors and product managers.

international@ora.com — For information about our international distributors or translation queries.
- For a list of our distributors outside of North America check out: **http://www.ora.com/www/order/country.html**

O'REILLY™

101 Morris Street, Sebastopol, CA 95472 USA
TEL 707-829-0515 or 800-998-9938 (6 A.M. to 5 P.M. PST)
FAX 707-829-0104

Titles from O'REILLY™

INTERNET PROGRAMMING

CGI Programming on the
  World Wide Web
Designing for the Web
HTML: The Definitive Guide
JavaScript: The Definitive Guide
Learning Perl
Programming Perl, 2nd Edition
Regular Expressions
WebMaster in a Nutshell
Web Client Programming with Perl
  (Winter '97)
The World Wide Web Journal

USING THE INTERNET

Smileys
The Whole Internet User's Guide
  and Catalog
The Whole Internet for Windows 95
What You Need to Know:
  Using Email Effectively
What You Need to Know: Bandits on the
  Information Superhighway

JAVA SERIES

Exploring Java
Java AWT Reference (Winter '97 est.)
Java Fundamental Classes Reference
  (Winter '97 est.)
Java in a Nutshell
Java Language Reference (Winter '97 est.)
Java Threads
Java Virtual Machine (Winter '97)

SOFTWARE

WebSite™ 1.1
WebSite Professional™
WebBoard™
PolyForm™
Statisphere™

SONGLINE GUIDES

Gif Animation Studio
NetActivism
NetLaw (Winter '97)
NetLearning
NetResearch (Winter '97)
NetSuccess for Realtors
Shockwave Studio (Winter '97 est.)

SYSTEM ADMINISTRATION

Building Internet Firewalls
Computer Crime:
  A Crimefighter's Handbook
Computer Security Basics
DNS and BIND, 2nd Edition
Essential System Administration,
  2nd Edition
Getting Connected:
  The Internet at 56K and Up
Linux Network Administrator's Guide
Managing Internet Information Services
Managing Usenet (Spring '97)
Managing NFS and NIS
Networking Personal Computers
  with TCP/IP
Practical UNIX & Internet Security
PGP: Pretty Good Privacy
sendmail, 2nd Edition (Winter '97)
System Performance Tuning
TCP/IP Network Administration
termcap & terminfo
Using & Managing UUCP
Volume 8: X Window System
  Administrator's Guide

UNIX

Exploring Expect
Learning GNU Emacs, 2nd Edition
Learning the bash Shell
Learning the Korn Shell
Learning the UNIX Operating System
Learning the vi Editor
Linux in a Nutshell (Winter '97 est.)
Making TeX Work
Linux Multimedia Guide
Running Linux, 2nd Edition
Running Linux Companion
  CD-ROM, 2nd Edition
SCO UNIX in a Nutshell
sed & awk, 2nd Edition (Winter '97)
UNIX in a Nutshell: System V Edition
UNIX Power Tools
UNIX Systems Programming
Using csh and tsch
What You Need to Know:
  When You Can't Find Your
  UNIX System Administrator

WINDOWS

Inside the Windows 95 Registry

PROGRAMMING

Advanced PL/SQL
Applying RCS and SCCS
C++: The Core Language
Checking C Programs with lint
DCE Security Programming
Distributing Applications Across
  DCE and Windows NT
Encyclopedia of Graphics File
  Formats, 2nd Edition
Guide to Writing DCE Applications
lex & yacc
Managing Projects with make
Oracle Performance Tuning
Oracle Power Objects
Oracle PL/SQL Programming
Porting UNIX Software
POSIX Programmer's Guide
POSIX.4: Programming for
  the Real World
Power Programming with RPC
Practical C Programming
Practical C++ Programming
Programming Python
Programming with curses
Programming with GNU Software
Pthreads Programming
Software Portability with imake,
  2nd Edition
Understanding DCE
Understanding Japanese Information
  Processing
UNIX Systems Programming for SVR4

BERKELEY 4.4 SOFTWARE DISTRIBUTION

4.4BSD System Manager's Manual
4.4BSD User's Reference Manual
4.4BSD User's Supplementary
  Documents
4.4BSD Programmer's Reference
  Manual
4.4BSD Programmer's Supplementary
  Documents

X PROGRAMMING
THE X WINDOW SYSTEM

Volume 0: X Protocol Reference Manual
Volume 1: Xlib Programming Manual
Volume 2: Xlib Reference Manual
Volume. 3M: X Window System
  User's Guide, Motif Edition
Volume. 4: X Toolkit Intrinsics
  Programming Manual
Volume 4M: X Toolkit Intrinsics
  Programming Manual,
  Motif Edition
Volume 5: X Toolkit Intrinsics
  Reference Manual
Volume 6A: Motif Programming
  Manual
Volume 6B: Motif Reference Manual
Volume 6C: Motif Tools
Volume 8 : X Window System
  Administrator's Guide
Programmer's Supplement for Release 6
X User Tools (with CD-ROM)
The X Window System in a Nutshell

HEALTH, CAREER, & BUSINESS

Building a Successful Software Business
The Computer User's Survival Guide
Dictionary of Computer Terms
The Future Does Not Compute
Love Your Job!
Publishing with CD-ROM

TRAVEL

Travelers' Tales: Brazil (Winter '96)
Travelers' Tales: Food (Fall '96)
Travelers' Tales: France
Travelers' Tales: Gutsy Women
  (Fall '96)
Travelers' Tales: Hong Kong
Travelers' Tales: India
Travelers' Tales: Mexico
Travelers' Tales: San Francisco
Travelers' Tales: Spain
Travelers' Tales: Thailand
Travelers' Tales: A Woman's World

International Distributors

Customers outside North America can now order O'Reilly & Associates books through the following distributors. They offer our international customers faster order processing, more bookstores, increased representation at tradeshows worldwide, and the high-quality, responsive service our customers have come to expect.

EUROPE, MIDDLE EAST AND NORTHERN AFRICA *(except Germany, Switzerland, and Austria)*

INQUIRIES
International Thomson Publishing Europe
Berkshire House
168-173 High Holborn
London WC1V 7AA, United Kingdom
Telephone: 44-171-497-1422
Fax: 44-171-497-1426
Email: **itpint@itps.co.uk**

ORDERS
International Thomson Publishing Services, Ltd.
Cheriton House, North Way
Andover, Hampshire SP10 5BE,
United Kingdom
Telephone: 44-264-342-832 (UK orders)
Telephone: 44-264-342-806 (outside UK)
Fax: 44-264-364418 (UK orders)
Fax: 44-264-342761 (outside UK)
UK & Eire orders: **itpuk@itps.co.uk**
International orders: **itpint@itps.co.uk**

GERMANY, SWITZERLAND, AND AUSTRIA

International Thomson Publishing
Königswinterer Straße 418
53227 Bonn, Germany
Telephone: 49-228-97024 0
Fax: 49-228-441342
Email: **anfragen@oreilly.de**

AUSTRALIA

WoodsLane Pty. Ltd.
7/5 Vuko Place, Warriewood NSW 2102
P.O. Box 935, Mona Vale NSW 2103
Australia
Telephone: 61-2-9970-5111
Fax: 61-2-9970-5002
Email: **info@woodslane.com.au**

NEW ZEALAND

WoodsLane New Zealand Ltd.
21 Cooks Street (P.O. Box 575)
Wanganui, New Zealand
Telephone: 64-6-347-6543
Fax: 64-6-345-4840
Email: **info@woodslane.com.au**

ASIA *(except Japan & India)*

INQUIRIES
International Thomson Publishing Asia
60 Albert Street #15-01
Albert Complex
Singapore 189969
Telephone: 65-336-6411
Fax: 65-336-7411

ORDERS
Telephone: 65-336-6411
Fax: 65-334-1617

JAPAN

O'Reilly Japan, Inc.
Kiyoshige Building 2F
12-Banchi, Sanei-cho
Shinjuku-ku
Tokyo 160 Japan
Telephone: 81-3-3356-5227
Fax: 81-3-3356-5261
Email: **kenji@ora.com**

INDIA

Computer Bookshop (India) PVT. LTD.
190 Dr. D.N. Road, Fort
Bombay 400 001
India
Telephone: 91-22-207-0989
Fax: 91-22-262-3551
Email: **cbsbom@giasbm01.vsnl.net.in**

THE AMERICAS

O'Reilly & Associates, Inc.
101 Morris Street
Sebastopol, CA 95472 U.S.A.
Telephone: 707-829-0515
Telephone: 800-998-9938 (U.S. & Canada)
Fax: 707-829-0104
Email: **order@ora.com**

SOUTHERN AFRICA

International Thomson Publishing Southern Africa
Building 18, Constantia Park
240 Old Pretoria Road
P.O. Box 2459
Halfway House, 1685 South Africa
Telephone: 27-11-805-4819
Fax: 27-11-805-3648

O'REILLY™

TO ORDER: **800-889-8969** (CREDIT CARD ORDERS ONLY); **order@ora.com; http://www.ora.com**
OUR PRODUCTS ARE AVAILABLE AT A BOOKSTORE OR SOFTWARE STORE NEAR YOU.

O'REILLY™

O'Reilly & Associates, Inc.
101 Morris Street
Sebastopol, CA 95472-9902
1-800-998-9938

Visit us online at:
http://www.ora.com/
orders@ora.com

O'REILLY WOULD LIKE TO HEAR FROM YOU

Which book did this card come from?

_____

Where did you buy this book?
- ❑ Bookstore
- ❑ Direct from O'Reilly
- ❑ Bundled with hardware/software
- ❑ Computer Store
- ❑ Class/seminar
- ❑ Other _____

What operating system do you use?
- ❑ UNIX
- ❑ Windows NT
- ❑ Macintosh
- ❑ PC(Windows/DOS)
- ❑ Other _____

What is your job description?
- ❑ System Administrator
- ❑ Network Administrator
- ❑ Web Developer
- ❑ Programmer
- ❑ Educator/Teacher
- ❑ Other _____

❑ Please send me O'Reilly's catalog, containing a complete listing of O'Reilly books and software.

Name _____   Company/Organization _____

Address _____

City _____   State _____   Zip/Postal Code _____   Country _____

Telephone _____   Internet or other email address (specify network) _____

Nineteenth century wood engraving
of a bear from the O'Reilly &
Associates Nutshell Handbook®
Using & Managing UUCP.

· POST CARD ·

NO POSTAGE
NECESSARY IF
MAILED IN THE
UNITED STATES

BUSINESS REPLY MAIL
FIRST CLASS MAIL   PERMIT NO. 80   SEBASTOPOL, CA

Postage will be paid by addressee

O'Reilly & Associates, Inc.
101 Morris Street
Sebastopol, CA 95472-9902